DAVE EDWARDS

LIVING MY DREAM

DAVE EDWARDS

LIVING MY DREAM

Dave Edwards
with
Paul Berry

ST DAVID'S PRESS
Cardiff

Published in Wales by St. David's Press, an imprint of

Ashley Drake Publishing Ltd
PO Box 733
Cardiff
CF14 7ZY

www.st-davids-press.wales

First Impression – 2017

ISBN
Paperback: 978-1-902719-64-1
eBook: 978-1-902719-65-8

British Library Cataloguing-in-Publication Data.
A CIP catalogue for this book is available from the British Library.

Typeset by Replika Press, India.
Printed by Gwasg Gomer, Wales.

Contents

For Emma, Jack and Evie, my inspiration in all that I do and my most favourite people, and all of my family and friends. Thanks for the continued support. I love you all.

Acknowledgements

I have many people to thank for helping me with the publication of *Living My Dream*.

Firstly to leading Welsh football journalist Chris Wathan and Wolves' head of media Paul Berry, for first talking to me about the idea, and then Paul for helping me write it! To Ashley Drake from St. David's Press, for taking the story on and publishing it. To Sam Dolan, my friend and colleague who helps me with off-field matters. To all the photographers who have provided images for publication – David Rawcliffe (Propaganda Photos) who is also Wales' official photographer; Matt Ashton (AMA Sport Photo Agency) who first started 'shooting' me at Shrewsbury Town; Sam Bagnall, Dave Bagnall and Stuart Manley/SM2 from the rollercoaster years at Wolves, Gareth Owen (Go-Photo) from Luton, and Jason Dawson (JASONP1PIX) from Reading. To everyone connected with Wales and all who looked after us at Euro 2016, and to everyone who has bought the book – I really hope you enjoy it.

Above all else, I would like to thank the managers and coaches I have worked for, the players I have shared a pitch with, and the supporters I have always given 100% for, week-in week-out. I have always been – and still am – *Living My Dream*.

David Edwards
October, 2017

Foreword

The tunnel at the Lens Stadium before England played Wales at Euro 2016 was a tense and passionate environment with both sets of players firing each other up ahead of what was a huge game. It wasn't just two 'home nations' and fierce rivals meeting on the biggest stage of all, but we needed the result for England, having been pegged back late on against Russia in the opening group game when Wales had beaten Slovakia.

In amongst all that tension, there was still time for a quick "hello" and high five to my old pal Dave Edwards, who has been one of my best mates in football all the way through my career. It is strange to think that there we were, ready to be involved in a game of such magnitude, not too many years on from when we were together at Shrewsbury, without a care in the world when life was a lot less complicated!

Even before we came through the ranks at the Meadow, we were on opposite sides in a big district cup tie, me playing in goal for Meole Brace School and Dave playing for Mary Webb School! I made a good save from Dave during the game, which he often reminds me of. The cup tie went to penalties, where we eventually won 11-10, but he was to get his revenge later on when Wolves beat Manchester City!

We went on to become good mates as we both broke through into the Shrewsbury first team, along with another young lad called Gavin Cadwallader, who has gone on to play in the Welsh League. They were good days, great times, and I wouldn't change them for the world.

Dave was both my chauffeur – he is older than me so passed his test first and would drive us into training – and also my landlord, as I rented a room off him for a year or so in those early days. He always tells me I was messy, which I would contest, but I had no excuse for one day taking a spade to the skirting board when we doing a bit of DIY decorating. I have to hold my hands up for the damage that was caused, although I was only trying to help! I have happier memories of our first lads' holiday together, when a group of us went to Zante for a first taste of going out for a few beers abroad!

Dave was actually with me at the life-changing moment I heard the big news that I was moving from Shrewsbury to Manchester City. We were down at the Quarry Park in Shrewsbury, by the river, both in our basketball tops (I promise that was the fashion of the time!) kicking a ball around, when I got the phone call from my agent, who also represented Dave.

It was quite an emotional moment for me, and I remember Dave being there to congratulate me and wish me all the best before I started phoning around with the good news! I had gone through a few tough times with all the speculation surrounding the move, and Dave was always on hand for a chat to talk things through, and was one of the people who I was leaning on for advice at that time.

You meet a lot of people in football, and lose contact with so many, but with our backgrounds and so many shared memories, I think myself and Dave will always be good mates.

He has a lovely family, and a desire to help other people, as shown by all of his charity work and the launch of his Little Rascals Foundation in Shrewsbury. His attitude to his football, and life in general, is a shining example for everyone to follow.

Going back to Euro 2016, and that game in Lens, although we finished up on the winning side, the tournament turned into a disappointing one for England, in stark contrast to Wales' fantastic run to the semi-finals.

This book from Dave offers some great behind-the-scenes insight into what it is like for a player at a major tournament, and some of the secrets behind Wales' spectacular success. It also offers a fascinating look at the journey made by all of us who set out as young kids with the dream of one day becoming a professional footballer, and all the obstacles which crop up along the way.

All the best with it, mate – and see you again on a football pitch somewhere soon!

Joe Hart
October 2017

1

The Nightmare Scenario

'Whether you think you can, or think you can't, you're right'
Henry Ford

As soon as I heard the crack I knew what it meant. The harrowing noise that any footballer dreads. But I didn't want to know. I didn't want to believe it.

Being injured is the worst possible feeling for a footballer. Worse than not being in the team, or having a bad game. That moment when the injury happens, you simply don't want to think about it and I certainly didn't. Not then. Not when I was in the Wolves team and we were on a decent run.

Whilst this wouldn't come into my mind until later, I was also thinking 'please not now, in this year of all years,' when I was aiming to be part of the first Wales squad in 58 years to head to a major tournament, the European Championships in France.

When I came to receive the ball from Kevin McDonald in the latter stages of our game at Queens Park Rangers in January, 2016, I tried to drag the ball away with my right foot and got challenged by Tjaronn Chery – a routine challenge that happens many times in a season. My left foot got caught under Chery's leg and, as everything went into slow motion, I heard the crack. I just didn't want to believe it.

Was that crack was the noise of my boot splitting? Was it was something else? Surely it wasn't a broken metatarsal, an injury I knew only too well having suffered it previously with my other foot. As Phil

Hayward, Wolves' head of medical came rushing to my side, I didn't want to confront that possibility, because I knew of the consequences.

"Eddo, Eddo.... Where's the pain?"

"Side of my foot, 5th met," I replied anxiously.

"Did you hear a crack?"

"No, nothing!" I instantly blurted out. Just a little white lie. I still wasn't prepared to believe it. "The pain is in my ankle now, it will be fine, just give me a minute and I'll run it off."

As I stood up Phil signalled to the gaffer Kenny Jackett that I was struggling, but to give me a minute. I was just hoping that my body's pain sensors were lying to me and I'd be ok. That the pain was caused by something else, something that would disappear once I ran it off, as happens so often on a football pitch.

When I got to the side of the pitch the Gaffer said: "Dave, are you going to be ok?"

"I'm fine, I'm fine," I quickly replied, and with that, I hobbled back onto the pitch.

It's amazing the difference that is made from adrenaline coursing through your veins. I had felt the agonising pain down the side of my foot when it happened, but now I was trying to get back into the thick of the action. Sadly, adrenaline can only last for so long and as I stepped into a jog, I just felt crunching in the side of my foot. I felt sick. I turned around straight away and started slowly limping towards the tunnel and signalled to the Gaffer I needed to come off.

I pulled my shirt above my eyes as I felt myself welling up. It's a bizarre feeling, I was angry. How could I let myself get into that position? I should never be going for a short free kick! Why did I drag the ball back? If I had scored a header a few minutes earlier when I'd had a good chance then that scenario would never have even come about. All pointless arguments I was having with myself but the frustration was raw. So very raw.

It was particularly raw because things were going well for me at that time. I had been involved with Wales in the qualifiers for Euro 2016 perhaps more than I expected. I had started a few games, including in the last few fixtures, and was really confident that if I could finish the season well with Wolves, I would be on the plane and have a chance of being involved in Euro 2016. Any footballer's dream, particularly a Welsh footballer given the wait of almost six decades to make it to a major finals. Maybe it was even a once-in-a-lifetime dream, especially as I was just a few weeks away from turning 30.

In terms of my form at the time, I had been feeling good after Christmas. We had won four games on the bounce after what had been a tough time so confidence was up. That run came to an end against Cardiff but we still headed to QPR in good shape. In the QPR game I felt really good, on a personal level, as well. After a poor start we had come back to equalise shortly after half-time and as the second half continued, I felt confident. The team looked confident. I had that header well saved, we were enjoying a lot of possession and it just seemed like a matter of time before we would get the winner. Then came the innocuous moment when it all happened, coming for that short free kick. I didn't need to do that, but I did it because I was feeling confident. Feeling good. Wanting to make something happen, which is a key part of my game.

As soon as it happened my initial thought was not about Wales, it was more about Wolves. I had been in the team, starting games, and I wanted to keep my place. That was the most disappointing thing for me in the immediate aftermath, but now I was limping off the pitch and towards the tunnel at Loftus Road with no real idea of what was to follow. Whether my season was over. Whether my Euro dream was over. From one innocuous moment, with no one at fault.

During those first few minutes when you get an injury like that you experience a huge range of emotions. It is crazy what goes through your head. You are trying to predict how long you will be out for, at the same time as dealing with the pain. You want to feel sorry for yourself and you want to blame someone, even yourself. Injuries like that are difficult to take.

At QPR the dressing rooms are reasonably close to the pitch so I didn't have far to go, and as I walked down the very small corridor and headed for the rickety massage couch in the middle of the room I tried trying to offload my foot as much as I could. Yet, with every step, all I could feel was that crunching sensation.

It is such a strange experience, going into that quiet, deserted dressing room which is normally such a loud and busy place. You get on the couch, and take your boot off. From a young age I'd been told not to take my boot off after getting kicked, because any injury would swell up and I wouldn't get my boot back on, but I took mine off and straightaway felt all the pressure release as my foot started to swell.

With Phil needed pitchside for the remainder of the game, it was our first team physiotherapist Jazz Sodhi who had escorted me down the tunnel and was now making his assessment. By this point I had accepted what had happened, and admitted to hearing the crack.

Jazz was keeping me positive - physios not only have to be experts in physiotherapy and rehabilitation but they must also have good people skills, be a friend, even a counsellor. Keeping a player's morale, positivity and work ethic at high levels during an injury is often key to how quickly and how well they return. A process that starts immediately.

Jazz started doing all his clinical testing and I asked him if it was broken. He said it seemed that way and all the symptoms were pointing towards that diagnosis, but we would have to wait for a scan. It was only then that I asked Jazz if he could go over to my peg and get my phone, only then that my attention turned towards not being involved with Wolves for a while but also wondering about Wales. Wondering about the Euros.

Jazz handed me my phone and I went straight to the calendar. Jazz suggested that if it was what he thought then it would be a 12 to 15 week injury. Looking at the calendar, my immediate thought was that there was no way I could allow it to be 15 weeks. I was going to come back in the shortest time, whatever that was, but not the maximum 15 weeks. Anything that was needed to do, anything that was within my control, I would do. The 15-week period would take me to the middle of April, and only give me a couple of games to come back for before the end of the season, and that would immediately reduce my chances of making the Wales squad. My mind was racing.

There was still about ten minutes to go in the game when I'd come off and I remember hearing a big cheer. Jazz and I thought QPR had scored but they'd actually hit the post. I wanted to get myself showered and ready before the lads came in. The last thing anyone would have wanted was to come in after a good draw, or even a win, all buzzing, and then have to ask me what had happened. It sounds quite unsociable but when something like that happens you are not in the best position to have any sort of conversation! You just want to get on the bus and go home.

4

THE NIGHTMARE SCENARIO

Getting in the shower was when the pain really kicked in. Yes there might be mental anguish, but there is also considerable, physical pain. All of a sudden, from being able to walk – or more accurately limp – back to the dressing room, I couldn't put any weight through the foot at all. It was really sore so I hobbled into the showers on crutches.

When the lads came in I shuffled to the corner of the room as the manager did his debrief. As a player, when you finish a game, the adrenalin is still pumping and when you get back in the dressing room you are talking about the 90 minutes and analysing the game. Then the lads noticed me and came to see how I was. I'd do exactly the same. Ask what has happened, and try and show some support. Unfortunately, as the injured player, you don't really feel like speaking to anyone so, after a few brief supportive words, I got out of there as quickly as I could. I hobbled down the corridor, saw the Wolves media guys and then just got myself seated on the bus. With my foot up on the back seat, we were soon heading back up the motorway towards Wolverhampton.

Phil came to the back of the bus with the Game Ready machine and to make sure my foot was elevated, and then Wolves' match analyst Phil Boardman came up to show the footage of the tackle so we could take a closer look at the actual mechanics of how I did it. After that I got my iPad out, put the headphones on and just tried to watch a few TV programmes and forget about it, for a while.

I had already rung my wife Emma from the corridor outside the dressing room. She was out with our two children at the time so had no idea how the game had gone. "Not good," was my answer to her enquiry. "I've broken a bone in my foot." She is great in those situations. Ultra-positive straightaway. "Don't worry – everything will be fine and you'll be back before you know it." All the comforting words that you really crave at a time like that. You want to get away from football and get back to your wife and children and speak to your mum and dad. Just be back with the family.

My brother is a massive Wolves fan and he keeps in touch with all the games even if he is not there. He is always really blunt with his messages. After a game it will just be: "How did you play?" He messaged me as usual just after full-time but this time it read: "What have you done?" My dad rang me after the game to see how I was and I spoke to my mum when I was on the bus on the way home. The news was quickly filtering through.

I remember that a few of the lads got off the bus at the drop-off point at Warwick. The journey back to Wolverhampton was a bit quieter from there, and that gave me the opportunity to have a really good chat with Tommy Rowe. Tommy had also once broken his fifth metatarsal. When I came back from breaking my other foot, I remember having a lot of trouble and it was about 15 weeks before I was back in training. Then I had lots of problems when it kept niggling away. I knew that 15 weeks would leave things really tight if I was to stand any chance of making the Wales squad.

Following his injury, Tommy had only been out for 11 weeks and hadn't had any issues afterwards so I was really picking his brains. He was a real comfort because he was talking me through it and giving me some pointers. I got on really well with Tommy when he was at Wolves and that conversation really helped me at a difficult time.

When we got back to the Compton Park training ground, Phil took me for an ultrasound scan. He warned me that it would only pick up anything blatantly obvious so we might need to wait for an X-ray on Monday. Within seconds though, Phil turned the scanner's screen towards me and said: "This white line running across the screen is your 5th met. It should be solid, but obviously it's not."

Even though I knew I had broken it, to actually see it on that screen – well, it kind of helped. It gave me clarity. There is nothing worse than maybe having a hairline crack and wondering if it might heal itself and having that decision to make. We knew there and then it was going to need sorting out and Phil phoned the surgeon James Calder. James is a foot and ankle specialist based in London, and I was immediately booked in for an operation on the Monday. Getting that organised so quickly meant I was already shortening the recovery period by two or three days. Not for the first time, I felt privileged as a footballer to be in a position for that to happen with getting the surgery so quickly.

A few hours earlier I was on top of the world looking forward to a Wolves game at QPR and at the back of my mind having an eye on Wales for the summer. Now I had broken a bone in my foot yet was somehow feeling positive. At least I knew what I was dealing with as I finally made it back home to Shrewsbury.

THE NIGHTMARE SCENARIO

Usually after a Saturday game, if we haven't got another game till the following weekend, I'll treat myself to a rare takeaway. This time though, straightaway, I was thinking 'no, I need to do everything right'. I wasn't going to do anything that might hinder my recovery and I even spent the rest of the night researching, scouring the web for information on anything and everything linked to the recovery, from what can help with inflammation to what helps with bone healing. Emma's help that weekend was really invaluable. She is really into nutrition and fitness, and was showing me different studies she had read.

Together we formulated a plan to take to the medical team at Wolves and once I had discussed it with them and we had set something in place, there was no way I was going to shift from it. Right from getting on the bus after the game, and immediately getting the ice on, if there was anything that I could do that could give me the slightest bit of help, then make no mistake, I was going to do it.

The kids do understand when something has happened like this. At the time my son Jack was five and my daughter Evie was three and were in bed when I got back from the game. Usually in the morning they will come in and dive on the bed but I'd had a light sleep because of the pain and just had to keep telling them: "Watch Daddy's foot, watch Daddy's foot."

As it turned out, I got through the whole injury without them knocking it at all. Apart from once that is. Jack had the TV remote in his hand and was swinging it around, and it hit the end of my foot. Ouch! That really stung! They were great and, despite being so young, they really understood. They were as good as gold.

Mentally I remained strong and didn't dwell on how I'd got injured. I had a spell in my mid-20s where I picked up a few injuries and I used to get really down about it. At that time I read a lot of books, self-help books mainly, which had a massive impact on my life as well as my career. In League One, when I problems with my foot, I had a long chat with Carl Howarth who was with our medical department at the time, before joining Everton. He gave me a lot of books to read about mentality and being positive. Thanks to Carl, my outlook and my mindset has changed, for the better. Now I don't let anything get me down, and I am a very positive person. Once the injury was done it was done, the only thing I could affect was how quickly I got back, and so I spun everything onto that instead.

I researched and investigated the available options and opportunities that could help me recover over that 10 to 12 week period, activities which I might not have been able to do had I been fit and been training. I explored other avenues, in all sorts of different areas. Anything that might give me a better chance of being as fit as possible for the summer. I knew immediately – I was going to need all the help I could get

2

Footy or the Farm?

'Saddle your dreams before you ride em'
Mary Webb

I probably had a different upbringing to a lot of footballers, growing up as I did in rural Shropshire. I was brought up in a little village called Halfway House, right on the Welsh border, maybe a mile inside England. I grew up with my mum and dad and brother Chris, who is three years older than me, and we had a family farm half a mile down the road which was owned by my uncle. As a child, I would spend a lot of time there with my dad, milking the cows, and helping out when I could.

My brother is a keen footballer but he was always really into his farming – certainly far more than I was. He is still in the farming trade now and works for a company called Pontesbury Tractors, which is involved with the sale and repair of tractors.

For me? I'm not sure I ever thought farming would be the right career. Sometimes I would try and convince myself that I could also get interested, so I'd get up with Dad at 5.30am and head over to the farm with him. Then, after 20 minutes standing in the milking parlour, I would quickly realise it wasn't for me. I just wanted to go home!

From then on, when we went to the farm, I would spend a lot time inside the house watching telly, or going to play football in the fields or inside a barn if it was raining. We were down there most days and I felt really lucky to grow up in the countryside with all this land to play on which was owned by the family. My dad fashioned a nice football pitch on a field behind our house, making some goalposts out of cut down logs! Yes, we played a lot of football growing up.

Mum and Dad split up when I was eight, and I then lived in different houses, although always close to Halfway House, and when I was 12, I moved to Pontesbury, a village to the west of Shrewsbury, which is where I've been ever since.

It goes without saying that football was always a massive part of my childhood. My dad managed my brother's football team, which started at under-8 level and, although I was only five at the time, I was desperate to play so I ended up joining a team the year below my brother, so two years above me. Worthen Juniors was that team, and I played with them up until I was ten. Playing with the older kids didn't really bother me – I was quite tall when I was young and I was close to my brother in terms of height.

We played in the Powys League so I was already playing in Wales against all the Welsh teams: Guilsfield, Llansantffraid and Llanfair Caereinion to name a few. It was a great experience travelling all over mid Wales at a young age, even if it meant playing in the occasional farmers' field! Then, when it got to under-11 level, Worthen moved into the Shropshire League. By this stage it had become the case that I wasn't allowed to play two years up – just one year – but I gave it a go anyway. What a rebel! That led to my first brush with the footballing authorities!

One day we were playing a game in Shrewsbury, and one of our opponent's parents complained that I was too young to be involved and I was forced to come off at half-time, ushered away like a naughty schoolboy, which I suppose – in a way – I was! I was only nine years old, though, it wasn't the case that I was so good that I was standing out. I just think the parent in question knew how old I was and was sticking to the rulebook!

As I result, I had to leave and drop down to my age group team, which was difficult due to the shortage of potential players. I was going to a school called Westbury, a couple of miles from Halfway House. It was such a small school there were only seven children in my year, five boys – none of whom were into football – and two girls. So at school I only really played football with older kids or younger kids. As a result I didn't have any friends in that under-10s team for Worthen Juniors and, when you are that age, it's not necessarily easy to go into that situation where you are a bit of a stranger. But, Mum and Dad took me along and I probably enjoyed my football as much as at any time growing up.

Now back in the Powys League we had a really good team, at times we were winning games 20-0, and cruised to winning that league before going onto the Shropshire League. We were in the 'B' league and still managed to get through to the County Cup final for Shropshire, which was a great achievement for a 'B' team. We played Shrewsbury Juniors who had won the Shropshire Junior 'A' league and we beat them 3-2, a game I still vividly remember to this day. That was confirmation that we had the best team in the county for our age.

I was playing centre midfield at this time, and was managing to chip in with a few goals as well. Usually, at that age, if you had quite a strong kick on you, then you'd beat most 'keepers if you could get it above their heads! That was generally my plan of attack. No messing about.

I had now started at Mary Webb secondary school and was playing alongside my teammates from Worthen Juniors, so our school team was very good as well. In Year 9 we won the Shrewsbury & District League, then beat the winners from the Telford area, and went into the national competition sponsored by Heinz Ketchup. We got through a few rounds then played a team from Middlesbrough in the last 16, where we lost in extra time, but it was a great achievement from a school out in the sticks with only 500 or so pupils – nothing like some of the really big secondary schools who progressed through the tournament.

When I was in Year 7 or 8 – playing a County Cup game for Worthen against Oakengates – I was spotted by a Wolves scout, Carlo Federico, known to everyone as 'Chico', who invited me to for a six-week trial. It was one night a week training on the astroturf at the Dome at Aldersley. I remember Keith Lowe, who went on to turn pro, being there and also Mark 'Sparky' Davies, who was playing above his age group. I also remember the red kit that they used to wear, the 'red mist' as Mick McCarthy used to call it.

After about three weeks of the trial with Wolves, the Shrewsbury scout – a guy called Charlie Walker – appeared unexpectedly and asked me to go there instead. Two of my school mates were already in the Shrewsbury set-up, and I was watching Shrewsbury's first team play every week, so that was what I wanted to do – go and play with my friends for the club I supported.

I stayed there for a couple of years but then it was getting to the point where there were so many players in my age group – probably about 30 turning up for every match – we would be split into three games of 20 minutes each, which wasn't enough for me. I just wasn't enjoying it and preferred to play with my mates so, at the age of 13, I knocked Shrewsbury on the head and returned to Worthen Juniors for another year or two. It was around that time that the team gradually disbanded, as can happen at that age, with some of the lads more interested in girls, or general boys' messing about, diverting their attention from the team and not really concentrating on football.

Football meant everything to me, so I finally left Worthen Juniors – with my brother – to join Hanwood United, a men's Saturday team in the Shropshire County League. It was quite a good standard of football and I had a couple of games in the reserves before getting into the first team, initially coming off from the bench, and then starting out on the wing.

On a Sunday I was playing for Pontesbury in the local Sunday League and while there was a fair bit of quality on the Saturdays, on the Sundays I generally got kicked to pieces! I didn't really mind that, it was quite good fun. Clocking the opposing full back stinking of ale from the night before, trying to get past them and knowing they were trying to completely clean me out. I was fit enough to be able to play back-to-back 90 minutes on a weekend – I just wanted to play as much football as I could, I loved it.

Going through school at this time, I was also doing really well at cross country – probably not a surprise to people who have seen me play football! Myself and one of my best mates, Ian 'Macca' McMillan, who was best man at my wedding, were really into it. We used to go running most mornings before school. I can't imagine too many 15 or 16-year-olds would have been into that sort of thing!

We were lucky to grow up in a beautiful part of the world and had all the Shropshire hills around, perfect scenery for a brisk early morning jog. We'd usually meet up at 6am and then head off from there, get back home to shower and then off to school. I used to feel brilliant at school in the mornings, really tuned in with all the endorphins flying around but, by the time I got to five or six o'clock in the evening, I was gone, finished! All my mates would want to go up the village and mess around and I was too shattered. It's fair to say I was a bit of a sports geek in that respect but they were really good times.

In addition to the Saturday and Sunday leagues, I was also playing football for Shropshire schools. Our county team was managed by Dave Perks and Steve Wilderspin and I used to really enjoy playing for them. We always got treated a lot better at county games and didn't have to wash our own kit. It would always be there for you in the dressing room ahead of a game, clean and tidy. We could pretend to be proper footballers.

I remember once we had a game against Cheshire at King's School in Chester. It was in January when I was in Year 11, and as I came off the pitch a guy came over to me who I sort of recognised. It was Ken Roberts, a previous Chester manager who had discovered Ian Rush, and was now chief scout at Shrewsbury for the first team and the younger age groups. He put his arm around me and asked if there was any chance I would reconsider going back to Shrewsbury. I'd been asked a few times to go back but hadn't really fancied it, but this time I said I'd think about it. I said I would have to speak to my parents.

The problem was that I was a reasonably bright kid, and I'd already got my future path all planned out: get my GCSEs out of the way, study Human Biology and PE at Sixth Form, and then go to Loughborough University and try to become a physio. Simple as that!

I went home and Dad said it was up to me. It was Dad, when I was at Shrewsbury, who spotted that I wasn't really enjoying it and told me not to feel that I had to carry on, there wasn't any pressure. That really helped me out. Now, with the chance to go back, it was Mum who told me I really had to consider giving it a go. There were boys in my age group already at Shrewsbury and likely to get scholarships and Mum said surely it would really annoy me if they got them and I hadn't even tried. She said I'd got nothing to lose. If I could sort my education out then it could be worth pursuing.

I knew I could go back to Shrewsbury until the end of the school year, without committing myself, so that's what I did. I rejoined the club at a time when Nigel Vaughan – a former Wolves midfielder and Welsh international – was the manager of the under-16s. It was a good decision for me because Nigel was to prove a massive influence on my career. From the moment I went back, it seemed to take off because Nigel took me under his wing and was focused on helping me improve as a player. I think he could see I had a desire to succeed, not just in football but also in life. He probably felt he had something to work with. A young guy called Joe Hart was also playing for Nigel's team, a year above his age group.

By the time May came around, Shrewsbury offered me a three-year scholarship, which was great news, but I wanted to make sure I could continue with my education so I had a chat with Alan Jones, from the Shropshire Schools and Colleges Football Association. He was very involved with Shrewsbury at this point, co-ordinating all the education programmes. They were excellent and immediately clicked with what I wanted to do.

The standard scholarship programme at that time involved the players studying for a BTEC in Sport and, for most of the lads who just wanted to play football, that was fine, but I still had the grand plan to be a physio, which I wanted to be able to fall back on if needs be. Alan agreed that I could get a tutor on Wednesdays and study for the necessary A-levels. That sealed the deal really. Knowing I could continue with my education as well as the football.

So, off I went for pre-season as a full-time scholar with Shrewsbury under-16s. I'd changed my mind slightly on the career front in the meantime and, alongside my football, I studied and achieved 'A'-levels in PE and Psychology and an AS-level in Business. At the start of the scholarship we were all told that, from the eight lads in our age group, two of us might get professional contracts and one might go on and play for the first team. Little wonder I was keen to get my education sorted out. It was also unique because all eight lads were from Shropshire and I'm not sure whether that had been done before or since. These days they might get players who'd been released from Wolves, Villa, Birmingham – local teams – whereas all eight of us then had emerged together and played in the same county team.

They were great times, and it was a great challenge. Going in every day to the club I had supported all my life and watched from the terraces. Life was good, but now was time for the next big step. Would I be good enough to make the grade and become a professional footballer? Only time would tell.

3

Operation Euros

'The true test of a man's character is what he does when no one is watching'
John Wooden

With the operation scheduled for the Monday, I chilled out at home on Sunday and watched the football all day with the Game Ready machine on. The Game Ready is a brilliant piece of equipment which supplies ice and compression using different body wraps.

Refreshed, relaxed but determined, I was up bright and early on the Monday morning to catch the train from Shrewsbury and meet Phil Hayward at Wolverhampton, *en route* to London for the surgery. We met with the specialist, James Calder, at his clinic around 1pm and after a quick X-ray we were in his consultancy room reviewing the scan. He said it was obvious there was a significant break, and the sensible option for me would be to have the surgery that day.

He briefed me on things I needed to do in preparation for the operation – all the usual like no food and drink – and we were then sent over to Cromwell Hospital in west London where a room would be ready for me. I would be his last operation of the evening so I knew it could be quite a while before I was taken down to theatre and I was already feeling hungry!

It was a long afternoon of waiting. I flitted between reading Steven Gerrard's autobiography and watching Netflix's *Making A Murderer* to pass the time. With having two young children at home I don't get to watch watch much TV, so away trips and unfortunate situations like this offer a good chance to get my fix of films and box sets. I finally got wheeled down to theatre just after 10pm. It had been a long day by this point but I was more concerned with how long a day it had been for James Calder, the man with the knife! I asked the nurse how James was feeling, and asked if he needed some Red Bull? She laughed, but I wasn't joking.

I then got prepped with needles and tubes ready for the anaesthetist, who started pumping different fluids into my veins. The first, he said, was a strong painkiller and said I would start to feel woozy in 30 seconds. I don't know what his definition of woozy is but I felt like I had just necked 10 pints. I felt steaming! He then put some general anaesthetist in my hand and said I might feel a cold sensation moving up my arm, and would start to fall asleep shortly. Anyone who has had this done before will know it's a strange sensation. I was determined to count to 10 and try to hold off going to sleep. I think I got to about four before I couldn't keep my eyes open any more.

I came around from the operation about 12.30am and then drifted back off until about 1.30am. When I woke this time, a nurse was in my room and asked how I was? I just replied, "I'm starving!" So there I was at 2am tucking into a big three-course meal. That food was amazing! I then drifted in and out of sleep until approximately 7am. I then had a huge breakfast. The service was second to none.

I was, however, still in quite a bit of pain and my foot was throbbing. The operation involved three main incisions along the outside of my foot. One at the fracture site, one at the base of my fifth metatarsal and one in my heel where a bone graft was taken. I also had some cells taken from the bone marrow in my pelvis, which, along with the bone graft, is used at the fracture site to encourage healing.

A screw was then inserted at the base of my metatarsal along the length of the bone. I was then stitched back up and that was it – done and dusted. So, after all that, the pain wasn't surprising and it stayed throughout the morning until I was discharged at around 1pm. It was an uncomfortable journey home as well which wasn't helped by breaking down on the M40. I had felt very fortunate with how quickly we had got the surgery sorted but maybe that was where my luck ran out. The breakdown turned my journey back to Shrewsbury into a six-hour trip. I was desperate to get home, desperate to see Emma and the kids, and desperate to get a shower and start to feel like a human again.

More than that I was desperate to start working on whatever I could to ensure a quick and complete rehabilitation. Even in the first few days, when there was probably very little I could physically do, I wasn't prepared to let any time go to waste.

4

Shropshire Lad

'Some call it the middle of nowhere, I call it the centre of my world'
Unknown

In my first year as a YTS trainee at Shrewsbury, there were under-19 and under-17 teams. I started with the under-17s, playing in the midweek floodlit league, having already made a few appearances whilst I was still in school. Steve Biggins was the manager of that team and Nigel Vaughan had moved up to the under-19s, alongside a guy called Jamie Robinson, which was great for me personally. Early in the season I broke into the under-19s and was playing regularly for them, until around Christmas when I started figuring for the reserves who played on Tuesday or Wednesday afternoons.

There was a mix of players in the reserves. The older pros who weren't playing in the first team and had been told to have a game, and in general didn't really want to be there. Then were the boys coming back from injury who were getting their fitness back, and a couple of young lads including me. Dave Fogg, assistant to the Welsh legend Kevin Ratcliffe at that time, was in charge of the reserves, and I really enjoyed the challenge.

What a life it was at that time. I was training every day and playing football. It was perfect. We lived in a place called Walford in North Shropshire, an agricultural college which had dormitories, and football pitches where the youth team trained. It was a great set-up but strange for me because if I'd still been living at home I could have got to the training ground quicker.

As the season went on, and I was training more with the first team, it would be a minibus journey over to the training ground and, after training, the YTS boys would still be expected to clean the facilities and the first team players' boots. They were long old days, and it could be a grind. The pitches weren't very good either, and always used to flood in the winter. From November onwards it seemed we were always looking for somewhere else to train, such as at nearby colleges, or indoors at RAF Shawbury, Shrewsbury College or Lilleshall. Although it was hard work, I was loving it.

I'd also started on the international road, being called up for Wales under-17s. I remember heading off to a tournament in the Faroe Islands, and playing centre half, a position I occupied a lot during my first year as a trainee. That was mainly because Shrewsbury had two really good central midfielders in the youth ranks so I think this was a way of me getting in the team. Peter Nicholas was the manager of the Wales under-17s at the time and I'd play on the left hand side of a back three.

Very quickly, still during my first year as a trainee, I was called up to the under-21s by Jimmy Shoulder, which was a bit of a surprise. Jamie Tolley and Darren Moss, who were first team players at Shrewsbury – playing week in week out – were also in the squad. I was on the bench for the game, at Barry Town, but being called up was a massive boost for me, and when I look back and think, so much happened for me during that season.

Yet there was still more to come. As the season wore on, the first team were really struggling. We had loads of games in hand because of having so many called off and we weren't winning any of those games. There had also been the famous FA Cup run, where we had beaten Everton 2-1. I was a ball boy for that game! We lost in the next round at Chelsea 4-0 and maybe that run just took everyone's focus away from the league. We just couldn't get a result and the games started slipping away. We were in freefall.

On the penultimate game of the season, we lost to Carlisle which confirmed relegation. Kevin Ratcliffe, whom I had got on well with during my first season as a YTS, was sacked so Nigel Vaughan and Mark Atkins, another former Wolves midfielder who had won the Premier League with Blackburn, took the team for the final game. Andy Thompson, another player very well known to Wolves fans, was also at Shrewsbury at that time.

In the week leading up to the final game there were four of us from the youth ranks training with the first team. A few of the older lads weren't too interested in playing and I think they just felt the management team wanted something fresh, to try and raise optimism for the future. During the week before the game it looked as though there might be two spaces free on the bench, which the four of us were battling for. I was the only first year, the others were second and third years, but Vaughany told me the day before, after training at SCAT (Shrewsbury College of Art & Technology) that I was going to be on the bench. I was petrified! So, so nervous. I couldn't believe it. I'd not long turned 17. It was my mum's birthday that Friday and I remember telling her the news. Not suprisingly, I had loads of people wanting to come to the game.

We lived on a *cul-de-sac* in Pontesbury and I remember at 10am on the day of the game I was out on the road, volleying balls against the wall, as I'd always done. We had the wall of the house, and then next to it the wall of a brick shed. I would use those walls to practise my half turn. Bang it against the wall, receive the ball, turn and hit it off the other wall, get it back, and repeat. At 10am on matchday I was just desperate to be out there on the road, kicking that ball against the wall. Slowly, finally, the hours passed and I travelled to the stadium, still feeling very nervous, to the point that I wasn't even sure I really wanted to play. I got to the ground and I remember really looking forward to seeing my shirt hanging up in the first team dressing room – for my potential first team debut – a huge moment. There it was, number 34, with my name on the back.

Thrilled, I walked straight up to the shirt and my first thought was, 'this looks terrible!' You could see where they had ripped the number 2 off the back and, next to the official Football League number 4, was a number 3 of a completely different size which didn't match. My name was on the back – EDWARDS – but you could see the black outline underneath of some faded letters of whoever had worn the shirt before. My shorts told the same story. They were number 4 shorts – which I think were a spare pair of Jamie Tolley's – with the number 3 next to it which was completely off-centre. You can look back now and never imagine that would happen anywhere. I guess it was the end of the season, and there were no new shirts left. I can laugh about it now, but on the day I remember it left me feeling really deflated. My big moment. Until I saw the kit.

The game was against Scunthorpe, who included the very well-known Peter Beagrie in their side – I bet his kit was ok! Anyway, we were 2-1 down, in front of a reasonable turnout – given the situation – of just over 4,000, when Mark Atkins shouted over, "Come on Dave, you're going to go on." I was petrified, but on I went, and I can still now close my eyes and remember my first touch in the Football League. Karl Murray, who played at centre half, had the ball and passed it to me. I turned a little bit, saw someone coming towards me, and just gave it straight back to Karl. Not spectacular, but I was off and playing in league football.

A vivid memory of that game remains with me to this day. It was getting a bit dark towards the end of the game and there was a goal kick to us. As the 'keeper kicked it out, I remember just looking at the Riverside terrace lit up by the floodlights and just thinking, 'This is so absurd!' There I was, 17 years old, playing in front of this crowd. In front of that terrace where I used to stand, week-in week-out. It almost felt like an out-of-body experience.

I had about ten minutes on the pitch and probably only touched the ball four or five times. I knew then, regardless of what happened afterwards, regardless of if I never stepped out on a football pitch ever again, I had played in the Football League. I had achieved my ambition. Even if I played a few games in the Conference the next season and we didn't get back up, I had made a professional appearance which could never be taken away from me. A huge moment.

We had been relegated the previous weekend but the fans stayed behind to the end to applaud us off. It seemed bizarre to celebrate having been relegated but I remember going out with my family for a meal to mark the occasion of my league debut. I may have had a couple of drinks, even though I was only 17! It was certainly a day that I would never ever forget.

The following season Shrewsbury brought in a new manager, Jimmy Quinn and in the pre-season I was still playing first team games to make up the numbers, but Jimmy brought new players in and I was soon back in the youth team and aiming to build myself back up. Shortly into the New Year I made my full debut in an FA Trophy win at home to Morecambe, and from then on I was in and out of the senior team, maybe starting 10 to 15 games and making about 20 appearances in total.

We had a decent season and made it through to the Conference play-off final. The top team went up automatically with the next four in the play offs. We were miles behind Hereford, who finished second, just a point behind the champions, Chester, and faced Barnet in the semi-finals. I was on the bench for the first leg, which we lost 2-1, and didn't get on. In the home game, however, we were 1-0 up thanks to Luke Rodgers, and when the former Blues midfielder Martyn O'Connor had to come off just before half-time, I went on in his place.

This was another massive game for me at that age and another vital opportunity to gain experience. So far, it is the only time I have been involved in the play-offs, and the Meadow was absolutely packed that day. The game ended up going to penalties, with me listed as the sixth taker. I, thankfully, wasn't needed as we won 5-3 with Darren Moss converting the decisive kick.

The final, against Aldershot, was held at the Britannia Stadium where I was again on the bench but this time didn't play. A huge following from Shrewsbury travelled to Stoke and probably made up three quarters of the 20,000 crowd. Again it went to penalties after finishing 1-1 after extra time. Luke Rodgers took our first penalty and blazed it over the bar, but then our 'keeper Scott Howie saved all their next three kicks and we scored our next three, making it a 3-0 win on penalties – we were back in the league at the first time of asking.

Jimmy remained in charge the following season and I began to regularly start in the team. By now I had also signed my first pro contract – on absolute peanuts to be fair – but it was a case of take it, or you go back in the youth team, and I was really enjoying being in and amongst the senior set-up. I played the first month of the season before falling out of favour a little bit, and it was getting to the point where I needed to play so considered going out on loan. Forest Green, who were then a Conference team, were interested in taking me so I spoke to Nigel Vaughan, who was still the youth team manager. He said he'd heard that the manager was under pressure, so told me to hang in there, and not to go out on loan.

What excellent advice that was! Everything went on hold for a couple of weeks and, as predicted, Jimmy Quinn left the club, with Gary Peters – a very well respected manager – coming in, and, fair play, he did an unbelievable job. We were poor, and we looked like we were on the way to getting relegated. Gary was ridiculously 'old school' with the training methods and tactics: "just get the ball forward, keep the pressure on." I remember in his very first session he didn't want a defender playing out and passing to a centre midfielder. That was banned. 'Just get it down the channel'.

During his first match in charge, Darren Moss played the ball from right back in to Jamie Tolley in the centre of midfield. The pass was cut out, and the opposition scored. Gary was furious! Overall, though, he was just what the club needed. He was a proper manager, he did everything from top to bottom. It was in the Alex Ferguson mould from that era. He would deal with training, contracts, games, analysis – everything.

He was good for my game as well and got me back on the bench as soon as he took over. He'd been scouting for Everton before coming to Shrewsbury and said he'd put my name forward to them a few times. I remember hearing some speculation that there'd been a rejected bid for myself and Joe Hart at one time. It may have been newspaper talk, but there was a lot made of it.

It wasn't long before I got in the team on a regular basis and it was under Gary that my Shrewsbury career really took off. I was playing week-in week-out, all-out action in midfield, a headless chicken sometimes! I was loving it. Living my dream. From that point I had a great couple of years and played a lot of games, and then it all came crashing to an end in somewhat controversial circumstances.

Towards the end of the 2006-07 season I had just turned 21, and Shrewsbury offered me a new contract. It was such a poor deal, only a minimal increase and miles away from what other players were earning. I felt I deserved parity as I was playing, week-in week-out, and playing well. The previous season I'd won the Supporters', and Players', Player of the Year awards and I was a local lad really enjoying my football.

As time went on there was a lot of newspaper talk about my future, and I was now a regular member of the Wales under-21 squad. I was getting some advice not to sign the contract and to see what would happen at Shrewsbury, as the club were starting to give it a real go to try and get promoted.

Towards the end of that 2006-07 season, however, my form was going through a dip. In April 2007 it emerged publicly that I had turned down a new deal and locally it was big news. It made the front and the back page of the *Shropshire Star*! I think it was bit of a push from Gary to put some pressure on but I was still waiting, wanting to keep my options open. It looked like we were going to get in the play-offs, and had we gone up, I would definitely have signed.

We got to the last game of the season, against Grimsby at home, and also the last ever league game at Gay Meadow. It was a full house, and a great day. I remember we had special commemorative crests on our shirts, a bit different to the kit I had worn for my debut a few years earlier! We drew the game 2-2, and were confirmed in the play-offs, and then it all got a bit bizarre after full-time. Gary wanted us to practise penalties, in case they would be needed, and so he asked the fans to stay behind and we mocked up a penalty shootout. A little bit strange – and I missed mine as well – but it was all part of the preparation for the play-offs which were to follow.

We got through the semi-finals, beating MK Dons over the two legs, but I'd picked up a knock in training and missed both those games. However, as I'd been a key part of that season's campaign, I knew that if I got myself fit I had a good chance of being involved in the final. I'd been close to making the second leg on the Friday but, by the Monday, I was definitely ready to train and stake my claim to be in the squad.

Monday morning arrived and we were stepping up preparations when Gary asked to meet me at the stadium after training. At the time I didn't really have any idea why he wanted to meet me. Did he want to talk about my contract, and try to get it sorted perhaps? I suppose it was. To a point.

I went in to see him and he just said: "The contract is there, I need to know if you are going to sign it." I repeated what I'd said before, that I wanted to wait and see what happened before making a decision. Win the play-offs, get promoted, and then see what was on the table in the summer. Gary replied by saying that was the offer, and that he was telling me now that if he didn't sign it, I wouldn't be playing in the final. I was gobsmacked. "Gaffer," I said. "This is the first play-off final at the new Wembley. Sixty thousand people are going to be there and this is a chance for me to play for the club I've supported all my life. I'm so up for it – I would give it absolutely everything."

He responded saying I needed to show I was committed, and that if I didn't sign the contract, then I wouldn't play. He wasn't budging. I said I needed some time to think. It was such a big decision that I needed to speak to my parents and would let him know the next morning. Mum and Dad both said that I shouldn't be bullied into signing it like that. There was a feeling that if I didn't sign it I would still play, but if I didn't sign and was dropped, it still wouldn't be as important as the rest of my career. My agent said exactly the same. As important as this one game was, and obviously I wanted to play at Wembley, there were many more games to come.

I spoke to Nigel Vaughan at length. He was my main mentor at this point. The first thing he said was: "Well it's not the Millennium is it?!" Cheers Nigel! Gary had said he knew people who would pay 10 or 15 grand to play at Wembley, and Nigel told me to go back and tell him it wasn't the Millennium! He was the same as the others and all the advice I got was that I shouldn't sign it just for that reason, however attractive the prospect of turning out for Shrewsbury at the new Wembley stadium.

I turned up to training as usual on the Tuesday morning. I didn't used to warm-up too much in those days. I'd arrive in my training kit, get out of the car, put my boots on, and go out and play head tennis or something similar before training. The gaffer would always go to the stadium first and then arrive for training. On this particular day he arrived around 15 minutes before training was due to start so I came in off the pitch to speak to him.

We went into his little office in the training ground and had a decent chat. I told him I was going to give it 100%, and was desperate to be part of his plans for the final, but I couldn't sign the contract at that time. I wasn't saying I would never sign it, and that if the club were promoted and if it was the right deal then I would be more than happy to commit my future.

I can still remember his words now. "You may as well take your boots off because I don't want you around the place." Clearly taken aback, I asked him what he meant and he just said he didn't want me interfering with training and that my Shrewsbury career was over. There was still Tuesday, Thursday and Friday training to follow before the game on the Saturday but I wasn't even going to be there. His mind was made up.

At this point I could really feel myself welling up. I was trying to persuade him but he wasn't having it and just said he didn't want me around the other lads. We'd been chatting for ten to 15 minutes by now and the lads had started the warm-up. They were stretching over on the far side of the training pitch. I said I was going to go and see the lads and say my farewells, to which he said he'd rather I didn't. I repeated that I was going to go over and see them and I walked over and told them that I was done. I wished them all the best of luck for the Saturday and shook everyone's hand.

There was only Stuart Drummond, who had played centre midfield with me that season, who was aware of the situation. I had spoken to him the day before, but none of the other lads had a clue what was going on. I wanted to tell everyone before I left. This was it. The end of my Shrewsbury career. I made sure I shook everyone's hands quickly and left, because I knew I was just seconds away from crying. I jumped in my car, still with my boots on, and immediately burst into floods of tears. I don't really know what it was because I didn't feel particularly mad or upset at that time. It was just the whole emotion of it all. I phoned Mum and Dad straightaway and they were very supportive, and told me not to worry about it.

So the week from there was all a little bit strange. The news came out towards the end of the week when I think the manager informed the media. I was on the back page of the paper again – 'Edwards will not play at Wembley'. He said he had players who wanted to be part of the club's future and he didn't want to give me a place in the team above anyone else. I was still devastated. I had played 51 games that season, 44 of which were starts, and the only game I think I missed, apart from the play-off semi-finals, was when I was away with Wales under-21s.

Did I go to the game? Of course I did. Above all else, I was still a Shrewsbury fan. I spoke to a couple of my mates who were going and booked myself on to one of the supporters' coaches. I had a few drinks and wanted to enjoy the day, although the tickets were awful, right at the back and high up. A bit different view of the proceedings to what I had been hoping for just a few days earlier.

Bristol Rovers were the opponents and when we went one up, I was buzzing. Genuinely, I was desperate for the lads to win the game and get promoted, but Bristol Rovers were a really good team, and too good for Shrewsbury on the day. We ended up losing 3-1, and that was that. For me it was the end, and there was no turning back. I was going to be leaving.

I didn't have anything else lined up. It wasn't like I was waiting on another offer. There was nothing on the table. I was going on holiday with my mates to Cancun that summer and it was just a case of hoping for some developments when I got back. I didn't go back to Shrewsbury again. It wasn't like there was anything there I needed to pick up. In those days you had your training kit and your boots and that was about it.

Football moves on very quickly, and the following season Gary actually rang me when my next club Luton were in administration. Because of my age they had to pay Shrewsbury compensation when they signed me, and the contract included clauses after I had played a certain number of games. I don't think they had paid too much by that point and Shrewsbury were trying to see if there was a legal way I could go back. I phoned my agent and he just said there was no chance it could happen.

I have seen Gary a few times since and it is all fine. As disappointed as I was at the end of it all, and with the way it turned out, I owe him a massive amount for what he did for my career. To be honest, I might not have had a career if it wasn't for him. He showed faith in me, trusted me, put me in the team, and I played a lot of games.

I probably saw Gary for the first time properly at a Shrewsbury game a couple of years ago when we had a good chat at half-time. We didn't talk about what happened at the end, more just what we had both gone on to do afterwards. He is a good guy, a proper football man, and I don't think I have ever known a manager work as hard as he did.

He had a bed at the stadium, and a bed at the training ground. He was that dedicated. It was before the days of analysis as we know now, and Gary would just watch video after video after video of matches. After every game we would have a DVD and a form asking us how we thought we had played and the opportunity to self-evaluate our performance. We would get those on a Monday and if we didn't bring them back Tuesday there would be trouble. It was like having homework!

Gary was a stickler in so many areas and he did so much for me despite how it all ended. There were three really good assistants in my time there as well. Mick Wadsworth, who had been at Newcastle and Carlisle, Leroy Rosenior and John McMahon – brother of Steve from Liverpool. I enjoyed working with all of those guys just as I did with Gary.

Playing for your home town club, it doesn't get much better than that and despite the circumstances of how I left, I still seem to have a really good relationship with the fans, which is something I am so grateful for. It wasn't just the team I had played for either. When I was 14 or 15, I used to travel to away games on the supporters' coaches, and play in the games they arranged as well. Play a game against the away fans, and then watch the match! I used to love that.

Social media wasn't around when I left so I don't really know if the fans were upset or annoyed, but I only ever get kind messages from Shrewsbury fans now. Whenever I go back I get a lovely reception from everyone I meet. I genuinely was a proper fan getting to play for his club. It was great, but in the end, it came down to a battle between my undoubted love for the club, and forging a football career. Hopefully the Shrewsbury fans have seen why I made my decision.

I will always be in debt to Shrewsbury, and hope fans will take it to their hearts that a lot of my success was nurtured in Shrewsbury and, you never know, I would love to go back and play for them again one day. It's my club!

5

Fighting for Fitness

'The pain of regret is far worse than the pain of discipline'
Nathan Whitley

Once I was back home after surgery the main aim was to reduce the swelling. James Calder asked me to keep me foot above my hip as much as possible so the fluid would drain, and that I shouldn't spend longer than five minutes every hour with my foot on the floor. Easier said than done!

Fortunately Emma was amazing with me, waiting on me hand and foot, and the kids were busy keeping me entertained with Jack showing me some football tricks and Evie her gymnastic routines. They didn't seem too keen on the idea of a board game or watching a film, or another similarly quiet pastime.

Nutrition was going to be vital if I was going to get back as quickly as possible. I am a bit of a chocoholic and do need to watch what I eat as my metabolism doesn't seem to be the same as my teammates. However, between the sports science team at Wolves, and Emma, who is a real nutrition enthusiast as part of her work as a personal trainer, we came up with a plan.

During the first two weeks it was all about reducing swelling so it was foods high with anti-inflammatory values and high calcium content to help bone growth – like kale and spinach – but no refined sugars. Towards the end of the first week post-surgery I went back into the Wolves training ground where Phil Hayward was able to assess the wound. I was impressed with how the scars looked when the bandaging was removed and that there wasn't too much swelling, so it had been well worth following Mr Calder's advice. From this point I was able to use the Game Ready machine at home, and an Exogen machine, which uses high frequency waves applied to the foot to encourage bone growth.

A diet of mainly rest, recovery and eating the right food, isn't the most exciting way to pass the time and it's fair to say that for a footballer, boredom can kick in fairly swiftly when you can't train or play. So I was looking forward to getting back into the training ground again on a regular basis to be back amongst the lads and the staff. Little did I know that after a week back I'd be struggling to manoeuvre my crutches out of the training ground due to the pounding my arms and upper body had taken in the gym. All football clubs differ, but at Wolves, when you were injured, you needed to be prepared for some very hard work!

For a so-called medium-term injury such as mine, it was important to keep fitness levels high and body fats down because when you've completed your recovery from the injury, you go into a conditioning period with the fitness coaches before returning to training. The better the shape you are in at that point, the more days you can potentially shave off that conditioning period. For me, with the Euros just a few months away, any time I could save was potentially crucial.

The work in those early stages centred around various different objectives. Restoring ankle range and movement, reducing inflammation, and then maintaining core stability. Also maintaining muscle bulk in key muscle groups, upper body power and cardio-vascular fitness. The days would always start with assessment from Phil, who would then start the mobilisations to try and restore some movement in my foot and ankle. Wolves' first team sports therapist, Matt Wignall, would then carry out my soft tissue work, moving the swelling away from the foot and doing some release work on any overloaded muscle tissue to keep me in as good nick as possible.

There would follow some more icing and compression, and one of Phil's dreaded core sessions before lunch. The afternoon would be gym time, with a structured programme over the week put together by the head of sports science, Tony Daley, and strength & conditioning coach, Richard Kirby. Three days of the week would involve a circuit-style session and on the other two, a high intensity session. Often you would find yourself working with another of the recovering players, and that does help with motivation, as it can get pretty hard!

To try and push me through these sessions I would put my earphones in, get *You Tube* on the phone and listen to some motivational stuff, which really helped me. A channel called *CJ Chan* was particularly good for some five-minute videos which were a mixture of music and motivational speaking. Also motivational speakers Les Brown and Eric Thomas, a former NFL star, all combined to help get me through those tough times.

Getting through the first week and into the weekend I could certainly feel the effects of the programme of fitness work. From the mental side, I was pleased that, even though I wasn't yet weight bearing, I wasn't feeling any pain in my foot. There is nothing worse than waking up every day with pain, something I'd experienced previously when suffering from a debilitating back injury, which left me in a really tough place mentally. While it was awkward being on crutches, the nature of the metatarsal injury meant I was still able to sleep perfectly well without any medication, and crawl around to play with the kids. Those positives made a massive difference to my mindset.

I also turned 30 during this time. As a kid or teenager I always felt 30 sounded really old, and in football terms it isn't a landmark you necessarily want to reach as it's the age when the clock is ticking down on your playing career. For me, though, I was determined to embrace it. I still felt very young both in my mind and in my body and was hoping that it would continue for a very long time. I had a great birthday – Jack and Evie were more excited than I was – and I enjoyed my first culinary treat since the injury, when 15 of us from the family went out to The Smoke Stop, just outside Shrewsbury, for a beautiful meal of good old American-styled barbecue food.

If there was one downer to those early weeks it was when the lads were playing and I was sat at home waiting for the scores to come in. As part of a team and a squad, you feel helpless when you can't contribute. I knew there was nothing I could do due to my physical situation, but it still hurt not to be involved.

During the rehab, I focused my mind and discovered a level of dedication and discipline I didn't know I had. If I had lived all my career as I did during those first few weeks after surgery, I know I would have been a better player. I'm just not sure I would have had the knowledge or mentality at the age of 18 to say 'no' to a weekly Domino's or a visit to the local chippy, or a couple of pints with my mates. Everything changes as you become more experienced.

All the way through, I knew that every single sacrifice would be worth it just to be involved in a major tournament with Wales. There are no guarantees when you are recovering from injury, but I knew that if I didn't do everything in my power to give myself the best possible chance then I would never forgive myself. Every morning, the first thing I saw when I walked downstairs and into the kitchen was a chalkboard on the wall with the words: 'Live a lifetime of DISCIPLINE or you will live a life of REGRET'. Never could those words have rung truer.

As the weeks passed, so my steady progress continued. Every step felt, literally, like I was moving in the right direction: starting to weight bear with the use of an air cast boot, having the stitches removed, and getting closer to the wounds healing so I could start to do a bit of swimming and just enjoy something different to the treatment and gym work. All the time looking slightly enviously outside, as the lads at Wolves continued to train and prepare for games.

The gym overlooked the first team training pitch at Compton Park and, when you were stuck in there working out, that could act as an inspiration. On other occasions, sadly, it could make you feel down. Two of Wolves' long-term injured players, Nouha Dicko and Razak Boukari, were in there with me one day and, in between one of our circuits, I sat down for a drink and caught Nouha standing there, gazing out of the window at the lads training in the sunshine outside. I had to take a photo of it because, to me, it symbolised how mentally tough it is when you are injured. I could almost sense Nouha dreaming about being fully fit and playing again. Footballers lead a privileged lifestyle, but there are also plenty of tough times as well. All the injured boys work hard, but to see how Nouha and Razak were going about their business with far worse injuries than me was actually very inspiring.

Another important part of the recovery process is to be able to do other things away from the intensive work to keep myself active and focused. My lad Jack is crazy about football and I had been due to take him to the Premier League game between Everton and Swansea the day after I got injured. He had written out details of the teams and memorised all of their names so he knew exactly who would be playing. He was as gutted about missing that as I was about the injury, so I promised I would take him to another game when my foot was on the mend and managed to get tickets for Manchester City against Tottenham at the Etihad. Jack was so excited and from the moment we watched the teams arrive, to when he flaked out in the car on the way home, he had the biggest smile on his face.

I'd also arranged that Jack would meet my old mate Joe Hart after the game – Jack hadn't met Joe before – and he was really looking forward to that. Joe was kind enough to give Jack his signed match shirt and also sign the teamsheet Jack had made for the game. Joe took him to the dressing rooms and pitchside for a photo. At the end of it Jack said: "Daddy, this has been the best day I have ever had." On the way home I did tell him that I had once scored against Joe when Wolves beat Manchester City at Molineux. He looked at me as if I was mad. Maybe that is what sent him off to sleep, but we had a magical day.

Later on in my recovery I went with Jack, my brother Chris and nephew Tom, to Shrewsbury's FA Cup Fifth Round tie with Manchester United – the first time the teams had ever met – and although United cruised to a 3-0 win it was a great occasion for my home-town club. We had been fortunate that as FA Cup fever hit the town, the Cup itself had visited our indoor soft play centre, Little Rascals. I even managed to have a hold of the famous trophy myself, which was a thrill, even for a grown man, and helped keep my dream alive of doing it properly at Wembley one day.

I was also invited back to Shrewsbury's next home game against Rochdale, as the club wanted to show some recognition to the squad who got promoted from the Conference into the Football League 12 years previously. It was a real privilege to be invited back and to see some friendly old faces. We got a great reception when paraded on the pitch at half-time.

It wasn't just football, however, which filled some of the gaps during my time on the sidelines. I also managed to get along to the Manchester Arena with two of Wolves' goalkeepers Carl Ikeme and Aaron McCarey to see Carl Frampton fight Scott Quigg. I love boxing, and felt fortunate to be part of an incredible atmosphere which saw Frampton edge the fight on a points decision. Fair play to any boxer – the nerves and the expectation they feel must be immense. It is a sport I have always loved watching, admiring their skill and dedication, but that moment walking to the ring knowing the guy in the opposite corner wants nothing more than to knock you clean out must be terrifying.

As I moved into the second month of rehab I was still meeting all the relevant targets and milestones, which were being devised each week, and it was always a major boost and sense of satisfaction to get through them when we got to the Friday. It was in week five that I started doing a bit of gym work in my trainers and without the protective boot. Initially this was working on glute activation, helping work those bum muscles which help your hamstrings, lower back and other muscle groups not to become overloaded. I was a bit tentative about it at first which I guess was only natural, but by the end of the week I was doing all the drills without a care in the world. That felt like real progress.

When recovering from an injury, at first it feels impossible that you will ever move with the same freedom that you previously had but, as the weeks go by, you break down each barrier ahead of you and gradually the confidence flows back. You can't even imagine being able to put your foot down properly at first, but then you get back to being weight bearing and it's hard to remember the initial discomfort and awkwardness of putting on a trainer again.

I had also started swimming again by this time, in the outdoor pool at Nuffield Health Club near Wolverhampton, I'd really looked forward to that, felt mentally refreshed after an early morning swim, and was raring to get over to Compton to start the gym and rehab sessions.

Not long afterwards I was also able to start making use of another amazing piece of equipment Wolves have at their training ground: an Alter G Anti Gravity treadmill. In simple terms this is a treadmill which uses air pressure to create a state of anti-gravity, enabling you to reduce your body weight whilst walking or running. It really cuts down on recovery time because you can get back into walking or running without having to be fully weight bearing and I was able to gradually add the load to my foot until I was ready to run outdoors. I was doing three-minute intervals without any pain at all which was great news and a sign that all the different treatments and exercises were working really well.

So much so that it was agreed I should have a few days off, just to shut off for a bit and make sure I didn't push myself too hard and end up regretting it. It had been a very intense six weeks and I had been very strict mentally on what I was doing, so I agreed with Phil just to have four or five days off where I would still have a reduced programme to follow, but would be able to switch off and give my body a rest.

Six weeks down, and hopefully past halfway, if I was to return to fitness in good time for the end of the season. Yes it had been really hard work, but I was feeling good, and everyone was pleased with how it was all going. When I came back after the short break, I was very hopeful the progress would continue. If so, then my Euro 2016 dream was very much alive.

6

Luton to Wolves

'Change brings opportunity'
Nido Qubein

Having left Shrewsbury at the end of the 2006-07 season I had become a free agent, waiting for my next move, and there were a couple of possibilities on the table. One of them was with Peterborough, so I met with Darren Ferguson and Barry Fry, after which they made me an offer.

It was obvious that they were very ambitious and they knew where they wanted to go. I really felt they had a good chance of getting promoted, particularly with the coaching staff they had, their facilities, and the players they were talking about bringing in, but for me to have left Shrewsbury to join another team in League Two wasn't my first choice, unless of course there were no other options from higher up.

After my lads holiday in Cancun, I returned home and quickly met with my agent who had some promising news. Kevin Blackwell from Luton Town – who'd just been relegated from the Championship into League One – had been in contact. This sounded better. Upon arrival at the ground I met Kevin and some of the Board and straightaway it just felt right. It felt very similar to Shrewsbury in terms of the size of the club and the stadium, and the way Kevin was selling the club made me want to go there and play for him. He had John Carver with him – JC as we would call him – who was a highly regarded coach, and an assistant in Sam Ellis, who had a wealth of experience in football.

The contract was offered and negotiated and I signed a three-year deal a couple of weeks before pre-season. Unfortunately, for reasons beyond my control, it was only to be a relatively short stay but I genuinely enjoyed my time at Luton. I bought a house in Flitwick, just north of Luton, and was playing in League One, a step up in standard, and getting a game every week.

For me, working with Kevin Blackwell was fantastic. He was a really good manager and, moving away from home as a single lad, he looked after me and helped me to concentrate on my football. I was in a hotel for nine or ten weeks before moving into the house and he just helped make everything a lot easier for me – I owe him a lot for what he did for me at that time.

The squad at Luton was quite an experienced one and a lot of the lads there had families. I got friendly with the 'keeper, Dean Brill, who had his own house where he lived with a couple of his mates. I had a great life with plenty of spare time – before I had any other business interests outside of football like I do now – so a lot of the time was spent either on a computer or watching films and box sets and stuff like that, as well as family and friends coming to visit.

Most importantly, on the field, it was all going well. I played a lot of games, and scored a few goals, a lot of the time from playing just off the striker. Darren Currie, who I used to watch and admire playing for Shrewsbury when I was a fan, actually set me up for my first Luton goal. We also had Paul Furlong and Paul Peschisolido playing up front, Chris Coyne was our captain, and other good professionals like Steve Robinson, who has gone on to manage Oldham, Chris Perry and Don Hutchison, who had plenty of Premier League experience. There were a lot of people in there to learn from, and that was an opportunity I made the most of. Our main problem was that we had a notoriously good home record, but a bad away one, where we just couldn't find that consistency.

Unbeknown to us, and as so often happens in football, there was upheaval just around the corner when, in November 2007, word got out that Luton were in financial difficulties and may be forced into administration. I was probably more fortunate than some of the other lads in that I didn't really have any responsibilities at the time. I had a mortgage to pay but I was on my own and didn't really have anything else in terms of outgoings. Some of the other lads had families depending on them and, if something like that happened to me now, I know it would affect me far worse.

As the club's financial crisis hit, we were getting paid 50% of our wages, which hit a lot of the boys hard. I have to say the PFA were great in stepping in to help players who needed loans and other types of support, but as we got into December, results on the pitch were starting to suffer. I had never been through anything like that before and I suppose I was still quite young and carefree. 'This is a football club,' I thought. 'It will all get sorted.' Realistically, however, it might not have got sorted, and we might not have been paid our money. While the uncertainty didn't bother me or affect me on the pitch, I can imagine it might have done some of the other lads who had very different personal situations.

During this period of uncertainty players were informed that they could go and speak freely to other clubs and that any valuable assets – anyone worth any sort of money – would be sold. I didn't go out and speak to anyone but it was certainly well known that there was a free-for-all at Luton and players were available. If teams were interested they could come in and take their pick. As the New Year approached there was some newspaper talk about teams supposedly being interested in signing me, but it wasn't concrete enough to waste time thinking about. Then came the FA Cup Third Round tie against Liverpool. It was a really good performance by the boys at Kenilworth Road – we went 1-0 down to a Peter Crouch goal but equalised soon afterwards and ended up drawing the game 1-1. Personally I also had a good game.

I firmly believe that in football there are key games when, even if you don't realise it at the time, the way you play gives you opportunities that you were totally unaware of. Playing well at the right time can open doors and there is a lot of luck in football in that respect. That game was one of those occasions because, with all that was going on at Luton, there were a lot of people watching.

The Liverpool team boasted household names like Riise, Benayoun, Hyppiä, Babel, Kuyt and Jamie Carragher, whose shirt I got after the game. It was the first time I had come up against a Premier League team and players of that quality. Early in the game I had a one-on-one chance which was saved and then, for the goal, I hurled myself at a left wing cross and managed to put the 'keeper off to the extent that the ball hit Jon Arne Riise and went in. Not quite an assist but close enough for me.

After that game I suddenly had options on the table, and four or five teams who wanted to speak to me. One of the keenest was Nottingham Forest. Forest were in League One at the time, but obviously a really big club in that division, with players like Grant Holt and Nathan Tyson on the books, but I can still remember to this day the moment when my representative said that I would never guess who else had expressed an interest. As soon as he mentioned Wolves, that was it for me – if the deal could be done of course. Knowing Wolves were such a big club, that the move would give me the chance to move back to Shropshire, and my brother and a lot of my friends being Wolves fans ... it all felt perfect.

I spoke to Kevin Blackwell, who said a fee had been agreed with Wolves and it was now just about personal terms. He also asked me if I would play in the replay against Liverpool, and make the move afterwards. As good as it would have been to play at Anfield, the risk of getting injured just wasn't going to be worth it. Fortunately I have since had the chance to be part of two winning Wolves teams away at Liverpool – but obviously I didn't know that at the time.

The only other hesitation I had prior to the interest from Wolves was that Kevin had become a very sought after manager, and it might have been worth hanging fire just to see where he went. Having such a great relationship with him might have provided an opportunity at his new club. Eventually he went on to manage Sheffield United, a big club no doubt, but Wolves was just too big a draw for me for so many reasons.

With a deal agreed, and just personal terms to sort, I remember arriving and meeting Mick McCarthy for the first time. I did my medical in the morning while all the boys were training and then went upstairs to the boardroom at the training ground where you can see out onto the pitches and I watched the end of training. Then Mick came up to see me. He is such a familiar figure. Everyone knows who Mick is, but it still felt strange to be meeting him in the flesh. I felt a little bit star struck with everything – meeting Mick, the quality of the facilities, just being at a club like Wolves. It was amazing and I was having to pinch myself that this was about to happen.

We started talking contracts and this was the first occasion, of many, when I realised how hard a deal the Wolves Chief Executive Jez Moxey could drive. I pitched up thinking I was about to go into the Championship and start to earn some decent money, but when the first offer came I was chatting to my representative and thought – just based on the numbers – it wasn't even worth me moving! With the amount I was going to lose on the house, it wasn't going to be worth it, at least from a financial point of view. We continued to negotiate and thankfully agreed on a package but, from the football side, I was never going to need any persuading.

So, on January 14th, 2008, I signed on the dotted line and was now a Wolves player, with absolutely no idea of the ups and downs that such a move was going to have on me over the next decade or so. That was all for later. Going into my debut, it couldn't have got off to a better start.

The team had been on a really bad run, without a win in seven league games, and the day after I signed, I looked on as we lost 3-0 to Crystal Palace. Sylvan Ebanks-Blake had joined the day before me and was eligible to play so made his debut. He played just less than an hour if I remember correctly.

We lost the game but I vividly remember my feelings about Molineux. I had been to watch a game there before – when I was about 12 years old – but hadn't visited during the transfer talks before I signed, so a long time had passed. It was a feeling totally different to what I had been used to at Gay Meadow and Kenilworth Road. They were both great grounds, and I had loved playing there, but they were just that, grounds. As I walked towards Molineux I knew this was different, this was a stadium. There was an aura about the place and, once again, I was star struck. I was there with my parents, taking it all in and it was just incredible. I was watching the game from the Directors Box and, whilst the result wasn't great, I was mesmerised by it all. I couldn't wait to get out there and play.

I was back in on the Monday, ready for a full week's training ahead of the trip to Scunthorpe, trying to push myself into contention for a first team debut. On the Saturday morning we were having a pre-match walk around the grounds of the hotel, when Mick came up to me and told me I was starting. We were going to be playing 4-4-2 and I would be alongside Karl Henry in the centre of midfield. I didn't really know Karl nor indeed anyone in the squad, apart from Kevin

Foley, who had been at Luton for pre-season before joining Wolves a few months earlier, but it goes without saying I was delighted to be starting the game, and it turned into an absolute dream debut.

Given our bad run, an early goal was going to be just what the doctor ordered. I couldn't have dreamed the goal would actually come from me. We were only eight minutes in as the ball broke down the left and came inside to me. I scuffed a shot – I didn't catch it cleanly at all but somehow it squirmed underneath the 'keeper. We were 1-0 up, and I had scored on my debut, so quickly as well. I had a really good game that day and also set up Sylvan for the second goal. It was a big win for us, given the circumstances.

For the next few months, towards the end of that 2007-08 season, I really enjoyed my football. Seyi Olofinjana had been at the African Cup of Nations when I arrived, enabling me to cement a place in the team and play in the midfield alongside Karl. Unfortunately, I picked up a bit of an injury at Preston and so missed a few games at the end of the campaign. We did manage to put some results together to mount a play-off push in those final stages but missed out by goal difference, and just one goal at that.

The next season was going to be huge for me, to try and build on that initial promise and nail down a place in the team. Coming back in the summer I knew I was going to have to work really hard to force my way in. Some new signings had come in during the close season including another central midfielder in Dave Jones, a defender, Richard Stearman, and strikers Chris Iwelumo and Sam Vokes, who I had played with in Wales under-21s. I was really looking forward to the season and was determined to come back, enjoy my football and get in the team.

Imagine my thoughts then, as the first game of the season came, away to Plymouth, and I wasn't even in the squad! I kind of knew I wasn't going to be playing from the week's build-up when Mick had been working with a team featuring Dave Jones and Karl Henry, but I thought I'd be on the bench. Lumes (Iwelumo) and Vokesey weren't starting and I didn't think they would both be on the bench – as a midfielder I thought I had a chance. The squad was named before the match and when I wasn't in there I felt really gutted, utterly deflated. We drew 2-2. In the following league match, against Sheffield Wednesday, I was named on the bench, came on, and scored as we won 4-1. From there, for quite a few games, I was starting on the bench and coming on to play.

We got off to a roaring start. After that draw at Plymouth we were relentless and putting teams away for fun. It was one of the those situations where you couldn't have any qualms about not being in the starting XI. The boys were playing so well, and Jonah and Karl were doing a great job in the centre of midfield. At the start of the season we made no predictions about winning the league, there are so many good teams in the Championship that at the start of the season most would feel they have a chance of promotion. So to be flying so high early on was great.

As the season progressed, I started a few more games, either in central midfield or wide right, and by the end of the season I think I had been involved in every game in some capacity, apart from missing out on the first day, and being an unused sub in another. There was a spell after Christmas where we struggled to get results but, luckily, the teams up at the top with us couldn't get a run together either. I remember the back-to-back wins away at Crystal Palace and Sheffield Wednesday in March – both 1-0 – which were vitally important. I played in both of those games, which were really battling wins and were pivotal in getting us back on track.

Then we went into the Easter period when we beat Southampton at Molineux on Good Friday and Derby County away on Easter Monday. Two key victories – scoring six goals in the process – and then came a truly amazing day against Queens Park Rangers. The best game I have been involved in at Molineux – it was incredible. The atmosphere was electric, and the noise when Sylvan scored just after half-time was unforgettable. It was such a great game to be involved in. I had all my mates at the game, and my partner Emma, whom I'd met on a January evening out in Shrewsbury just before I joined Wolves.

We knew that a win against QPR would seal promotion, but as we also had two more games left there wasn't really a great deal of tension about it. We played well and I had an early shot and a header saved. Like many games that year, we never really looked uncomfortable. I suppose there was a little bit of anxiety about the place, just wanting to get that goal, get the job done, and it was goalless at half-time. Straight after the break, however, Andy Keogh made a tackle in the corner then ran in and laid the ball off for Sylvan to score. The five minutes or so after the goal is something I will never forget. The sheer level of the noise created by the fans was breathtaking. It was like an out-of-body experience! It was a joy to be out there and, from that moment on, we knew we were going to win the game.

The final whistle went and the fans came storming onto the pitch. I wasn't far from the tunnel so, while I did get mobbed, at least I didn't have too far to go. There were some great scenes in the dressing room after the game and then we went up to the Directors Box where we could see all the fans on the pitch singing *We Shall Not Be Moved* which had become the anthem of that season. Such happy scenes. An amazing day was followed by an fantastic night, as the players, staff and our friends all went out for a huge celebration.

The following week we headed to Barnsley, with the chance of becoming champions. It was a really scrappy game and they took the lead before Kyel Reid equalised for us, which sparked another pitch invasion as that point in our final away game was enough to seal the title. Another mad celebration was sparked when the final whistle blew at Oakwell. Wolves were not just promoted, but we were the league champions. Just when everyone else was happy and enjoying the moment I remember Mick coming into the dressing room fuming. Apparently one of the fans had jumped on his back and Mick had come close to giving him more than a piece of his mind!

We knew then that the final home game of the season against Doncaster would be a parade of sorts. A day we could all enjoy and then lift the Championship trophy at the end. For me it was a hugely significant personal achievement. I had been part of a Shrewsbury team which had gone back into the Football League via the play-offs, but to win the Championship with Wolves, at the age of 23, was something really special. In my first full season at the club as well. I also now had the chance to play in the Premier League. It was a progression I'd dreamt about all the way through my career. Initially it was, 'could I make an appearance in the Football League?' then, 'could I win an international cap?' and now, 'could I just play one game in the Premier League?' That would be amazing. It was now the next aim. The next rung on the ladder. All in all, it made for another enjoyable summer holiday before attentions quickly turned to getting ready for the new campaign. It was probably the most I have ever looked forward to a pre-season.

All of the boys in the Wolves squad felt we had a chance of playing in the Premier League. Some new signings had arrived, but it was clear that Mick was going to give all of us an opportunity. There was always that safety net as well. Obviously we all wanted it to work out for the club and individually we all wanted to prove ourselves in the Premier League, but equally, if it didn't happen, you could end up back in the Championship if it didn't quite work out.

For me, I just wanted to play in the Premier League, complete with the fanfare and the circus that comes with it! The media interest, the spotlight. Just being seen on *Match of the Day*. Incredible.

7

Back in the Game

'Patience, persistence and perspiration make an unbeatable combination for success'
Napoleon Hill

On returning to Compton to continue my rehabilitation after a few days away, it was back onto the Alter G Anti-Gravity treadmill. If I could get myself running at 90% of my body weight, then I would have ticked off the last bit of rehab before being allowed outside to run on the grass. The Holy Grail, and I achieved it.

At the same time I was also doing some plyometric work in the sandpit at the training ground – Costa Del Wolverhampton, eh? This felt really good as I was starting to load my foot in more multi-directional jumps and hops, although finishing the sessions with three sets of 30 seconds high knee running wasn't quite as much fun!

All of this meant that, on a Monday morning in March, I was able to get the boots back on, and get outside for a run on the grass, which is always a huge milestone during such a lengthy recovery process. I had already been for an early morning swim before the session of four sets of four minute runs at jogging pace, with some early stage agility and ball work in between.

I did feel apprehensive, but just to be running outside in a pair of boots again felt incredible. From there things gradually built up and by the end of the week I was doing some slalom runs over 80 metres, loading more through the outside of my foot and at about 80% of my maximum pace. The agility work was also becoming more intense, and I was picking up speed through different ladder and hurdle drills and, with that, the ball work was also increasing.

All the signs were good, and mentally it was all positive as well. Through the highs of the outdoor rehab, the medical staff were all still working really hard with me in the gym and treatment room. Balance and proprioception work, upper and lower body conditioning sessions, high intensity interval training, the sand pit plyometric sessions, and still the early morning swims. I'd actually got to the stage of doing 50 lengths straight off – 1000 metres – in less than 20 minutes, perhaps raising hopes of a new career as a triathlete!

It's key for footballers to have other interests and activities to stay mentally stimulated during a period of inactivity such as an injury. During this spell on the sidelines I was also delighted to be able to get involved in some media work, an industry which really interests me. First up came my debut in the Molineux press box to commentate on the Wolves against Birmingham game alongside commentator Mikey Burrows and a former team-mate in Matt Murray. It was a typically tight derby game, very enjoyable to watch but it felt very different to be in the top tier of the Billy Wright Stand rather than in the dugout. It looks a lot easier from up there, like you have so much more space and time than the reality on the pitch in the thick of it all. It does give you the opportunity to accurately see what is happening, tactically, and I really enjoyed giving my thoughts and opinions on the game.

I was also a guest of BBC Wales for their coverage of Wales' fixture against Northern Ireland which was another great chance to pick up some more media experience. I joined presenter Jason Mohammed and former Wales assistant manager Kit Symons on the show, which was really exciting, albeit nerve-racking, knowing it was all going out live. Everyone involved made it really comfortable for me, and we were on air for the build-up, at half-time and then again at full-time. I would much rather have been out on the pitch representing my country but it was really enjoyable and time absolutely flew by. The game wasn't the best, it has to be said, but Wales fought back well to get a draw against a tough and resolute Northern Ireland side.

On top of that I joined former England midfielder Steve Hodge, also more recently a coach at Wolves, on Talksport 2's *Up The League* programme with presenter Geoff Peters, and I was a guest on the

BACK IN THE GAME

Saturday Sport Show on *Sky News*, discussing the international programme which involved travelling to the Sky Studios. From the moment I arrived, the whole place was really impressive. Being a genuine sports fan I was chuffed to discover that the show would be aired in the Sky Sports studios and even more so when the producer took me on a tour and I was able to see the Sky Sports News set as well. It was huge, and there was so much going on.

I met the presenter Arron Armstrong and chatted about the show, and even got to go through make-up! Having someone apply foundation and anti-shine to my skin was certainly a new experience, but after the initial shock wore off, I began to see the miracle of what make-up can do. I looked about five years younger and more like that young and carefree person before the dark eyes and sleepless nights that my children have given me. Not that I would change that for all the world, but when the make-up artist offered me some wipes to clean it all off after the show I said, "No way". I wanted to show Emma my new eyes!

I really enjoyed all of these different experiences and it showed me how talented all the presenters and staff are who work on these shows. The amount of work that goes into the broadcasts is incredible, and it's not just about the voice, the presenting and the interviews but also managing the timing and content and messages from colleagues. Hugely impressive stuff. A great experience.

Nevertheless, my main focus was on my recovery and, as I closed in towards being able to join in with full training again, came the dreaded Conditioning Week. When I say dreaded, that is very much tongue in cheek, because it is still much better than being in the gym or treatment room. It is also positive as it suggests a return to full training is just around the corner. Conditioning Week also meant that I knew my legs and lungs would be screaming out in discomfort every single day. There had been a real mix during the sessions to make sure I was working hard in every aspect of my recovery, from short and sharp multi-directional sprints with little rest, to longer repeated runs of over 100 metres. At the end of every session I was at the stage of near physical exhaustion and there is never any hiding place, as a GPS system and heart rate monitor tracks every movement.

These systems have become very important to football clubs as they allow staff to accurately measure everything that each player is doing during training and matches. From there, all of the data collected can be used to modify training sessions to ensure the optimum amount of physical work and recovery time is programmed in. It was a really important tool for me, having suffered a foot injury, as it meant my loads could be monitored live throughout sessions, so when I hit the targets set for me by the medical, strength and conditioning departments, I could finish the session without the risk of being overloaded.

Along with all of this was the continued preparation I did before every training session, including post-training recovery work with Phil Hayward and Matt Wignall. I'd also do my own warm-up in the gym for 20 minutes or so before the squad did the team preparation. It was a routine I'd been doing for a few years, involving different dynamic movements and stretches to make sure my body was completely ready to go into the warm up. Since starting this routine, and along with my post-training routine, I've been able to avoid any serious muscular injuries.

Conditioning Week went well, and prepared me for the more specific football work ahead, that final step before returning to full training. By now it was week 10 of the rehabilitation, and I was working on football-specific drills with Phil to make sure my foot would be able to deal with the different exertions that the movement patterns playing football would expose it to. Thankfully, I came through that without any issues and also joined in with the first team for a bit of non- contact work and some passing drills. By now I was desperate to rejoin full training.

First, though, came a CT scan at the 10-week stage, which had always been on the agenda. Just to make sure the bone was healing well and that the screw in my fifth metatarsal was still in a good position. I was 99.9% sure everything would be ok, as the rehabilitation had gone so well without any pain, but it was still a massive relief when the radiographer and surgeon both came back with positive reports and gave me the all-clear to return to full training. Even better was having the surgeon tell me it looked like I was 14 to 16 weeks post surgery rather than 10. That just confirmed to me that all the sacrifices I had made and the dedication shown over the 10 weeks had all been worth it.

BACK IN THE GAME

There were many other factors involved in why it all went so well. For starters, the medical and sports science staff at Wolves, who were excellent, and all the work they took me through in the gym and treatment room. They went above and beyond to make sure I returned in the best, possible condition. My nutrition programme was also vital, as I think my food choices played a big part. Also all the anti-inflammatory processes of elevating my leg at every opportunity, massage and all the icing and compression through the Game Ready machine. I calculated that in the 10 weeks since the operation I had used the Game Ready 250 times, amounting to 84 hours, which is three-and-a-half days! No wonder I had no pain in my foot, it had probably been numb! It was certainly a positive recovery programme as, apart from the first 24 hours following surgery, I hadn't taken one tablet or painkiller, which is quite incredible when you think about it.

So I finally I got back into full training – a great feeling. I first joined in on a Friday, and then over the weekend, building up the intensity each time. Thankfully, there was no pain in my foot, and no hesitancy, whether in striking the ball, sprinting full out, closing people down, or going into tackles. The following Monday I was included in the travelling squad for the trip to MK Dons the next day – another big breakthrough. I love the matchday routine, and the chance to be back in the dressing room helping the boys to prepare for a game was something I had been longing for during the previous two months.

Even better, I was named on the bench and, better still, got the call to go on, with us 2-1 ahead and just five minutes to go. Normally that can be quite a difficult situation for a substitute as there isn't really anything to be gained, only something to lose. Of course, for me, it was fantastic and I was dreaming of returning with a goal. I managed to get one touch, a headed flick-on to Adam Le Fondre, so I was claiming a 100% pass completion rate! Joking aside, it was great to be back out there, and an incredible feeling coming just 73 days after leaving the Loftus Road pitch in agony with a fractured metatarsal. It was also my 250th appearance for Wolves which is another landmark of which I was extremely proud.

With over a month of the season remaining, I was back in action, with the chance to stake a claim for the Welsh squad and remind Chris

Coleman that I was there – ready, willing and able. I managed to make four starts, including scoring a goal at Hull, and another appearance off the bench. I felt good and I felt fresh. It had been hard work getting back, but mentally and physically I was in really good shape. I had given it everything, and now it was pretty much a waiting game to see if I would make it onto that plane.

8

The Premier League

'Keep your eyes on the stars and feet on the ground'
Theodore Roosevelt

Preparations for the start of my first Premier League season with Wolves in 2009-10 included a pre-season tour of Australia – ever so slightly different to Scotland the previous year. We spent just under two weeks in Perth, which was amazing. I had never been to Australia before and it was their winter so it wasn't too hot. A lot of the tour was spent training or in the hotel but we still managed to get out and see parts of the country.

Perth was beautiful and we trained at the WACA, which, as a cricket fan, was particularly special for me. We went up against some of the Western Australia players in a practice match, and that is when you realise how good some of these guys are. We also had a go on the indoor bowling machine. We stood behind it to start off with and they set it to the speed that Brett Lee bowls at, something in the region of 95 miles per hour. It was frightening. You couldn't even see the ball. Clearly we couldn't try it at that pace so they slowed it down to 55 miles per hour, the speed which Shane Warne bowls at. When you watch his leg spin on the television you think, 'it's not that quick!' Well, I didn't see the first three balls, and they were bowled straight. With Shane Warne drifting it and turning it and doing all sorts of things with the ball, facing him must have been very tough.

Amidst all the other experiences we were enjoying, the training was still really hard work. It was the toughest pre-season I'd ever had. Tony Daley and Steve Kemp were in charge of the fitness side and insisted we did some runs in Kings Park. They were adamant they'd done these runs before and so we should all be able to do them. As soon as we started to give it a go, none of us could believe they had done it in the times they'd claimed. I'm quite a fit boy, but it was horrible. It was a 600 metre run, gradually uphill. You had to run it in a certain time, jog back down in a certain time, and then run back up again. There were six of them, one after another and no one was getting back down in time to start again. After the third run, all the boys started claiming it was an impossible challenge. It was quite a warm day, and players started throwing up and getting quite ill.

We had been split into groups with the better runners in the final group. George Friend was the fittest, and then I was probably after him in the fastest group. I remember on the third run up the hill, looking to the side to see Bobo Balde – the big defender who was out with us on trial – sitting with his back against a tree, head in between his knees, pouring with sweat – he looked so ill! Needless to say he didn't get a contract. I can't imagine he was overly disappointed after that sort of initiation.

I think the session was eventually cut to four runs but every player who was on that trip will tell you they have never run as hard before, or probably since. We had been doing repetitive 800 metre runs at Compton before we left, and the targeted time was getting lower and lower, and the rest time in between also getting shorter and shorter. We all used to hate it. At the WACA Tony had measured out 800 metres, which was just over two laps of the outfield and none of us could understand why we couldn't finish below the targeted time. It had been hard at Compton, but we had been making it, yet now, in Australia, we were nowhere near. We were pushing each other harder and harder but making no real progress, so we assumed it must have been our tiredness from the training or the weather. We couldn't work it out. The run was being rotated with an attacking and defending session, and it was certainly taking it out of us.

Finally, I remember we spotted one of measuring wheel devices and one of the boys went out and measured the track. It was 870 metres! Everyone was raging! It was an accident and wasn't deliberate, Tony had just made a mistake, but you can imagine the reaction from the boys.

Mick McCarthy just wanted us to be as fit as we possibly could be and who can fault that? I remember seeing a Sean Dyche interview when Burnley returned into the Premier League and he commented that his team could not be technically better than some of their opponents such as Arsenal, but there were areas where they could be superior – like fitness. We were certainly fit when we came back from Australia. It was really tough, but very worthwhile in preparing us for the start of the season.

The first game was against West Ham and I was on the bench. It was disappointing, and we lost 2-0, but I got on with ten minutes to go. We had made all three changes, and then Sylvan got injured, leaving us down to ten men. We lost, but the atmosphere that day was immense. Wolves were back in the Premier League. For me, it was another massive achievement. I had played in the Premier League. No one could ever take that away from me.

Despite the loss, it got better. I started the next game at Wigan, when Andy Keogh scored a header in the first 10 minutes and we won 1-0, the first time Wolves had ever won an away match in the Premier League. It was an amazing night, and this Premier League life all seemed like a fairytale. In the first three or four months in the Premier League I was playing every week, and absolutely loving my football.

I was playing wide right for most of the time. In the Premier League, if we were going to play two strikers, up against some of the quality we were facing, you couldn't play two wingers. I know that's what fans want to see – two strikers, two wingers, going full out – but in that league, in any league, it is difficult. We'd done it in the Championship when we got promoted but there was no chance we were going to be able to do it against the superior quality in the Premier League.

It was clear that I was the one who was going to have to tuck in and do that defensive job on the right, make sure the full backs didn't get out and also to be that third central midfielder – not to mention creating some width when we did have the ball. I was never going to be one who would jink past people but I could get wide and get crosses in and also then drift into the box for anything coming over from the left.

I was really enjoying it, and I got a goal early in the season against Fulham in a game we won 2-1. We were on the break and Keogh cut it back to me just inside the box and I struck it into the top corner. Scoring in the Premier League – another thing to tick off the list. A fantastic experience to win that game as well and another special personal moment.

Everything was going swimmingly well up until we played Tottenham away from home. They had won their previous home game 9-1 against Wigan, but Kevin Doyle scored early on for us and we were 1-0 up. Things were going well with an hour or so gone. Then, Benoit Assou-Ekotto – their left back – got the ball, cut inside into the centre of the pitch and did a big chop back onto his left foot. Sold me completely, and as I tried to change direction, my foot just collapsed completely from underneath me. There was a really sharp pain through my ankle and pins and needles shooting right through my leg. At first I thought I'd broken it.

Steve Kemp came on and did his initial assessment. It didn't appear that anything was broken but I couldn't put weight on it and it was clear I was going to have to come off. I went into the changing room and Kempy thought it was something called a syndesmosis – there is a ligament which goes across your ankle between your fibula and your tibia and he thought that was the injury. He told me that if I pressed my ankle, and felt an excruciating pain, then that would be it. He did it, and I had never felt pain like it. Horrendous, and it backed up the initial prognosis that I had either sprained or torn my syndesmosis, or maybe even snapped it.

When I was young, an injury didn't feel like the end of the world to me. Obviously I wanted to play football but it was more a case of 'I'm injured, I'm out, but I'm going to get back quickly and I'll be fine'. That one, however, was the first really bad injury I'd suffered in my career. We got the scans back and it confirmed that I had snapped the ligament and was going to be out for about 12 weeks. I also had to undergo surgery to have some wire put across my ankle. It was disappointing, because I'd been in the team and felt I was doing well. Andy Keogh had been out with a problem with his ankle so we were re-habbing together at the time, along with Michael Kightly. I was back in 12 weeks but my ankle was still really sore. I'd come back into training a couple of weeks earlier and it clearly wasn't quite right to the extent that it kept me out for a bit longer, but I did make it back for the last six or seven weeks of the season by which point I'd made 16 starts that season which was great, but my contract – signed at the start of the season – had a clause stating that if I made 20 starts

THE PREMIER LEAGUE

I'd get an increase in my wages. As I returned to fitness I was sure I had a chance of hitting that 20-start target. In my first game back, at Arsenal, I came off the bench when Karl Henry was sent off and we agonisingly lost in the very last minute. Karl was then suspended for three games and I started all of them. We drew a couple, 0-0 against Fulham and Stoke, and then also drew 1-1 against Blackburn – a result that ultimately kept us in the division.

However, I still needed one more start to make it to 20 but, in the last two games against Portsmouth and Sunderland, Karl was back in and I was a sub both times, leaving me on 19 starts. The bonus payment I'd have received was minimal to the club and it wouldn't have been a reason for Mick not to start me. I doubt he even knew and, even if he did, it wouldn't have made any difference. He was always going to pick the team he felt had the best chance of a result. So, I missed out by one, but it didn't matter all that much. I was buzzing with how we had done in securing our Premier League status.

It was an amazing achievement to stay up and be in there for another year. It's the only place you really want to be, and to do it with a couple of games to spare, in our situation at that time, it felt we'd done it quite comfortably. It had been a good season and now I was back feeling healthy and feeling ready for a second go at the Premier League.

We went into that 2010-11 campaign full of optimism, like we had something to build on. A few players came in, including Steven Fletcher, who was a big signing, and Stephen Hunt, who was coming back to fitness at the time but added a lot of experience to the dressing room. Everyone was confident we could have another good season.

We started fairly well, beating Stoke on the first day, and then getting draws against Everton and Newcastle, but from there we started to struggle and we went on a bad run. We lost a fair few games and had gone a while without winning before welcoming Manchester City to Molineux at the end of October. The money had arrived at City – they had Roberto Mancini in charge and some top players in the team like Silva, the Toures, Balotelli and Adebayor.

It was a game that turned into a real career highlight for me, because here I was, coming up against goalkeeper Joe Hart, a good friend of mine from those Shrewsbury days. I'd played against him when he was at Birmingham but this was the first time against

City. We went a goal down, to an Adebayor penalty, before Nenad Milijaš equalised with a low shot into the bottom corner. We were playing really well, especially given the pressure we were under because of the run we'd been on and our position in the table.

My big moment arrived just before the hour mark, when the ball broke down the right and Kevin Foley lifted a cross in. Kevin Doyle went up for a challenge and I was there, ready to pounce. Yaya Toure is a fantastic player, but on that day he didn't seem too interested in tracking back and I'd managed to get away from him. The ball landed just in front of me and I sent Joe the wrong way with the finish.

What a feeling! I can still picture the scene of me and Matt Jarvis running off to celebrate the goal – which proved to be the winner – in front of the North Bank. I remember Joe coming up to me at full-time and congratulating me, it was all fairly light hearted. I think he was saying that if they had to lose, and if anyone was going to get the winner, it didn't hurt him so much that it was me! It was a great day, one of the best of my career.

We were in the middle of a crazy spell of fixtures at this point. Before the City game we had lost 3-2 to Manchester United in the Carling Cup and then 2-0 at Chelsea in the league. Then it was back to Old Trafford, and Arsenal at home.

The league game at Manchester United is another I don't think any of us will forget, but for very different emotions to the win against City. United made a few changes, and we were always in the game. Park Ji-Sung had put them in front and then – just after the hour – we made a double substitution, with myself and Hunty making way for Sylvan Ebanks-Blake and Steven Fletcher. Within a couple of minutes Sylvan, back at the club where he'd started his career, had equalised. It looked like we were heading for a really good draw, and to have taken four points off the two Manchester clubs would have been massive for us at that time. Then Steven Fletcher lost the ball on the halfway line, United summoned one more attack, and Park Ji-Sung scored his second of the game, in the 93rd minute.

Mick McCarthy was furious. He went berserk in the dressing room and it was one of those occasions where I felt a bit sorry for Fletch. I know how difficult it can be, trying to keep possession in the closing stages at Old Trafford. They still had a lot to do to score from the position where he'd lost the ball, but we all understood why Mick was so angry. It was the same frustration that all of us were going through – we had been so, so close to getting a point, and emotions were running high. Mick was telling us we had to manage the game better and that you couldn't yield possession like that in the 93rd minute at Old Trafford.

No one said anything – you learned not to say anything back to Mick when he was in full flow. The only time I ever saw anyone try was Gary Breen in my first season, after a game at Molineux. He said something back and it got quite heated. Mick didn't actually lose his temper all that often, most of the time he was very controlled, but when he did, you soon knew about it. It happened once with me, about the time of those games, just as winter was approaching. Mick was always a stickler for what he called housekeeping, and had this great ability to spot when standards were slipping, even slightly, at the training ground. Whether it be timekeeping, or people leaving their kit around the place he would soon be onto it. He always stressed the need to show respect for the club and our teammates.

These housekeeping lapses always seemed to coincide with us hitting a poor run of form so Mick would call a meeting to remind us of the rules, with a 'right lads, this is how it is' session. One evening we got a text from Mick's PA, Fay, telling us to be in at 9am the following morning for a housekeeping meeting, but because of the congestion around the training ground at that time in the morning we all knew we needed to be in for 8.15 just to be completely sure. Well, that was my plan.

Our goalkeeper Wayne Hennessey, couldn't drive so I'd often pick him up from Telford on my way in from Shrewsbury, and this particular housekeeping meeting was one of those occasions. We were slightly ahead of schedule and, after I picked him up, we ended up getting stuck in Telford, in heavy early morning traffic. The pressure was now on and we wanted to ensure that we weren't going to be late – the players would always speculate as to who would miss the start of meeting and incur Mick's wrath – but the longer the hold-up went on, the more it looked like we were going to be struggling to beat the clock. Having come off the M54 and onto the A41, I was starting to panic, contemplating trying to overtake people at traffic lights and all sorts.

The clock was ticking and, as I expected, there was a big queue of traffic heading for the local schools by the training ground. It was now 8.45am and Wayne and I were looking nervously at each other. We were very close to just dumping the car in a shop car park and running the last bit into training – probably a mile and a half! – but we kept our cool, the queue gradually moved and we turned into the training complex, flying over the speed humps, with the clock at 9.02am and raced into the building.

I knew we were in trouble, and it was also November – or naughty November – when, whatever the misdemeanour, fines were doubled. Mick was in the reception as we raced past but we didn't say "sorry we're late" or anything like that as we still thought we just might have made it in time. We sat down very sheepishly and looked around to see pretty much everyone else in their training kit, having obviously been in very early and ready to go. Kevin Doyle was in the same situation as us, and said he'd only been there a couple of minutes. I felt a bit bad for Wayne, as I was the one picking him up, but not that bad, as if I hadn't had to pick him up I'd never had got stuck in Telford. A real *Catch 22*!

Then, a big sigh of relief as five minutes later Nenad Milijaš walked in. At least we weren't the last. Mick was still in reception, waiting. I then caught sight of our defender Ronald Zubar, sat at the back of the room, with his brand new sparkly trainers absolutely covered in mud! He'd made the dash across the fields from the same queue we'd been in. That was the sort of impact Mick could have on a player!

Mick came in and, although he wasn't exactly angry, he told us in no uncertain terms, "You can't be like this, people being late, this is the housekeeping I am talking about." I just sat there thinking, 'Please don't look at me, please don't speak to me!' as he continued: "This is going to cost you as well – how much is it for being late?"

"It's 250 quid, gaffer," someone replied.

"Well that's 500 quid then isn't it?" said Mick.

For pity's sake – or something much stronger – I was thinking. This was seriously going to cost me, and Wayne as well. I felt horrendous. There were three or four of us who were late and we were going to cop it. That was a seriously expensive couple of minutes. Shortly afterwards Mick collared me directly. I thought it was all over and done with and had got changed for training when I saw Mick talking to Nenad. He looked in my direction and shouted, "And you, you knob." I glanced around. Was he talking to me? Yes. Yes he was. Mick McCarthy had just called me a knob. "What's your excuse then?" he barked. "You must have an excuse for being late. What is it?"

"No excuse," I replied. "I thought I'd left enough time to get here but I got stuck in traffic. No excuses."

"I can't believe it," he said. "You're back in the team, you're doing well, and then you go and do this!" With one or two expletives thrown in for good measure. 'Oh no,' I thought. Please don't let me get dropped on Saturday for this! He didn't drop me. It was just him setting his standards.

I have to say that was the only time I had a disagreement with Mick, or when he had a go at me off the field. Although he has that fierce reputation, for the majority of the time he was very controlled and measured. Honest, yes, and he got his point across, but he was fair and it would always be forgotten about once he'd had his say. For me, that day was as bad as it got – particularly as I've always been such a stickler for being on time - but it cost me 500 quid before Christmas.

During that season I was starting to pick up some niggles, one or two groin injuries, and was getting really frustrated as I missed a few games. Playing a midweek game against Arsenal, on a freezing cold night, I cleared the ball in the early stages and felt a twinge in my quad, and had to come off. It turned out to be a tear which kept me out for the best part of a month. I was back in the team for the derby game against Birmingham, which we won 1-0, but then found myself in and out of the team over the Christmas period which was very frustrating. One notable highlight was when I came off the bench towards the end of our 1-0 win against Liverpool at Anfield. That was an amazing night, with Stephen Ward grabbing the goal. We were down there and in trouble but just kept nicking results at exactly the right time to stay in the fight.

The same thing happened at home to Chelsea at the start of January, just after we'd lost at West Ham. We went 4-4-2, brave as anything, with me and Kev Foley in the centre of midfield. We worked so hard that night after taking the lead, following an own goal from Jose Bosingwa from Stephen Hunt's corner, and we held on to get the win. We then faced Doncaster in an FA Cup tie a few days later but my legs were knackered after the Chelsea game after all the chasing back and covering. On the Friday before the game, the gaffer spoke to me and said he wanted to keep the team reasonably similar and would I be able to go again? "Yes. Yes, I'm fine," was my reply. Of course you always want to play. Even though my hamstrings were screaming.

I started the game really well but then, after about half an hour, my hamstrings really started to tighten up, so I came off again. Another niggle. I was having so many of them now and just didn't know what was causing it. The harder I was working to try and stop it, the worse it seemed to be getting.

I was in and out of the team after that but played as a number ten in the game at Bolton in February, a game which turned out to be another where Mick wasn't best pleased at full-time. Despite some of the fantastic results we'd enjoyed, beating the likes of Manchester City, Liverpool and Chelsea, we were still bottom of the league. Being in touch with a fair few of the teams above us kept our spirits up and we kept battling away. I started against Bolton but came off after 75 minutes, with Jamie O'Hara – who'd arrived on loan from Spurs at the end of the window – coming on for his debut. We had done ok, Wayne Hennessey had made some great saves, and it would have been a decent point against a team in the top half.

The game was now into injury time and we had a throw-in just inside our half. Zubey, instead of throwing it down the line, threw it into Karl Henry, which put him right under pressure. Karl actually did really well to get it back to him, but then Zubey looked to pass it straight back to Wayne, but sold him short. Too short. Daniel Sturridge nipped in and scored in what was the third minute of injury time. Game over. What a disaster.

The flipchart, with all the pre-match tactics, was still up in the changing room when Mick appeared. It didn't stay standing for long. He volleyed it across the room while screaming at Zubey. He was more angry with the throw-in than the back pass and questioned why on earth Zubey would do that. Zubey didn't say anything. He knew what he'd done and was devastated. A lot of the time Mick wouldn't say too much after a game and wouldn't be too analytical. He would normally watch the game the next day and then give the team his thoughts, but this occasion was different. It was such a hammer blow.

We had Manchester United at home in the next game and, Mick being Mick, he picked Zubey. Showed his faith in him. Zubey then repaid that show of confidence, had a great game and we won. United hadn't lost all season and were on a 29-match unbeaten run. Not anymore! We beat them 2-1, with goals from George Elokobi and Kevin Doyle, although George tried to claim both. I probably wouldn't have argued with Big George to be fair.

I wasn't involved in that game. I was on the bench but didn't get on. Jamie had come in and he started. Another of the good things about Mick and his man management was that if he knew that you weren't playing, he would always pull you over on the Friday to tell you and explain his reasons. That being the case, on a Friday morning you never wanted his assistant TC (Terry Connor) to come and find you and say the gaffer wanted to see you. Everyone knew what that meant.

On this occasion he hadn't said anything to me. We all went out and trained as normal and were just about to do some set pieces at the end when Mick called me over. He told me I wasn't playing and I'd be on the bench. That hacked me off. For one, it was Manchester United at home, but more so because I was only being told now. I just felt that if Mick was leaving Kevin Doyle out, or Sylvan, or players like that, there was not a chance he would leave it until right at the end of training to tell them. Because I was a quieter character than others, and still quite young at this point, I just wondered if Mick thought he could get away with it. I was furious but didn't say anything at the time. I felt I had to stand up for myself and say it was wrong he hadn't told me earlier, especially as Mick was generally always so fair with everyone.

It felt wrong, so I went to speak with him after training to make my point and to say that if it had been anyone else, there is no way he would have left it so late.

Fair play. He was genuinely apologetic – you could always have a really honest conversation with Mick – and he assured me that he didn't see me like that, as the 'easy' one to leave out. It was purely what he believed in terms of the best team for the game. I think he accepted he got that wrong and it was great that I could speak with him like that, as Mick always preferred people to tell him what they were thinking. That was one of the rare occasions I probably stood up for myself in that way.

In terms of the game itself, there was a reason I didn't get on. In the half-time warm-up I went to whip a ball and I just felt my groin go. Yet another niggling injury to add to the list. A groin earlier in the season, a hamstring, a quad, a groin again. It just kept happening to me. Then came the usual dilemma. Do I shut up, sit on the bench, and then come on if I'm asked. I couldn't do it. We were winning 2-1, and it was a huge game. As always the team has to come first. We knew Jamie wasn't going to last all game, but if I came on after an hour and broke down it would be to the detriment of the team as well as my own fitness. So I told the physios, and didn't come on. When Jamie came off it, was Kevin Foley who went on in his place as we picked up a famous result, still while occupying bottom spot in the league.

That injury kept me out for another three weeks but, when I came back for the Blackpool game, it was probably my best performance of the season. We started very strongly, with myself and Jamie playing more advanced roles in front of Karl Henry, and supporting Kevin Doyle. We were all over them. We were 1-0 up just before half-time when a cross came in from the left and popped up just in front of me. I volleyed it with my left foot but Richard Kingson made a good save in the Blackpool goal. Not scoring was bad enough, but I felt a massive pain shoot through my back. 'Get through to half-time, get some treatment and then I'll be ok,' I thought to myself.

With all the niggles I'd suffered that season, this was the first time I'd felt real pain in my back. My intention was to loosen it up at half-time and then give it five or ten minutes of the second half to see how things went, but by the time I was out for the second half I could barely move – it had seized up. I had to come off, which was a huge disappointment as we'd played so well, and went on to win the game 4-0.

The Wolves physios said the left side of my back appeared to be having a spasm and all the muscles had contracted to protect it. We'd just have to wait until it had settled down before they could properly assess what was going on. I was given some tablets – muscle relaxants – to take that evening and hopefully get a good night's sleep, but I woke up on the Sunday morning, and could hardly get out of bed. I was in absolute agony. I'd never felt a debilitating pain like it. Every little movement was excruciating, with shooting pains up the side of my back.

Mick came to see me early the following week. Tottenham were our next opponents, and he said if I could get back into training on the

Friday, the day before the game, I'd be fine. He was impressed with how I was playing and obviously I was really motivated to get right and be fit. You don't want to miss any games when you feel you're doing well, especially the big games in the Premier League. There are so many times in your career when you play at only 90%, even 80%, of full fitness, and just make sure you get through games.

To have a chance I needed to be outside and running on the Thursday, so I did absolutely nothing for the first few days of the week and just rested to give myself the best possible opportunity. My back was still really sore, but I was desperate to give it a go. On the Thursday I tried to do some strides but it was complete agony. I could barely move. I knew now there was something seriously wrong.

It was obvious I wasn't going to be fit and, as my back wasn't settling down and improving with the treatment, I went for a scan, which showed a stress fracture. It was between vertebrae L4 and L5 in my lower back on the left hand side. The disc below had degenerated and caused the two bones to collide. They must have been wearing away gradually, with the impact of my awkward body position whilst volleying against Blackpool shutting the joint down completely and causing the crack. As soon as someone tells you that you've broken your back – in any sort of physical sport – you have to be hugely concerned and I began to wonder what was going to happen next.

Well, I can only describe it as the hardest seven or eight months of my entire life. Honestly, it was horrendous. I know all things are relative, and people in life have to go through far worse things than a football injury but, as a relatively young guy hoping for many more years in football, this was as bad as it could get. The stuff I went through to try and get things right, with no timescale set for recovery as we didn't know if a recovery was possible, was huge. Because of the nature of the injury it was impossible to predict what was going to happen, which was something I found hard to comprehend. It was tough not having a target to aim for or work towards.

I went to see specialists who told me to just rest it for a month and see how it felt, that surgery was an option, but a very tricky option and one that was to be avoided at all costs if that was possible. So it was a case of resting the back and just working on my core. Pretty much every day! I'd go back to see them and they'd ask how it was feeling. "Yes, it's ok, a little bit better," I would say, and then I'd try and do a little bit more work, feel the pain straightaway, and resume the resting for another month. That's exactly how it went for the first three or four months. It was horrible. Mentally I was all over the place. I was really struggling.

My physical condition now began to affect my mental wellbeing and I started to feel really low. Steve Kemp, an absolutely top physio who has since gone on to work with the England senior team, was taking me through the rehab, but during this period I just didn't want to be around the place. It is always hard to come in when you are injured and see the boys training and going about their business, but when you know what your injury is, and how long it is going to take to get back, it's bearable, and you can use it as a motivation. The nature of my injury, however, meant I had no timescale and no targets. I was coming in and doing my core work, and that was hurting. I couldn't see any improvements. I have never been one to avoid rehab and when I know what I need to do I'll work as hard as anyone to get back. Yet, at this point, I just wanted to go on holiday, to get away. I was struggling and, to be honest, I was depressed.

My little boy, Jack, had been born in the previous July, so he was now at the stage when he was crawling around, but it was simply impossible for me to play with him at all. He'd be playing on the floor and I'd be sat in a chair. Emma would pass him to me so I could hold him, but that was about it. Once he became fidgety, I had to hand him back. My family life has always been great and I've been very fortunate in that respect but rather than enjoying the first year of Jack's life, I was in complete agony. I couldn't even play with my son and share those special early moments, which added to my general feeling of depression.

In terms of football, I didn't want to be anywhere near a pitch. I couldn't see my injury getting be tter. I was in my mid-twenties, and was seriously wondering if I would ever play football again. By this point I knew this was the cause of all the other injuries I'd been picking up. The imbalance in my spine had caused me to overload in all manner of different areas, creating other problems, yet it was still proving difficult to get to the root cause of why the recovery was so slow. There was no sign of any improvement. The fracture was healing, but it was still so sore and tender.

An international week appeared on the horizon, and Mick gave the lads Friday, Saturday and Sunday off. I thought I would get the same, which would give me the chance to get a couple of days away to feel refreshed, but I had just been allocated the Sunday. When I was told I remember just welling up. I was hating being in, and now I wasn't even going to get these couple of days off, so I went to see Mick and told him my head was all over the place – that I was really struggling with it all and just needed some time off. Mick was as good as gold and spoke to the medical department. He told me to make sure I did what I needed to do with my rehab while I was away, but that I should get off and get my head right. He was always really good in that respect.

At this time every single treatment I was getting was just making me feel sore. I knew the medical staff wouldn't have thought this, but I was struggling so much with my mental state that I was convinced they believed I was faking the pain. I was being asked to do basic stuff but I just couldn't do it because my back was so sore. My mind was telling me they just wanted to say, 'C'mon, man up', even though that was patently not the situation. I ended up feeling bad for the physios as well as me because we just weren't making any progress. Sometimes I'd really push myself but then wake up the next day in absolute agony. It was getting to the stage where, once again, only complete rest was seemingly the answer.

After Mick had agreed to my weekend off I went straight home and said to Emma that we needed to get away. We rushed through a passport for Jack and flew to Dubai and stayed there for four nights. It was the first time I had ever been to Dubai – I just wanted to go somewhere warm, just to feel better mentally and be able to lie on a sunbed and relax. We had a lovely time, but when we returned my back still wasn't getting right and the whole thing just turned into a slog again with no light at the end of a seemingly endless tunnel of despair.

We now started to consider surgery and there was the possibility of having a spinal fusion, although Steve said it really wasn't ideal for someone involved in sport. Spinal fusion is when two bolts are inserted in between the levels of your vertebrae and lock them together. That might not sound too bad in terms of just two vertebrae, but the amount of movement you lose at the central point of your body, would potentially lead to problems in life, not just football. Understandably, I was desperate not to have it done so we put surgery on the backburner and tried the more moderate approach to the rehab which is usually the best way to go about it. Over that summer the rest had started to work a little bit and I was feeling a bit better. I went over to Ireland for pre-season where we started to step things up but then, whilst playing head tennis with the lads, I raised my left foot to get the ball back and that awful pain started shooting through my body again. I was furious and immediately felt really down.

Desperate for improvement, I then had an epidural injection in my back but that just made me feel really ill. The doctor said it was due to all the steroids in my back hampering my immune system, which had been weakened. One morning I woke up and couldn't see anything out of my eye. It was completely closed. Emma looked at me and was shocked. She it looked as if I'd been punched and had a black eye. I had some swelling in the other eye, as well as a cyst, but at least I could still see through that one. As if that wasn't bad enough that was the day for the pre-season team photo day at Molineux. I put my sunglasses on and went to see the doctor, who managed to get an appointment with the specialist the next day, but there was no way I could be in the team picture.

Mick said I'd be alright if I stood at the back. I thought he was winding me up! Thankfully, the Doc came to the rescue. Given we didn't know what was wrong with my eye, we couldn't be sure it wasn't a contagious infection, so it wasn't wise for me to be with the other lads. I was to miss the line-up on doctor's orders. That certainly wouldn't have been a team photo for the scrapbooks!

My eye got worse as the day progressed, with the swelling getting bigger and the throbbing was very painful. 'Everything is going wrong,' I thought. 'My back is knackered, my eyes are knackered. What more could go wrong?'

Well, the treatment wasn't exactly something to look forward to. The specialist said there were two ways of dealing with it. The first option was to have a course of antibiotics which would settle it all down within six weeks, with a difference after a week. "What's the other option?" I asked hopefully. The answer was a scalpel to the cysts to let all the pus out, from both eyes. Lovely! He told me it was a painful procedure but my immediate response was: "I don't care, let's get it done!"

The first step was a local anaesthetic – a needle being inserted right next to my eye – which was agony. I then lay on the bed, with my eye clamped wide open. It was the first time I'd been able to open it for a couple of days. Initially it was horrible not being able to blink, but when you then see this huge scalpel coming towards you and nothing you can do about it, and no way of not seeing it, it was a horrible experience.

The pain itself was agonising. He nicked the cyst and there was all this yellow liquid gushing out of my eyes. The procedure took 20 minutes and was excruciating. I must have looked quite a sight as I headed out to Emma in the car park, with sunglasses on, loads of tissues in my hands and my eyes constantly weeping – as they did for two or three days afterwards. Yes. Things were going really well for me at this particular moment in time. My head was all over the place. Again!

The team were still in the Premier League, having stayed up on that dramatic last day of the 2010-11 season, despite losing to Blackburn on the final day. I had watched everything unfold from the home dressing room which was an incredible experience. We were watching different games on the different screens and getting messages out to the gaffer. For a long time it looked like we were struggling to stay up, but then there was Stephen Hunt's goal – and it all worked out well in the end.

I was ecstatic that we'd stayed up. It helped me as, despite my injury, it gave me the security of knowing that if I could get myself right I would have another shot at the Premier League. I had also spoken to Wolves' club doctor Matt Perry about my depression. I was in such a lonely place. Obviously, I had the support of my family, which has always been there, but it is very difficult when you can't do your job and have no idea when you might be able to do it again. The other lads are great and will always ask how you are and keep in touch but it is very difficult for them to help. I was struggling to shake myself out of it.

One day I spoke to Ben Herd, who had been at Shrewsbury with me. I was telling him how I was making little progress and that we were now considering the operation, which was clearly going to be dangerous in terms of my future career. Ben told me he had been going to see a guy who he called The Guru. Because, quite literally, he fixed people! He said this guy did a lot of soft tissue work but you wouldn't call him a masseur. He didn't have a title as such but had done loads and loads of research and gone out and learned everything he could. At this time he was working in the City, specialising in back pain, but had just started moving into the football world. Ben and another lad from Shrewsbury called Dave Hibbert had been to see him with chronic problems and they'd both been sorted within a couple of sessions. At that point I would have tried try anything, so I ran it all past Wolves, was given the go-ahead and gave The Guru a call.

His name was Ronan McCarthy and I briefed him on my problems and the treatment I'd received: the scans, the injections everything. "No worries," he said. "Come down and see me and we'll get that fixed in a couple of sessions!" Unbelievable! "Who is this guy?" After all, I had been suffering torment for about six months and he was now suggesting he would solve all my problems almost immediately. I wasn't really having it to be honest. I was looking at everything through a prism riddled with pessimism but, I also thought, there was nothing to lose. To hear someone saying they could fix it gave me a glimmer of hope.

Steve came down with me to see Ronan, who said he didn't really need to see the scans we'd brought – he would do his own assessment. He asked me to do a few simple tests like squatting and bringing my knee to my chest. He was measuring the angles in relation to my pelvis and just looking closely at my posture and all my movements.

The physios at Wolves were great. So intelligent and forward-thinking – always looking to better themselves, but no one had really done this – it had all been about the treatment and trying to get me right. This was totally 'leftfield', but Ronan was so analytical about it all. When he'd finished his assessment he told me I had zero movement in my left hip. Nothing there at all. He asked me to try and do the motion of the volley which had sparked it all off. I knew it was really going to hurt but I did it all the same. Ronan explained that every time I raised my left leg, my back was shutting down because I had absolutely no range in my hip. My muscles were so overloaded that they had basically switched off.

He told me he hadn't really seen people in a condition as bad as me and that the treatment would be painful. It was also going to take more than the two sessions he'd originally suggested. It was going to be like kneading dough and would have to carry on until the elasticity had come back. It wasn't a case of rubbing a particular muscle. It was release work, and Ronan was a specialist in neural symptoms.

I had been getting a lot of pain down my left hand side, down to my sciatic nerve, which comes out of the back and travels down your glute – where your muscles are rock hard – through the hamstring and into the calf. It was why I had been suffering so many niggles, with so much overloading of my groin and hamstrings. They were having to work so hard to compensate for the muscles which had basically shut down.

So, I started going to Ronan for treatment and, not for the first time, I was going through complete agony. It got to the point where I was thinking I didn't want to get fit anymore. Just leave me alone! It was that sore. I saw him six times in the space of a couple of weeks and, despite the pain of the sessions, I did start to feel the improvements. I felt the back pain reducing, and my hip was feeling brand new. It felt like progress. Ronan told me it would take some time to get used to a new series of movement patterns and I would have to make sure that, my core stayed as strong as it could be. At last, I started feeling better. Day by day I was gradually improving.

With my previous niggles, I'd got to a certain stage of my rehab and then broken down, but now I was keen to give this a go. I was still aware of protecting my back as I stepped things up but it was nothing like it was before, and never enough to halt my progress. I got more and more confident and eventually got back into full training. The pain in my back disappeared, probably a month or so after the sessions started, and never came back. All these years later, I have never felt it since.

Due to my treatment, I missed the first month of the season but came in for the Cup game against Kenny Jackett's Millwall. It was such a good feeling to be back, and I scored after just three minutes. What a return! And what a relief. It was going to be another tough season ahead but, on a personal note, after experiencing genuine fears as to whether I would actually ever play again, I was determined to make the most of it.

9

Young Dragon

'What's important is Welsh football and that it progresses'
Gary Speed

Becoming an international with Wales has been a huge part of my career and, of course, helped me play at a major tournament at Euro 2016, but the beauty of Bordeaux was a long way away from those early days when I was coming through the different age groups as a youngster.

I got my first under-21 call-up when I was a 17-year-old at Shrewsbury and Jimmy Shoulder was in charge of the U21s. I didn't get to play in that game and then I had to wait a fair while for another opportunity. Some of the local media were suggesting it was because Brian Flynn – who had strong links with Shrewsbury's rivals Wrexham – was in charge, but that definitely wasn't the case.

When I was selected again, I grew into being quite an important player for the under-21s. Flynny had a lot of confidence in me and I think he saw me as a leader – I captained the team on quite a few occasions. Then, after playing Northern Ireland away, and winning 4-0, Flynny informed me that I was ready to move up. Brian was working, with the Welsh manager John Toshack, to provide a conveyor belt of players going from the under-21s to the seniors and I was the next player in line to make that leap. My first senior call-up was for a game against the Republic of Ireland at Croke Park. It was still the period when teams would only have a squad of 18 on a matchday, so five or six players called up into the squad of 23 or 24 would miss out on a place on the bench.

70

YOUNG DRAGON

My first time at the Wales camp at the Vale hotel, ahead of training at Ninian Park, I was absolutely terrified. There were some big characters in the squad at that time including Ryan Giggs and Craig Bellamy, and quite a few others who were playing right at the very top. Then there was me, a young whippersnapper pitching up from Shrewsbury Town in League Two! John Oster, who used to play for Everton, hadn't been picked. He did a piece in the media saying it was a farce that someone from Shrewsbury Town was in the squad. I felt a little bit unworthy of being there, not because of that comment, but because I was a League Two player going in alongside some of these really big names and top players. All of a sudden I was due to train with Ryan Giggs, one of the best players in the world. Wow!

When I first arrived at the camp who should be the first person I should bump into? Yes. Ryan Giggs, outside leant up against the wall, on his phone. He probably didn't know who I was, even though I had my Welsh gear on. He told whoever was on the phone to hang on, came over straightaway and said, "Nice to meet you, I'm Giggsy!" "Yeh, no shit," would have been my response if I could have got my words out. That always sticks out in my mind, to get that first welcome from someone like him. It meant a lot.

I was petrified about the first training session as well. We were doing crossing and finishing and, as the young lad, I was the one sent over to put the crosses on for the other lads to finish off. So, there I was, crossing balls in for Ryan Giggs. What dreams were made of! He was coming towards his last Welsh cap so I only trained with him a few times, but I remember Giggsy scoring a wonder goal in training. It was a five-a-side and his team got a free kick, almost right in the corner. The 'keeper came out a little bit to the six yard box to organise the defence and Giggsy just put the ball down on the wing and struck it so sweetly that it faded away and beat the 'keeper at the near post. It was ridiculous, and very much a 'what am I doing here?' moment for me. I just knew that I was nowhere near that sort of level. Perhaps I didn't look as out of depth to the others, but I certainly felt it. I knew I could work hard but it didn't feel as if I was at international level.

We had two or three training sessions and then the squad were travelling over to Ireland for the game. John Toshack called me in, said it had been great experience for me but I wasn't going to make it onto the bench and, with League Two games not automatically getting called off for internationals, I could go back and rejoin Shrewsbury for their fixture. I thanked John for the opportunity and then went back and played a couple of games for Shrewsbury as the internationals took place.

I'd moved to Luton before making my full international debut, on the bench against Slovakia. We won 5-2 but I didn't get on. The team were excellent and Bellers (Craig Bellamy) in particular was brilliant that day. He scored a couple of goals and I remember John Toshack coming in and telling everyone that there were 21 players out there on the pitch – and Craig Bellamy. He was out on his own, and made the difference.

I was in the squad for the next camp, in November 2007, and was on the bench for the first time at the Millennium Stadium as a player. We were up against the Republic of Ireland, and Carl Robinson went down with quite a nasty injury. There was no hesitation from the manager: "Come on then Dave, you're going on." Wow! Was I nervous? There's a photo of me talking to the manager on the touchline and I look as white as a ghost.

The crowd wasn't big by international standards – around 25,000 – and we drew the game 2-2. It was an amazing feeling to get my international debut, and I felt I did quite well. I didn't do anything spectacular but, equally, nothing spectacular went wrong either. There were a lot of young players in the Welsh side at that time such as Chris Gunter, Neil Eardley, Joe Ledley, with players like Andrew Crofts and Craig Morgan on the bench.

It was another one of those highlights of a career when you stop and think that you've now played international football. Even if it never happens again afterwards, you have a senior cap, and in a competitive European Championships qualifier as well. What a moment.

Then to go onto the next step, the following game, when I started away against Germany in Frankfurt. Another qualifier, and we drew 0-0. It was in an unbelievable stadium – almost 50,000 – and my first start at the age of 21. Up against a German team involving household names such as Lahm, Mertesacker, Hitzlsperger, Podolski and Klose. It was a huge day for me on a personal level and, despite missing our big players, we went there and got a result.

From then on I soon became a regular in the Welsh squads. I got my third cap at home to Norway in Wrexham off the bench. I came on and did really well. I was starting to think I'd arrived at this level – playing for Wolves in the Championship and now for my country – and I was here to stay.

It was great for me personally, but Welsh football was really struggling at the time. However, John Toshack has to take a lot of credit, along with Brian Flynn, for what they did in blooding so many young players who'd go on and play a part in the future. Eight years later you turn up at the Euros and there are experienced and established Welsh players from 26 to 30 years old who have 50 or more caps. They must have seen a generation coming through that they felt could achieve something and, for us, that was huge. Toshack got a lot of stick during his time as manager and, yes, results weren't very good at the time, but he was laying strong foundations for Welsh football, something solid that Gary Speed and Chris Coleman could build upon in the future.

Even so, at that stage we weren't that good a side and would get outplayed quite a bit. It was a strange time. I was playing for my country – which was incredible – but we were turning up at places and there was hardly anyone there to watch us. It did take a little bit of the magic away. For me, going onto the Premier League and playing, week-in week-out, for Wolves in front of massive crowds, and then going to Llanelli to play for Wales in front of a few thousand – yes it was a strange time and, to be fair, we did nothing to win those fans back. Results and performances weren't good but, when Gary Speed came in, thanks to Toshack we were ready for him.

It was a tough start for Gary and he certainly wasn't an overnight success – results wise – losing his first five games on the bounce, but he had changed absolutely everything. Under John it was a bit of a traditional old-school set-up. Very relaxed. There would be video meetings where you'd watch clips and games but there was no real structure behind the session. Training was always ok, but away from it there was nothing like the sort of professional outlook to it that you would get today. Players who lived locally would just go home from day to day rather than stay in camp.

I was a culprit for not doing things properly, like everyone was. If training was at 10am I'd get up at 9.30 to 9.45, put my boots on, grab a crumpet or a piece of toast and eat it, walking down to the training pitch. It seems crazy now but it was that relaxed. There were no set times for breakfast or real detail on the nutrition. That was John's way, and also how he had worked in Spain, where the culture is very different. He'd won the Champions League with Real Madrid and was a top, top manager. It was also, perhaps, before the time when the game became as professional as it is now, with so much reliance on fitness and sport science.

When Gary took over, with the number of younger players we had and the way football was evolving, it was a lot more professional and a lot more analytical. He brought in Raymond Verheijen as assistant manager, who was popular with some and disliked by many others. I, for one, thought he was brilliant in what he did for Wales. I know a lot of fans wouldn't agree with that, and he could be quite derogatory to people, but the quality of what he brought to the table was exceptional. He used to be a player before he got injured when he was young, and from there his background was in fitness and sport science.

Gary was the one making the decisions, but you knew that he was relying on Raymond behind that. He made Aaron Ramsey captain which was such a big shout at an early stage of Rambo's career. Speedo also brought in Osian Roberts, who was a massive influence and is still a key part of the Welsh set-up now. Gary had done his coaching badges with Osian and they were really close. The two of them and Raymond were the trio who really changed Welsh football. The work Osian has done not only with the senior team but also behind the scenes with all the age groups, the FAW and the FAW Trust has been nothing short of magnificent. He is highly respected and well thought of everywhere.

The new regime encapsulated everything that is part of modern football now. Just little things, such as everyone getting down to meals at the right times and not starting until the captain said everyone was present. There were no flip flops at dinner! Everyone wore the same polo shirts. It was all very professional, and that attitude spread to the pitch.

We started doing video meetings, where the play would be broken down into the different positions. Training would also be filmed and reviewed. I loved it. We were also doing it at Wolves, but not to the same level of detail and approach. I am very much into analysis and believe the more you know the better. Although I know other players don't necessarily share that view and, for some, it's about the freedom of going out to play without thinking too much, but those analysis sessions were giving out the information in bite-size chunks from which it was easy to concentrate and learn.

There was a feeling that it was just a matter of time – backed up by hard work – before the new Wales set-up would start to generate success. The system Speedo played – a 4-3-3 – really got the best out of everyone. Gareth Bale and Bellers were on fire, and on the counter attack we were so dangerous. I had missed a lot of the campaign for the 2012 European Championships through injury, but I was involved at different times. I was injured when Gary first took over but he rang me to introduce himself and have a chat. Those sort of touches always mean a great deal to a player. He invited me to the first camp to say hello even though I was injured. A great leader.

Furthermore, Gary Speed was one of my heroes growing up. Probably the main one to be honest. I was a big Shrewsbury Town fan but I also followed Newcastle as well and Speedo was a legend up there. He was a goalscoring midfielder, and the sort of player I aspired to be. I had so much respect for him and that just increased when he became the Wales manager.

I got involved towards the end of the campaign for Euro 2012 and it was always about building for the following one and the World Cup qualifiers for 2014. Our chance of reaching the Euros had gone and so we were using the opportunities that games and meet-ups provided to think about what we were going to do in the next series of qualifiers. We also started to hit some good form.

We played Norway at home and the lads were absolutely magnificent, winning 4-1. It was one of those games when absolutely everything that Gary and Raymond had worked on with the squad came together in one 90-minute display. Everything they had drawn on the tactics board. Everything they had shown on the video. Every bit of messaging. It was all perfect. It all worked.

We had spells of keeping the ball which pulled Norway apart and one of the goals was a real beauty from Bellers, which followed one of those spells of possession that lasted over a minute. It was brilliant. Myself and Andy King only came on in the 90th minute but it was just an incredible night to watch and be involved in. It was a night when everyone thought, 'Right, Welsh football's got a chance now.'

It was such an exciting time but, so sadly, it ended up being Speedo's last game in charge. Just over a couple of weeks later he was gone.

It was one of those moments – those horrible moments – when I think everyone remembers where they were when they heard the news that Speedo had passed away. It was on a Sunday and I was in the car with my wife and young son Jack, driving on the inner ring road in Shrewsbury where I was living. Emma was driving and my brother rang and asked me if I had heard the news. "No," I replied, whilst realising from the tone of his voice that it was something serious. He carried on: "Gary Speed has died." It was one of those thunderbolts of news that takes several seconds to comprehend and digest.

I simply couldn't believe it. I definitely couldn't understand it. My brother said the news had been on the radio so it had to be true. I finished the call, shell-shocked, and talked with Emma. I idolised Gary Speed. Everything about him as a human being. He had this beautiful way with words, in the way he would talk to people. He had this wonderful, childish laugh which everyone loved. I can still hear that laugh even now.

I didn't play either with him or against him too often, but I'll always remember a game Wolves played against Sheffield United. He was coming to the end of his career and, in the tunnel, he was asking, "How are you doing Dave," and being chatty, even though I'd never met him before. Then, when I was injured, he went out of his way to ring me for a chat – make it feel like I was still involved. He was an absolute gentleman, everything you would want to grow up to be like or you would want your children to be like.

The aftermath of the dreadful news left everyone wondering why? Why would it happen? I guess you never know the ins and outs of it and that is probably the way it should be, out of respect to Gary's family. There was his wife Louise and their two young sons left behind, and it was so, so sad. You can only hope that they found some peace after it all. It was sad enough for football, and for Welsh football in particular, but for his family and friends it was far worse – such a terrible loss.

Somehow, the Welsh lads had to carry on. There were matches still to come including Gary's memorial match against Costa Rica. It always seems strange in those situations to be talking and thinking about football but Welsh football had been on such a high with Gary in charge. We felt we were going to do it. We believed we were going to make it to the World Cup. Then the question became, 'who on earth could take over from Gary Speed?' What would they do? Keep everything that had worked so well the same, or make changes?

I thought Raymond might want to take it on, but would he be a big enough name? Perhaps the FAW would want a Welshman to take on the mantle. It was always going to be difficult. Chris Coleman had wanted the job all his life, but he'd been really good mates with Speedo. What a difficult situation he now found himself in. He decided to take it, and he kept Osian on, which I know was a good thing. He had a really sticky start, losing four or five on the bounce, and that World Cup qualifying campaign, about which there was such hope, was over before it had begun.

He wasn't after anyone's sympathy and he knew what he was getting into but I felt for the gaffer. He was under a fair bit of pressure. He had seen how well we had done under Speedo and everything that had been put in place. I think he just tried to carry it on at the start. Before realising he needed to put his own stamp on it. He had to do it his way. He realised that quite quickly, and we started building again. There are still things in place which are very much from Gary's era. He was ahead of his time in implementing innovations that are in most football clubs now. When Chris came in, he made his own changes and his own improvements and put his own sparkle on it, and that is what he took into the qualification for Euro 2016.

10

The Wolves Relegations

'Adversity introduces a man to himself'
Albert Einstein

As the 2011-12 season continued, I was back playing for Wolves which was a massive relief after what I'd been through with the injury, but I was still very sceptical about my body and was doing everything in my power to stay fit.

At times it was almost to my detriment because I was doing too much compared to what I do now, including too much worrying. Doing so much before training to make sure my body was right to train, and then so much after training to try and protect myself. At the time though I had got myself back playing and was delighted.

My first game back was the Carling Cup win against Millwall, when I played the first half and came off at the break. The half-time substitution wasn't planned but Mick said he was thinking ahead to the Liverpool game the following Saturday. I'd played as a number 10 in a 4-4-1-1 against Millwall, as the gaffer was looking to tighten things up a bit in the league. I was a bit annoyed to come off in what was my first game back but the gaffer suggesting I was going to play at Anfield a few days later certainly softened the blow.

The pattern of me coming off at half-time was repeated against Liverpool. We were 2-0 down and getting the runaround. I was out of the starting XI for a few weeks after that but was back in for the next Carling Cup game against Manchester City at Molineux. We were actually 1-0 in front but went on to lose 5-2. We then got a massive win in the League against Wigan and I managed to get a goal, always nice in the Premier League.

After the international break when I came off the bench in the closing stages as Wales beat Norway 4-1, it was back to Wolves where I was back in the team, but we were enduring mixed fortunes – winning a game and threatening to go on a decent run, then losing games and leaving ourselves in trouble. We really struggled to show any form over the Christmas period and we went into January needing some results.

The home game with Aston Villa is one which really sticks out. We were 1-0 down but hit back to lead 2-1 and I scored the second goal with a header. We were playing really well and the first half performance was very good, but everything then conspired against us in the second half. Manny Frimpong had come in on loan from Arsenal, and was doing really well for us, but we lost him to an injury as he got kicked in the face going for a header. Then we lost Karl Henry to a red card after an incident with Marc Albrighton. By that point Robbie Keane had equalised before scoring a late winner. Talk about coming back to haunt Wolves!

That was the moment the players knew we were in big trouble and we really needed to pull something out. Our next game was Liverpool at home, which we lost 3-0. Andy Carroll hadn't scored in a while but he put Liverpool ahead early in the second half. It seemed to be that sort of season for players who were on a bad run. Come to Molineux and score a goal and put it all right!

After the game, the chairman Steve Morgan came into the dressing room which attracted a lot of publicity. It's always difficult for a player when other people criticise you for a lack of effort. Not the chairman on this occasion, but generally in football. A bad performance is never for a lack of trying and that can be very hard to get across to people outside the game. People can ask, 'why didn't they do this?' or 'why didn't they do that?' For a footballer it is never for a lack of trying.

Mentally, there is so much that goes on within a football game, and confidence has so much to do with it. At that time we had zero confidence and once we went behind in a game it felt like a mountain to climb. Against Liverpool, it was the second and third goals which followed, but, from our point of view it was never for a lack of trying.

There was certainly a lot of talk about the chairman coming in post-match, especially as we were now heading to an huge game against QPR on the Saturday. We were fighting for our lives and went behind in the first half. Then there was a big altercation between Djibril Cisse and Roger Johnson with Cisse being sent off, which was to prove a big turning point in the game. We got through to half-time without really hurting them, but after the interval Mick took a very attacking line – he knew we just had to win this game.

We went 4-4-2, and a very attacking 4-4-2 at that. It was me and Jamie O' Hara in the middle of midfield, Kevin Doyle on the right, Matt Jarvis on the left, and Steven Fletcher and Sylvan up front. Sylvan had come on for Frimpong who had unfortunately damaged his anterior crucial ligament in the first half.

Looking at that front six you had an out-and-out winger in Jarvo, Doyler on the other side who is a striker, Fletch and Sylvan who are strikers, Jamie who was an attacking midfielder at that time and myself, another attacking midfielder. I was the one who was going to have to play the holding role. So yes, very bold from Mick and very attacking, but it worked. Jarvo and Doyler got the goals, a 2-1 win and a vital three points. You could just sense the relief – it was incredible. It felt like we were ready to get ourselves back on track.

Then came the West Bromwich Albion game at Molineux. I had never previously played against Albion and, at the time of writing, I haven't played against them since. Playing in a Black Country derby had always been an ambition. Previously, just before Christmas the previous season, I'd been told I'd be playing but the game had been called off, and then, for the rearranged date I was injured.

I had been really desperate to play but, at the start of the week, Jamie was struggling with his groin and, out of nowhere, my knee had just started giving way in training. It was a bizarre sensation and left me as a doubt for the weekend. Eventually, me and Jamie got strapped up on the Friday just to try and get through and be available for the game, and we played.

It was another very attacking line-up. Because of what had happened in that QPR game, I think Mick just thought, 'right, let's go for it', but Albion had three in central midfield against our two. That is always difficult because it gives the opposition an overload. If our attacking formation worked, it would be a dream and, if it didn't, a potential disaster.

Albion took the lead just after the half hour mark. The ball was cut back to Peter Odemwingie and I closed him down, trying to get my body in the way. It came off my backside, which wrong-footed Wayne Hennessey, and we were a goal down. We weren't playing well at all, but thankfully, Fletch grabbed an equaliser just before half-time, and we were right back in it.

Fletch had another chance in the second half, but Albion then got their second goal and, all of a sudden, everything just started to collapse. Having struggled with my knee for most of the week I came off at this point and sat with the other lads on the bench watching it all fall apart. It's bad enough being on the pitch in those situations but even worse being on the sidelines without any chance of being able to affect it. We lost 5-1. A complete disaster. The post-match dressing room was a scene of devastation. I had waited so long to play in a big derby game and we'd lost 5-1. It was gut-wrenching.

We knew that Mick had been under pressure and had heard whispers he'd been called to see the chairman at Carden Park after the Liverpool game. The heat was definitely on, but even after that Albion game, surely he wasn't going to get the sack. Not after the job he had done. We were still outside the bottom three at that point. Hopefully the previous win at QPR would prove enough?

After losing in that manner, however, and to our fierce, local rivals, we knew there was going to be a reaction. At this time the fans were giving Mick a lot of stick. He'd done such a great job and masterminded three successive top flight seasons, something which hadn't happened for maybe 30 years, and hasn't happened since. The players were still behind him – 100%. We'd been in worse positions the previous seasons and were still confident we could stay out of that bottom three. I thought Mick would be given until the end of the season. If we did go down then, or even if we stayed up, it would all be considered then.

We came in the next day and were all called into the meeting room at the training ground. That was when we started to click that something had happened. Mick came in. You could see he looked upset. Not crying, but you could see he had maybe been welling up and was emotional. He looked at us all and very light-heartedly smiled in that way that he does. We knew this was something big.

"Look lads," he began. "This is the end of the road for me." He said he was absolutely gutted and devastated, but retained a smile throughout. I don't think he wanted the lads to think of him as being upset or angry. He is a proud man, and stayed proud to the very end. "Regardless of what is happening to me, it is all about you guys now," he continued. "I have every faith in you. You have all done such an amazing job for me and I am sure you can stay in this league." He went on to thank us all for what a pleasure it had been for him over the previous six years or so.

It was tough. Mick had done so much for pretty much everyone in that room. He walked out for the final time and everyone just turned to each other. The palpable feeling was: 'What now?' Mick was all that a lot of us had known at Wolves and that made things really difficult to take. Chief executive Jez Moxey then came in and informed us that, for the time being, TC (Terry Connor) was going to take over while they looked for a new manager. I think Jez was very fond of Mick, and whether he wanted him to go or not, you could tell the decision had hurt him.

All of the boys wanted to go and see Mick again on that Monday before he left. He was up there clearing out his office and the boys popped by, in twos and threes, to say their farewells. I went with Kevin Doyle. We all wanted to thank him for what he had done.

For my part he had transformed my career, signed me from Luton, turned me into a senior international, and played me in the Premier League. You could tell Mick was upset by this point, which is no surprise. You live and breathe a football club every day and I think he was still confident he would have kept Wolves in the League. I remember phoning him a few days later, just to re-iterate my thanks and appreciation and I know he went to Molineux after leaving the training ground to say goodbye to all of the office staff there as well. A class act from a man who always tried to do things in the right way. This was the first time in my career I'd seen a manager leave who had done so much for me. I was very young at Shrewsbury when it happened before with Jimmy Quinn, and at that time I wasn't playing and was nowhere near the first team.

TC was a very well respected figure on Mick's staff, and a great coach. We all knuckled down in training to work together for him and were waiting to see what would happen. There was a lot of talk about

Steve Bruce taking over and it got to the stage where the whispers had us convinced it was a done deal. Then, arriving for training on the Friday before a trip to Newcastle we were told by Jez that TC had been given the job. The lads were a little shocked at first, but we were also very happy. We all knew how good TC was on the training pitch and as a person and, once he was given the go-ahead, we were desperate for him to succeed. We thought it would be great if we could do it for him.

His first game at Newcastle turned into a really good one. We were 2-0 down after 18 minutes, which wasn't the best of starts, but we got back into it and drew 2-2 thanks to Jarvo and Doyler. That performance, and a point gave us a real high. We felt we had to give it a right good go, and that we still had a really decent chance of staying in the division.

I'd got a nasty kick against Newcastle so I missed the next game at Fulham – a bit of a reality check with a thumping 5-0 defeat. I got back to fitness fairly quickly, just in time for a couple of really tough weeks. A 2-0 home defeat to Blackburn, and then another 5-0 thumping, at home to Manchester United. We actually started that game really well, before Ronald Zubar was sent off just before half-time when we were only 1-0 down and it all went downhill from there. We were playing 4-4-1 against Manchester United who were at the top of their game, highlighted by an absolutely magnificent performance by Paul Scholes.

He was a couple of months into his return from retirement and was superb. After the match his stats were put on the wall: passing percentage – 99%; passes attempted 101; completed 100. That game, he was – hands down - the hardest opponent I have ever played against in my whole career, after having retired for six months! I tried to close him down but he was so quick, just flicking it around the corner. So I stood off him and he was spraying the ball everywhere. I just didn't know how to play him. If I really tried to press him he was just far too clever, and with the time and space he created, he was cutting us wide open. Little wonder we lost 5-0 when we had ten men and the opposition had a player like Paul Scholes pulling the strings.

The buzz from our draw at Newcastle had ebbed and, whilst we remained determined, we realised we were bang in trouble. A 2-1 defeat at Norwich was followed by a 3-2 home defeat to Bolton, during which Roger Johnson and Wayne Hennessey had a bit of an on-field disagreement. Roger also gave away a penalty. Everyone was still trying as hard as they could but there was the sense that things were falling apart. Whatever we did, nothing seemed to work. We just needed a spark. Anything to try and get things going.

A trip to Stoke was next, where we played quite well. We went in front when I tried to get on the end of a Michael Kightly cross and, although I couldn't reach it, the 'keeper was distracted and the ball crept inside the far post. Despite being ahead, we were really short on confidence a nd couldn't hold on, losing 2-1. Our season was falling apart and, when Sebastien Bassong was sent off after just eight minutes into our next game, a 3-0 home defeat to Arsenal, we knew our indiscipline was giving us an impossible mountain to climb.

Relegation was signed and sealed at home to Manchester City when we lost 2-0, on a day when it just seemed to pour with rain throughout the whole match. Quite a fitting end to a sad season. Everyone knew it was coming but it didn't make it any less difficult to take. We were gutted.

Our season was over but we still had games to play. At Swansea we were 3-0 down after about 15 minutes, with the players sensing a humiliation, but we showed some great character -even with no league position to play for – and dug in for a 4-4 draw, which hopefully gave the fans some small crumbs of comfort. I got our third goal and our game was shown first on Match of the Day that night, which didn't happen very often for us.

We finished the campaign with a few 'nothing' games, a 0-0 draw against Everton and then the final day trip to Wigan when I think most people were more interested in what was happening at Manchester City with Sergio Agüero's goal winning them the title.

For us it had been a tough, tough year. We were all hugely disappointed that our three-year Premier League adventure had come to an end but, as we were heading to Wigan for that final game, we knew who was going to be our new manager. News has broken that Terry Connor would be stepping down and Ståle Solbakken coming in. The speculation had been rife towards the end of the season with Paul Franks, on his BBC WM show, talking about how Ståle was the front-runner. Franksy went on to say if Ståle had got the job he'd run around Molineux – naked! Well, a short while later, after the managerial announcement, and wearing a Mankini to spare his blushes, Franksy completed his stadium run, but that radio discussion was, however, the first I had heard of Ståle.

At the time it was quite an exciting appointment. Something a bit different and a manager with a decent track record in Europe with Copenhagen. We were pleased that he had kept TC on, to help with the continuity, although as time went on that didn't really work out and Terry left a couple of months into the season.

During the pre-season we went over to Ireland and Ståle started to get his ideas across. His approach was probably the polar opposite to what I had been used to and I think the other lads felt the same. It was a 4-4-2 system but it was compact and he didn't want too much space in between the lines – he wanted to make us hard to break down. It was a bit alien to a lot of the lads and what we had been used to. He didn't necessarily want us to go out and press the ball. He was happy for us to get into our shape and sit off a little bit, wait for them to give the ball away and then we could start our attack.

I have to confess, I had my doubts about the system in terms of home games in particular. At Molineux our fans were not going to want to see us sitting off opponents and letting them have the ball. They were going to want us to be pressing at a high tempo and trying to make things happen. As good as the system might be, at home in the Championship you have to try and get on the front foot and go out and try and win the game. All managers have their own ideas and their own tactics, however, so we were trying to follow what Ståle wanted to do and playing as he wanted us to.

Training was very tactical. We weren't on the training pitch for too long under Ståle – we were done inside an hour on most days. He was very big on keeping players fresh and not getting injured and so we weren't allowed to do much extra work either. Some days I felt like staying out there and doing some extra training, but I couldn't. It was the philosophy.

We'd lost Steven Fletcher and Matt Jarvis as the season started – with Michael Kightly having previously left - and we signed quite a few new players, a few from overseas, and they certainly had a lot of quality. For me, Ståle was probably the one manager at Wolves I didn't get on with, in a football sense, in terms of what I had to offer. It was nothing personal, he was a good and affable guy, but I'm not sure the way I played really suited what he was looking for, which can happen in football with players and managers.

The first game of the season was actually a League Cup game, against Aldershot at Molineux. Ståle named the team and the bench the day before the game, and I wasn't included. He pulled me to one side and said because I had missed a little bit of pre-season through injury he wanted me to come in on the Saturday morning and train, rather than be on the bench and perhaps not even get on. So, I went in on that Saturday morning, a little bit annoyed not to be involved, but also determined to make the most of the training session and get myself into a good shape ahead of the start of the league campaign. Halfway through the session, the head of medical Phil Hayward came out and told me that I needed to get to Molineux to be on the bench. Someone had been sick in the night and was no longer available.

I'd been told I wasn't ready, and wasn't fit enough, and now because someone was ill I was being asked to go and sit on the bench. As I was halfway through the session and wanted to get myself fully fit, as I'd been told, that is what I wanted to do. A far better solution would have been to put one of the young lads on the bench instead. I couldn't understand how I was now fit enough to be on the bench but I hadn't been the day before. This didn't make sense, so I made a call to Ståle. It was my first real difference of opinion with him but I think he understood where I was coming from and I was able to go back out and finish the training session. As I walked back out to finish the session, Eggert Jonsson was coming back in. He'd just been called, and was heading to Molineux to sit on the bench!

We started the League season away at Leeds, losing 1-0, and I think that was a bit of a wake-up call for the way things were back in the Championship. Neil Warnock was the Leeds manager, and they produced a typical Championship performance to clinch the points. I was on the bench at Leeds and came on in that game, but from that defeat we went on a bit of a run. The next game was at home to Barnsley, and I was on the bench again, going on after an hour when we were 2-0 ahead, with the instruction to help the team see the game out.

I came on in centre midfield and the ball went out to the right. I could see their midfielders weren't going to track me, and there was a gaping hole to run into. So off I went, before hearing a shout from the bench: "Edwards – where are you going?" I was on my way by now so there was no turning back! I got into the box and headed home a cross from Jarvo in what turned out to be his last game for Wolves before joining West Ham. Even though I scored, and we won the game 3-1, the manager brought it up with me when I came in after the game. It wasn't something he wanted his central midfielders to do – he wanted them to sit in there, something that didn't really suit my way of playing.

That was the first time in my Wolves career I thought I might have to move on. I was still playing though, when there were injuries to other players, so I was still getting plenty of time on the pitch, but it was a bit in and out for my liking.

I was captain for the League Cup tie at Chelsea when we were beaten 6-0. It was my first time wearing the armband for Wolves and I was immensely proud – even considering I wasn't the first choice and the result which followed. It was one of those games where the opposition were absolutely magnificent. They had the likes of Cahill, Terry, Ramires, Mata, and Fernando Torres was unbelievable. The gulf in class was, well, it was miles. After the game I spoke to Tim Nash, a reporter from the local newspaper, and I could see he was trying to get me to apologise to the fans because we had lost 6-0, but the truth was there wasn't really anything to apologise for. It wasn't a lack of effort or anything like that. They were just unbelievable that night.

It took me a while to get back into the team but then I had a good run of starting seven or eight games leading up to the festive period. I'd played wide right a little bit before moving into the centre but I was having to be very disciplined and not really getting forward into the box very much. If I'm honest I wasn't really enjoying my football. It wasn't how I was used to playing.

Then came the game away at Bristol City which was to prove eventful for several different reasons. It was in early December, and we were due to have our players' Christmas 'do' in the evening after the game. It was fancy dress, and I'd got my costume all set – Bret Hart, the famous wrestler. I'd been into wrestling as a kid and loved Bret Hart so I'd got the full works with the black wig and the pink lycra pants. I had the belt, everything, even the pink glasses. Ten out of ten for preparation. I was really excited for the Christmas do as the game came around. We weren't in great form, losing to Millwall and Forest in the build-up, and when you're about to have your Christmas party there is a real desperation to win the game, otherwise you don't really feel you deserve to be going out.

Leading up to the game there'd been a bit of a dressing room discussion around Bakary Sako, who was doing really well for us but would never get taken off, even though he was struggling to see out games. The more he played the stronger he got in the League but at that stage, in his first few months, after 60 minutes or so you could see he was struggling yet it was always other players who were substituted. I'd been speaking to the captain Karl Henry about my own situation and had told Karl that I'd always follow what my manager wanted me to do – that was how it worked - but in playing that way he just wasn't getting the best out of me. If that was what he wanted, he may as well play someone else.

We'd all been brought to Wolves for a reason and we all had different strengths to bring to the team. For me, that was getting forward, making runs into the box and scoring goals. For Karl, it was about pressing, getting stuck in and winning the ball back. Mine and Karl's natural instincts were to go out there and win the ball back but we were being told not to do that and not to press. We were really struggling with the way the manager wanted us to play.

The manager's new system and demands had really affected our morale and Karl sensed that something needed to be said. Out on the pitch, at Bristol City, we got into our usual pre-match huddle. Normally it was the final opportunity to confirm the game plan and to fire us up for the match, but this time we were all quiet. "Right," said Karl, "let's just play our own game now. Forget the tactics. If you want to run forward then run forward. If you want to press then press up. If you think it is right to stay back then stay back." He said we knew what our strengths were, and we had to use them so don't stick in the rigid 4-4-2 because it clearly hadn't worked so far. He finished with, "Go and express yourselves and enjoy the game."

It was of a bit of a surprise to hear that from the captain, but to be fair to Karl, he was a character who always said what he felt and was always willing to stand up for what he believed in. The boys really appreciated those words and I could sense the belief and determination flowing back amongst the players. We knew he was right, and we were going to give this everything we had, right from the start.

A minute into the game, I got the ball, looked up and Karl had made this forward run right into the far corner. That was unusual as it wasn't part of Karl's game, but he was gone, sprinting forward right into the channel. He was making a point and leading from the front. I played it up to him and we were immediately on the offensive, taking the game to Bristol. Within minutes we were playing free-flowing, instinctive football. Sylvan Ebanks-Blake scored, Kevin Doyle got two, and Bjorn Sigurdarson bagged another – we were 4-0 up by half-time! Despite playing brilliantly and being 4-0 up, we went in at the break not really knowing how the manager was going to react, because we weren't sticking to his game plan. His only comment was that as we were now 4-0 ahead, it was essential for us to keep our shape and not get broken down. The game was won pretty much and we were all set for our Christmas do. It was going to be a good night.

Not for me though. In fact it was to turn into the complete opposite of a good night. With about an hour gone, the ball got cleared from one of our corners and they started to break away. I was sprinting with a Bristol City player in what was a 50-50 situation and, just as I planted my left leg to make a tackle, the player barged into me and my left leg completely seized up. It felt like someone had shot me – one of the worst pains I have had in football. Straightaway I thought I'd torn my hamstring. I had never had a muscle injury that severe before and it was agony.

The challenge had looked innocuous enough, but I was lying on the floor beating my fists on the ground in terrible pain. You could hear the Bristol fans shouting at me to get up. At 4-0, they probably thought I was wasting time. I wish I had been! I had to come off and I knew the injury was bad. The Christmas 'do' was certainly off the cards for that evening. The Bret Hart costume would have to go back into the wardrobe. Another time maybe. But not tonight.

It turned out I had a grade two tear, which was to keep me out for almost two months and proved to be my last game under Ståle. My agent didn't tell me at the time, due to the fact I was injured, but I might well have been on my way shortly afterwards. A lot of new players had arrived, the club planned to get rid of a few in January and Ståle felt I was one who could move on, providing something came up which was right for everyone. My agent knew this but was waiting for me to get fit. As it turned out I got injured, and Ståle didn't really have too long left at Wolves.

We had two horrendous results over Christmas. Having won at Blackpool, thanks largely to a superb performance from Carl Ikeme, we had two home games against Peterborough and Ipswich. First up was Peterborough, and we lost 3-0. The funny thing about this was that I knew a few of the Peterborough players. We'd won at their place earlier on in the season when we were doing well and, after the game, Ståle had told their manager Darren Ferguson that if he needed some players we had some in the under-21s or youth team who might be able to go and do a job for him. In his defence, I think Ståle was only trying to be helpful, but it was perceived as being disrespectful as Ferguson went back into their dressing room to tell the players he'd been offered a load of Wolves kids because they weren't good enough! The Peterborough players certainly didn't need motivating for the return fixture after hearing that.

Lee Tomlin played in that return game and was brilliant. He scored the first goal, followed by Tommy Rowe and Dwight Gayle. It was a convincing defeat. Then Mick McCarthy returned to Molineux for the first time with his Ipswich team, and left with a 2-0 victory. We then lost at Crystal Palace on New Year's Day, before travelling to Luton in the FA Cup. Luton were in non-league football at that stage, and I was gutted to be missing the chance of going back there for the first time. We lost the game, and Ståle lost his job a few hours later. Dean Saunders was very quickly appointed in his place.

The change of manager gave me a boost of confidence and, just as I'd been at the start of the season, I was full of enthusiasm. I knew I hadn't been Ståle's type of player and our system wasn't getting the best out of my natural game. We were now bringing in a Welsh manager who I had worked with whilst playing for the national team. Deano was a really good coach with Wales, he was always really bubbly, had great fun with all the lads and I got on very well with him. He came in, we had a good chat, and I felt this was going to be positive. And I was.

After working exceptionally hard for six or seven weeks, my fitness returned and I was back in the team – but it had proved a tough start under Dean. We didn't win for nine games, which now made it a run of 13. We'd picked up a few draws, though, so a few points had been won. My first start under Dean was a 0-0 draw at Derby, followed by a really big midweek night at Barnsley.

THE WOLVES RELEGATIONS

We went 1-0 up and were playing really well, with Jamie O'Hara hitting the bar, but in the second half we capitulated, and Barnsley came back to win 2-1. They were close to us in the table, so it was a big result. By now we were really struggling. At Oakwell you come off the pitch right next to the away fans, and we were getting absolute pelters. That is one of the worst experiences you can have as a footballer – walking off after a really disappointing game and getting abuse from supporters. It is difficult, especially when it's particularly vitriolic and directed towards you as an individual. You just try and block it out as much as possible. I realise that fans pay a lot of money to come and watch football, and are always entitled to voice their opinions but, at the same time, I'm not sure they are entitled to call people vile and disgusting names. I'd been at Shrewsbury, as a supporter, and can understand the strong feelings and emotions among fans if things don't go well, but I do find it difficult when it is so personal and to your face. It wouldn't happen in any other line of work!

In those situations we, as players, just have to bite our tongues. No footballer ever wants to lose a game or not play well. It's never, ever for a lack of effort that you don't get a result - certainly on my part and pretty much with every teammate I have ever played alongside. No one plays badly on purpose. We play on confidence and, if it's not there and you're struggling, then maybe that gives a perception of a lack of effort.

After Barnsley, we lost at home to Cardiff then grabbed a last minute equaliser against Watford. Still no win. I had been an unused substitute for those two games but came back into the side for the midweek trip to Millwall. I was playing wide right, as I did a fair bit under Deano, but 'tucked in' so I could drift into the number ten position as well. I scored early on and then Sylvan found the net with a great overhead kick. We won 2-0, and everyone felt, and hoped, it could be a turning point.

There was a bit of payback after the Millwall game as well. When we'd lost the home game earlier in the season, and Andy Keogh had scored the winner, their big centre half Danny Shittu had come down the tunnel making loads of noise, cheering and banging on our dressing room door as he went past. That really stuck in our memory so, after we'd won away, Roger Johnson went down their tunnel, doing exactly the same, screaming and banging on their door just to rub it in a little bit!

With that win we thought things could turn for us, but we went to Nottingham Forest that Saturday and lost 3-1. Personally, I felt I had quite a good game that day, and as a team we didn't do too badly, but we were leaking goals, lost the game, and that was all that mattered. We were right back in trouble.

Next up was what became a bit of an infamous game against Bristol City. In more ways than one. It was a huge game as they were down there with us at the wrong end of the table. After the Millwall game, I'd got some pain in the outside of my foot. I didn't think too much of it at first but it lingered on and I could feel it in training. I got through the Forest game and then decided to scan it on the Monday, thinking it might be a bit of irritation on my fifth metatarsal.

We were terrible, right from the start, against Bristol City. It was just one of those games when nothing went right. We were so nervous, and the atmosphere at Molineux was exceptionally edgy. I don't think any of us were having a good game. Midway through the first half, David Davis played a back pass to Carl Ikeme, who tried to control the ball, but it bobbled, he missed it and it rolled over the goal line. 1-0 down.

Then we had an injury with Sako - one of our key players – having to come off and then, not long before half-time, I brought the ball out of defence and had a run up the right-hand side towards the dugouts. There was no one in front of me, so I checked to turn back inside then felt a tackle right on that sore point of my foot, where I'd been struggling. It was extremely painful, but I carried on, and a minute later I turned really quickly and I felt another really sharp pain in the side of my foot.

I was really struggling by now, and didn't really want the ball anywhere near me as I knew I needed to come off, but the ball was bouncing in the middle of the pitch. I had to clear it. As I turned to volley it, my foot was totally limp and just hanging there. I fluffed it about ten yards because I couldn't get any strength behind it at all. Then came the boos from the crowd who obviously didn't know what was happening. The physio came on and I told him the pain was excruciating and I could hardly walk.

My brother was watching *Soccer Saturday* at the time and

remembers the guy summarising our game saying about how things were falling apart for Wolves: "Dave Edwards has just come off. I'm not sure what is wrong with him – I just don't think he fancies it!" I was raging later when I heard about that. Especially when the extent of the injury became clear.

I went into the dressing rooms and my foot was feeling really sore. The diagnosis, which followed later, was that I'd broken my fifth metatarsal. The diagnosis for Wolves was about to get just as bad. Having already made two first half substitutions, we were about to lose someone else at half-time. There were a few words exchanged about the Bristol City goal and, as Carl himself explained later on, he lost his head. The way he decided to release his anger was to punch the tactics board, situated in the middle of the dressing room. Unfortunately he caught it a treat, right in the middle which is reinforced with steel at the back. I was in the treatment room at the time and the door was shut, but I heard the commotion and then Carl came through and the doc had a look at his hand. It was massively swollen already – there was no way he could continue.

So there we were – 1-0 down, playing rubbish, and having made all three substitutions. Could it get any worse? Well, no, because the lads went out there and showed real character to come through. Sylvan and Doyler got two quickfire goals about 15 minutes from time and we won the game 2-1.

The lads then gave it a real go and won the next two games as well, against Middlesbrough and Birmingham, but Sylvan – the one player who looked like he could get us out of trouble – broke his ankle in that win against the Blues. We'd already lost Sako, who didn't get back until the last game of the season, so we'd certainly had our share of bad luck.

Unfortunately, as the season continued and our form dropped again, a second successive relegation was starting to look inevitable. I was still in for treatment, feeling massively disappointed and frustrated that I couldn't contribute. Going into the last day at Brighton, it was going to take a miracle – in terms of other teams' results – if we were to stay up. Still injured, I had been given permission to go to a mate's wedding, so kept an eye on the score through the afternoon and, sure enough, relegation was confirmed. Another bitter, bitter blow.

News came through fairly quickly that Dean would be leaving.

Results may not have gone his way but he didn't fail through lack of effort. He worked very hard, and wanted all his players to do the same. He was so passionate. I just wonder whether he took over the team at the wrong time, when we had no confidence, and were on a downward spiral. The injuries didn't help either. At that time, the club needed a general clear-out and to start afresh. Maybe he could argue he had a rough deal but, at the same time, with everything that happened, the Board probably didn't have too many options. As a person he was always bubbly, always trying to keep everyone's confidence up, and wanting it to work. Unfortunately it didn't. It always seemed as if the harder Deano tried, the worse it all got. He would probably have done a good job in League One. He'd done well there with Doncaster, but hindsight is a wonderful thing, and when you look back now, the appointment of Kenny Jackett was everything that Wolves needed. A perfect fit at the time.

For me, the club had an option for an extra year on my contract and I was waiting to hear if they were going to exercise it. At that stage, I was just concentrating on trying to get myself fit. After the two seasons we'd gone through, this was probably my lowest point as a Wolves player and with my relationship with the fans. Maybe a change of scenery wouldn't have done me any harm, but the club decided to exercise the option, and did so prior to Kenny being appointed. That focused the mind on trying to get myself back fit for pre-season, and trying to do my bit to help the club to halt the slide of the previous years, and move back in an upward direction. I was now looking ahead, feeling positive. There was going to be a new gaffer to impress.

11

The History Boys

'Unity is strength...when there is teamwork and collaboration,
wonderful things can be achieved'
Mattie J. T. Stepanek

The qualifying campaign for Euro 2016 began with an away game in Andorra. The game took place in September, 2014, just as Wolves had started the season after returning to the Championship. I wasn't in the squad for the game, having not been involved with Wales while Wolves were in League One. I was a bit disappointed as I had started the Championship season quite well, but it was understandable that I was going to have to do a bit more to get myself back into Chris Coleman's thoughts, but I certainly made sure I watched the game on television.

I had spoken to Sam Vokes on the day of the game and he told me about the new system they were going to play, which was something no one had ever heard of before: three at the back; a box in midfield with two holders and two tens; wing backs who almost play as wide midfielders; and one striker up front. I remember wondering just how it was going to work, but it was a masterstroke. It was a formation that became synonymous with Wales, but has also since been used successfully by so many other teams, Chelsea being a prime example.

As it transpired, there were reservations about playing it against Andorra because they were only really going to play one up front and were more likely to line up as two banks of five. The gaffer was insistent however, and felt it was important to get used to the formation because it was the way he wanted to go against the other, stronger teams in the group qualifiers to follow.

We went behind early on to a penalty. What a start! Maybe, when it comes to Wales, it's natural to feel concerned but my mind raced to previous qualifying campaigns where – when we started with a bad result, especially against a team regarded as one of the weakest in the group – we were almost out of contention after one game. Losing against Andorra would have been horrendous! They hadn't scored a competitive goal in four years – until that penalty – and had lost 41 successive European Championships qualifiers.

The state of the pitch didn't help either. It was a brand new artificial pitch and the rubber crumb had only just been laid. Even watching on the television it looked terrible, and the boys said it was one of the worst surfaces they had ever played on.

With a tremendous header from a Ben Davies cross, Gareth Bale drew us level but time was running out, quickly. A draw would have been a disaster. Then fate stepped in. With ten minutes to go it was 1-1 and the gaffer was getting a load of stick from the Welsh fans. We got a free kick in a good position but Baley stepped up and hit it straight into the wall. The referee blew and said the wall had encroached so it needed to be taken again. This time was completely different. Baley replaced the ball and pinged it straight into the corner.

Cue the Welsh fans going mad behind the goal and massive relief for the country to get off to a winning start. Now the fans were singing the gaffer's name. It was such an important win. As difficult as it was, it set us up nicely for the new campaign with this new system.

Next up came the back-to-back qualifiers in the October, for which I was delighted to be back in the squad. We played Bosnia at home, and did really well, against a team we knew were going to be right up there in the group. We looked solid in the new formation, and the game finished goalless. Four points from the first two games is something that we were relatively happy with.

I was an unused substitute in the Bosnia game, but did get on the pitch in the follow-up, at home to Cyprus. We made a great start with two goals inside 23 minutes from David Cotterill and Hal Robson-Kanu. They got one back, against the run of play, not long afterwards but we were playing really well and went in at half-time 2-1 up. Then Andy King got sent off right at the start of the second half. As I'd been warming up at half-time, I'd just popped back into the changing rooms and was now heading back through the tunnel to the dugout when I saw Kingy walking towards me. I wasn't aware of what had happened and just presumed he'd taken a knock. He had a face like thunder, and carried on walking past me. I asked him if he was alright and he just shook his head and carried on walking. Not the best time for any form of prolonged conversation!

The head of performance, Ryland Morgans, came into the tunnel and told me I needed to get warmed up quickly. They left it for a few minutes to see how it went, but then made the change and I went on just before the hour mark. We were starting to get over-run in midfield so I came on for George Williams, who'd been playing out wide. It was my first competitive game for Wales for some considerable time, and quite a situation to go into. Down to ten men, and trying to see the game out for a vital win. It was great to be back involved and we did indeed see it out for the victory which was great for me and great for Wales.

By the time of the next game, in November, I was out with an injury I had picked up for Wolves at Ipswich. It was even more galling because it was such a big game, away at Belgium – the favourites to win the group and one of the best teams in the world – and what a night that was. The lads dug in and really did a job on them, coming away with a 0-0 draw. With eight points after four games, we'd made a very good start and I thought we had a really good chance to break the long-awaited absence from a major tournament.

Next up was Israel away, when I was an unused substitute. The boys played well, and Baley and Rambo (Aaron Ramsey), in particular, were brilliant. Rambo scored a header, and Baley got a couple as we won 3-0. We had really dominated the game and they had a man sent off in the second half when it was 2-0. Israel, Belgium and Bosnia were the teams we thought would be battling it out with us for the two qualification spots so that was a really good result for us.

Belgium, at home, in June soon came around, but I was really disappointed not to make the squad. Wolves had enjoyed a good season in the Championship, just missing out on the play-offs, and I'd played a lot of games. I knew it was going to be tight and that if everyone was fit I might have a battle to get in the squad, and so it proved.

It was the end of the season and I'd booked a holiday in Vilamoura in Portugal with Emma and the kids. My family were coming over for the first week before coming home, and then my friend, his wife and their little girl for the second week. If I was in the squad, however, I would fly home after the first week and Emma and the kids would probably come back as well. I knew when the squad was going to be announced and I didn't get a heads-up. So there I was, sat on the beach at Vilamoura, constantly checking my phone. If I was ever not going to be named in a squad, and to have that disappointment, then this was probably the best time. I was on holiday, with my family, enjoying the sunshine, and I would be able to relax. That's was how it panned out. I wasn't named in the squad, I stayed out on holiday, and the boys got an amazing result by beating Belgium 1-0.

That moved us on to the 2015-16 club season and, from not being in the squad at all, I went on to start the next qualifier away against Cyprus. Such is football. It was a huge game for me personally, to get back in the squad, but then also for two games where we knew if we won both we were really close to clinching our qualification.

I wasn't expecting to start, but Joe Ledley tweaked his hamstring right at the end of training the day before the game, so the gaffer told me I was starting – it was me and Andy King holding, behind Gareth and Aaron. It was really hot out in Nicosia, but I had one of my best games in a Wales shirt.

The pitch wasn't great, but it felt more like a Championship game than an international. It was all a bit frantic, which suited me. I even scored with a header – right in front of the Welsh fans -in the first half but the goal was disallowed. I was wheeling away to celebrate but the referee disallowed it, supposedly for a foul by Hal Robson-Kanu who had jumped with a defender just in front of me. Looking back it certainly didn't seem like a foul.

The game ebbed and flowed but Baley popped up in the closing stages with a great header from a Jazz Richards cross to win the game and give us a huge result. We knew that if we could win at home to Israel then we had qualified and ended that decades long wait. Surely it was all set up for us?

The gaffer kept the same team so I was starting again, and we played really well, keeping possession and dominating the ball, but we just couldn't get the crucial goal. I think it was the most passes I have ever made in a game – something like 100 overall – but Israel played five at the back, four in midfield and put a block on us. We just couldn't break them down. Andy King had a good chance in the first half and Simon Church had a goal disallowed late on, but it just wasn't to be. It was another point closer, but a bit of an anti-climax given we knew we could have booked our place had we won.

After the game we went back to the hotel, the St David's in Cardiff Bay. We were a little bit disappointed but still happy with four points from the two games. Bosnia away was going to be tough, but we also had Andorra at home still to come. Belgium were away in Cyprus that night, if they failed to win we would have qualified. We didn't expect Cyprus to hold them but, with half an hour or so to go, it was still 0-0. As the news spread around the hotel, the rest of the lads headed to the TV room to join the hard core who'd watched the whole game. As full-time loomed ever closer, it was still goalless, and the boys were buzzing. It looked like it was going to happen.

Our bubbling excitement fizzled out when, in the 86th minute Eden Hazard popped up to score and win the game for Belgium. That put a dampener on things and meant we were going to have to wait another month or so but we still knew we were in a great position. I guess it was just a mixture of frustration and impatience at this point.

We travelled to Bosnia, now needing just a point to qualify, and were beaten 2-0. I came on late on when we were 1-0 behind and pushing everyone forward. It was a huge game for Bosnia who also needed a result to get themselves into the play-offs. It was a disappointing result, but we also knew that events elsewhere might still have a bearing on things. Israel needed to beat both Cyprus and Belgium to stand any chance of overhauling us, and the first of those games was coming to an end in Jerusalem.

The tunnel was on the other side of the pitch from me, so while we were getting bits of information we were never completely sure. Bryn Law from Sky Sports was rushing around letting us know the score when he could. Cyprus went in front then Israel equalised, so we still didn't know what was happening as full-time approached.

Then we heard cheers and roars coming from the Welsh fans – Cyprus had won 2-1 in Israel. Wales had qualified! For a while though we didn't know that for sure, but everyone was celebrating, so we just joined in! It was nice to share the moment on the pitch with the Welsh fans who had followed us all over Europe for so long without any real success. It wasn't the most luxurious of places to have sealed the deal, but in a way that made things even better.

We had a few beers in the dressing room and then went back to the hotel. They gave us a conference suite for us to use to have a get-together and toast our qualification. Owain Fôn Williams got his guitar out and played some tunes and we even got the gaffer to give us a song. Chris Gunter stood up in front of everyone to give us his rendition of one of the famous inspirational speeches made by Wales rugby star Scott Quinnell: "You feel those butterflies in your stomach? They're not butterflies. They're dragons!"

It was a really good night and we had a great sing-song. There wasn't really anywhere we could have gone in Bosnia to carry on the celebrations, but it was still a special night. We also knew we had the Andorra game to come a few days later, when we really wanted to finish things on a high, so we didn't go stupid on the celebrations.

It was a strange couple of days leading into that Andorra game, which we knew was going to be a bit of a parade, and I probably didn't prepare to the absolute best like I usually do, which contributed to me picking up an injury during the game. I was also a bit unfortunate. Usually, as a substitute, having done your pre-match warm-ups, you tend to wait 20 minutes or so on the bench before getting up and doing a bit of running to keep yourself ticking over. It was about that 20 minute mark, that Hal Robson-Kanu suffered an injury and I was called upon to go on without really having had a chance to get warmed up, and by this time it was 30 to 40 minutes since I'd been active.

I went straight into it, on the left hand side of midfield, which was a position I'd played a lot for Wolves at the start of the season. I was really pleased to get on and thought I'd be able to get forward from there and definitely, against Andorra, had a chance of getting a goal, but when I got the ball and tried to explode away from someone I just felt my groin tighten up a little bit. I carried on until half-time but it wasn't getting any easier. There wasn't really anything left to play for with Wales – second was the best we could finish – so at that stage it was a case of protecting myself for Wolves. I spoke to the physios and it was agreed I would come off.

Fortunately, in the second half, Rambo and Baley got the goals to make it 2-0, with Rambo doing a Joe Ledley dance by the dugouts after his goal, and we finished on a winning note, having achieved history – the first Wales side for 57 years to qualify for a major tournament.

There wasn't really any chance for any further celebration in Cardiff as we all had to get back to our clubs, me especially given that I had come off with an injury and, to be honest, from the moment the qualification campaign finished, I was thinking about the tournament itself, as I'm sure all the other lads were as well. It was all going to be about doing everything possible to book a place on that plane for France.

I was delighted to have played a part in the qualifying, especially in the final four games, when I'd started two and come on from the bench in the two others. That made me more confident of my chances of making the squad than maybe I was in the middle of the campaign. All roads now led to France, and I was desperate beyond belief to be a part of that journey.

12

The Wolves Revival

'Most great people have attained their greatest success just one step
beyond their greatest failure'
Napoleon Hill

From what I knew and had heard about Kenny Jackett, I thought it
was a really good appointment and just what Wolves needed after two
very difficult seasons. Dean Saunders had already told me he wanted
to take up the year's option on my contract and the club followed that
through before Kenny was appointed. I had a holiday in Portugal in
the summer but the rest of the time I was at the club, making sure I
was fit and ready for the first day of the 2013-14 pre-season.

Kenny had a tough job coming in to a team which had gone
through successive relegations, and I'm not sure if it was him or the
board, but the decision was made to freeze out some very established
players from the first team, including Roger Johnson, Jamie O'Hara,
Karl Henry, Stephen Ward, Kevin Foley, and Kevin Doyle for a time. I
think Kenny was just looking to change things around and plan for
the long-term. Doyler got back into the team, as did Kevin Foley, and
Jamie O'Hara for a time. For guys I'd played with for a long time it was
strange – they were coming in to train at different times and our paths
weren't really crossing. It seemed a bit much. If they weren't part of
the plans, fair enough but it wasn't something that had happened at
Wolves before during my time.

Initially, it didn't really look like I was going to be in Kenny's starting
line-up, just as with Ståle 12 months earlier. We went to Scotland for
pre-season and I was involved in the games, but it wasn't until we

came back and played Chesterfield that I properly staked my claim. I played in the number ten role for part of the game, scored, and did fairly well, which seemed to push me forward, and I started the first game of the season at Preston. It was a weekend which marked the 125th anniversary of the Football League, with two founder members playing each other, and there was a big game atmosphere at Deepdale, helped by 5,000 really loud and passionate Wolves fans who had made the trip. It felt like an important day for us, given everything that had gone on over the last couple of years, as well as the difficulties we'd endured during pre-season.

Deepdale was bouncing, with both home and away fans making it a real occasion. At the end of the warm-up Joe Gallen – the gaffer's assistant – got all the team together to applaud the travelling fans, and the response to that was incredible. The Wolves fans behind the goal really got behind us and, despite all the disappointments of the previous two years, they were fantastic and the players definitely appreciated their full-blooded support.

In contrast to that wonderful reception, the game itself was quite drab. I don't think either team could really get the ball down and get things going. I was on the fringes of the game and couldn't really get into it and, at half-time, Kenny told me that I needed to get more involved. In the second half I started making some good runs and was becoming more of a threat, but then disaster struck. I got the ball, hurdled over a challenge and, as I landed, I felt a shooting pain in the same foot I'd undergone the surgery on. More agony, and huge frustration. I had come through all pre-season absolutely fine – the training and the friendlies – but then, one innocuous leap over an opposition player and 'bang', that sharp pain had returned with a vengeance. I tried to carry on but it was just too sore. I had to come off.

I thought I'd broken my foot again. Suffered a re-fracture. There was a screw in my fifth metatarsal so maybe I had sustained a partial fracture. Back in the dressing room after the game, I was devastated. I also had a painful journey home.

Normally, we'd have travelled the night before to prepare for a game like that but due to budget cuts the team was due to travel by coach the morning of the game. I wasn't a big fan of sitting on a coach for more than an hour or so on the day of a game so I'd spoken to Kenny and asked him if I could drive up myself the day before, and book myself into the hotel – where the team would have a pre-match meal and teamtalk – at my own expense, just to make sure I was completely prepared for the game. My plan had now backfired as I had to drive home with a damaged and painful foot. I stopped at a service station and chatted with a few Wolves fans who would have seen me hobbling around. I was pretty distraught and genuinely thought I had done something really bad again.

Thankfully, the scan showed there wasn't really any major damage but the pain was still fairly severe – I could barely walk and was back in an aircast boot. It took me a month or so to get over that. Even when I got back into training I was still feeling a fair bit of pain but, based on the scan results, I tried to battle through it.

This was the prelude to probably the most difficult time I had at Wolves. I fought my way back and was desperate to be involved in the game at Shrewsbury. With my history at that club, being a huge Shrewsbury fan, and never having played against them in a competitive game since I'd left, it would have been an amazing experience. I'd been back in training for a couple of weeks without being in a matchday squad, but I was selected on the bench for the trip to Gay Meadow. I came on – on the right of midfield – with about 15 minutes to go, and I was given a great reception. There was a standing ovation, maybe even more so from the Shrewsbury fans than the Wolves fans. It was really special and meant a lot to me. I'd left the club under a bit of a cloud, so it felt nice that the supporters still seemed to respect me, as a Shrewsbury lad and a big fan of the club. It was important for me that they had understood my reasons, and this was the first real opportunity for me to see whether they did. I came on just after Curtis Main had missed a great chance for Shrewsbury and, late on, Bakary Sako scored a penalty for us to win the game 1-0.

I was desperate now to build on that and get a sustained run in the team. I started the following weekend – playing right midfield – at home to Sheffield United, and felt like I had a half decent game. We were 1-0 up and I scored with a header with about 15 minutes to go, but it was disallowed for offside – though it was never offside. If that had gone in then what happened afterwards might have been different but, there you go, that's football.

Five minutes later I came off and just presumed that, with this being my first start after about six weeks out, I'd be given another chance a week later. How wrong I was! We were heading to Colchester the following weekend and, on the day before the game, Kenny called me to see him in his office. I assumed he was going to tell me he was leaving me out and that I'd be on the bench, but he said he wasn't going to take me to the game at all. I was gobsmacked. I felt I'd done ok since coming back into the team the previous week. We'd won 2-0 and I'd had a goal disallowed, but James Henry had just arrived at the club on loan from Millwall, so it looked like I wasn't going to get a look in.

Looking back, Kenny was great for me for my career, but there were one or two times – and with other players as well as me – where one of his decisions would take you completely by surprise. This was certainly one of them, and it took me into one of the toughest times of my Wolves career.

We were playing in League One and I was fully fit, but I wasn't getting a sniff at being in the team. Kenny believed I wasn't fit enough and that hurt me because I pride myself on my fitness. I'd not long come back from six weeks out and there wasn't much I could say. I just asked to be allowed to play in some reserve games to keep myself going and get into good shape. Previously, the gaffer had said not to play in those games because of the risk of being injured but now I was going to have to and he said he had no problem with it.

Steve Weaver, who was in charge of the under-21 team, said playing with his squad wouldn't be a problem, and Arsenal away at the Emirates was the first game I played in. We performed really well, and it's a great stadium, but it wasn't really where I wanted to be. This went on for a couple of weeks and I began to feel I was drifting away from first team football at Wolves.

I don't believe there was anything else going on, in terms of the club wanting to push me out or anything. The money I was on was pretty miniscule compared to a lot of other players at that time, and rather than think about leaving, my first reaction was: "I'm going to prove you wrong." That is always my reaction when I am left out of the team rather than throwing my toys out of the pram and wanting to leave.

I was still training with the lads but wasn't getting close to a matchday squad. As they were playing well and picking up results, that was understandable. A training ground game against Notts County on the under-18s pitch was organised so I asked to play and, after the game, their assistant manager came over to me and asked if I'd been injured. "No," I replied. "I just don't think the gaffer fancies me at the moment but I'm trying to get back in the team." Being in the last year of my contract, I knew I needed to be playing and he asked if I'd thought about going out on loan. I said that it was certainly a possibility and he asked if there was any way I would consider going to them. Notts County are a good club but it illustrated where I was at the time, a couple of years after playing in the Premier League I was now looking to get out on loan.

After that game, and weighing up my options with Emma, I decided that I really needed to play some games and perhaps a loan period would help me. I realised that as a player struggling to get into a League One side I certainly wasn't going to get a Championship club so I started wondering if I could get a loan move to Shrewsbury. Perhaps they'd be willing to take me back until January and I could get some football under my belt. I spoke to my agent who told me not to rush into anything but he would scout some possibilities.

Once I'd had that conversation I went to see the gaffer and told him I needed to get out on loan. I was 27 years old, and needed to play. I said I wasn't happy sitting around and picking up my money. Kenny said he'd have a think about it and that if there were teams interested to let him know.

Over the following days, Kenny spoke to me again and revealed he could see I was looking sharp again in training and was thinking about getting me back involved, which was good to hear. I wanted to play, but more than anything I still wanted to play for Wolves.

Kenny picked me on the bench at Oldham, where I came on fairly late in the game, and I was on the bench for a couple of games when Jamie O'Hara came back. Although I was pleased to be back I still had a feeling that Jamie's return might be another nail in my Wolves coffin. Jamie is a terrific footballer, and was top drawer in training, but seeing him coming back in after being initially frozen out felt like it was another push towards the door.

We played Oldham again, this time in the FA Cup, and I was picked to start, playing the number ten role, where I had quite a good and effective game. Then – during an international break when we had players missing – we went to Notts County and Ethan Ebanks-Landell scored late on. On this occasion I played in central midfield in what was a really good win. Finally, I was starting to get back into it, playing well in a top-of-the-table game with Brentford and then getting my first goal of the season against Tranmere. Richard Stearman got sent off in the first half but then there was a horror tackle on Ethan and a Tranmere player saw red as well. We came in at half-time and the gaffer asked me if I could do a job at right back? "Yes of course," I replied! A ball came in from the left and I'd made a break forward from right back, a bit like Matt Doherty for Wolves in recent years. I arrived on the edge of the box and hit a volley down into the ground past the Welsh 'keeper Owain Fôn Williams. It was one of my better goals, and we got a draw – a decent result.

On a really windy Friday night, in horrific conditions, we lost at Gillingham when Aaron McCarey came in as 'keeper. We played ok, without creating too many chances, but ended up losing to a goal in added time. The gaffer was also busy reshaping the squad with a few players leaving and others coming in. It really freshened things up, and our season started to take off. We played Preston at home in the following game and I was now bang in form, playing alongside Lee Evans as advanced midfielders. I had a few chances before scoring a one-on-one just before half-time. I could have had a hat trick. I felt in really good nick and everything was going really well again. I was full of confidence.

Cue another setback! It was in training the week following the Preston game and we were playing a small-sided game. I was trying to take the ball past a few players and Danny Batth put in a strong tackle on me. As I went through, my foot got caught in the grass. It was my bad foot which rolled. Bam! Exactly that same pain as at Preston on the first day of the season. Once again I had a scan, which didn't reveal anything, but I was sidelined for about four weeks before getting back into training.

This stop-start stage was incredibly frustrating for me, and I was desperate to be back involved at a time when the boys were really picking up form. Once again I started getting back into the action from the bench, including a good win at Brentford when Michael Jacobs was absolutely brilliant. The team had just broken a club record run of wins, which came to an end on a really difficult pitch at Crawley. I was recalled against Sheffield United at Bramall Lane, which signalled a really good spell for me under Kenny as I finished the season with six goals from nine games. The big one was in the game which clinched promotion away at Crewe, with all my family watching.

Kevin McDonald got the first goal via a deflection and I scored the second as we won 2-0 and clinched an immediate return to the Championship. That goal meant a lot to me considering that a few months earlier it looked like I might be surplus to requirements. We were flying at that point, winning games well, and it was great to be a part of a successful Wolves team getting back up to the Championship. There was a different sort of pressure on us that season, with a lot of expectation on Wolves as a big team in League One, but there was still that feeling of excitement and satisfaction at winning promotion.

There was an added pressure for me at that time as I was soon to be out of contract, so was effectively playing for my future. I was delighted the club had been promoted, and that I had contributed, but I was also hoping my performances would help secure my own future as well. In an ideal world I had impressed enough to earn a new contract at Wolves, but if not, at least I'd have put myself in the shop window. That run of form certainly came at the right time for me.

More drama was to come that season, with our home game against Rotherham the following Friday night, and surely one of the most incredible matches ever played at Molineux. Rotherham had been good all season and they took the lead. Nouha Dicko then hit back to score a couple for us, and I found the net from a one-on-one, but they fought back to 3-2, then we scored – 4-2 to us – before they grabbed a brace, making it 4-4 with a couple of minutes left. It looked like we'd blown it!

My fellow Welsh international Sam Ricketts had other ideas, as he picked the ball up right of centre just inside the Rotherham half and fired it in to me. I waited for him to arrive, laid it back to him and he bent one into the top corner! I think he was the only outfield player who hadn't scored by that stage of the season, and he'd had a terrific season. Sam was a great signing by Kenny, and was one of the main reasons we got promoted. It was great for him to get the goal. The fans poured onto the pitch in celebration. Then Kevin McDonald got another goal in injury time to make it 6-4. Game, set and match to

Wolves! Cue more mayhem in the stadium with fans running all over the pitch. What a fabulous occasion.

From there it was to Leyton Orient for a lunchtime kick-off where we put in a solid performance to win 3-1 and, on the bus on the way home, we found out we'd won the League title which sparked more scenes of celebration.

We had two games left, against Coventry and Carlisle – the only teams we hadn't beaten during the season. I scored at Coventry on 84 minutes but we conceded shortly afterwards to draw, then we beat Carlisle on the final day before the trophy was presented and we enjoyed a parade around the pitch. It had been a fantastic finale to the season and one which all of us thoroughly enjoyed. A couple of days later we did it all again for Jody Craddock's testimonial, a fitting tribute to such a top, top professional. For me, the run of form I had enjoyed as part of a successful team was set to take me into some of the best years of my career.

However, my future was still very much unclear. It was really disappointing I hadn't heard anything about a possible new deal, but the gaffer spoke to me at the end-of-season awards dinner and said that Jez Moxey would contact me with an offer and we'd get something sorted. Great news and the end of a great season, or so I thought.

As the days passed, I went out of contract and it all went quiet. My agent confirmed that nothing had come in from Wolves and I didn't want to go and beg. Firstly, there was no need to as I'd already been given the nod, but also that would put me in a bad position for any bargaining. So I began to wonder if there was anything else on the table. I definitely didn't want to leave, but had to consider other options in case an offer from Wolves wasn't forthcoming.

My agent confirmed there'd been interest from other clubs. Some were waiting on other targets, but the one that stood out as being really keen were Bristol City who'd enjoyed a really strong finish to the season in League One. Steve Cotterill had taken over when they were struggling at the bottom of the table, and had masterminded a terrific run which saw them finish in the top half. They were going to give it a real go in the following season and I was convinced they would get promoted.

Having heard nothing from Wolves, and as you are allowed to do when you are out of contract, I arranged to go and meet Steve, and also the chief executive John Pelling. I'm not sure if word had spread, but my agent then received an email from Jez with the new contract offer, which I have to say I found insulting. It was only for one additional year. It may have been prompted by my recent injuries, but it was difficult to take. I had played 31 times, and scored nine goals, and part of my absence from the first team was a selection issue with the manager. I was 28 years old, coming into my prime as a midfield player and having had a good finish to the season. The money in the contract wasn't great either, especially compared to football in general and what the other lads were earning, so I decided to go and speak to Steve anyway.

I popped down to Bristol, met with Steve and he made me feel wanted. It was the first time since signing for Wolves that I'd actually spoken to another team about the possibility of moving. Steve and John sold me the club and convinced me I'd be a key part of what they were trying to do. They spoke about what they could do for my family, as our two children were very young at the time, and how they could help us settle in the area. John actually told me he had a place in Bristol which I could use for a couple of months until we found somewhere to live.

They were bending over backwards for me. It felt nice. It felt right. In stark contrast to Wolves, where the club appeared to be hinting that I'd been there a while and they would do me a favour by offering me a contract. Bristol City were offering me three years on slightly more money than Wolves but, if they won promotion, it would increase considerably.

With a decision to make I spoke to Kenny, who told me I was a big part of what he was doing at Wolves, he valued my experience of Premier League and Championship football, and felt that I now knew how to manage my body, look after myself and stay fit. I told him the money wasn't the big thing. It was more about the club showing some faith in me and getting that extra bit of security. "Give me two years and I'll sign." I said. Kenny told me it would get sorted. He seemed genuinely surprised at the deal that Bristol City were offering me even though they were a league below.

I'd told Steve Cotterill that I needed some time to think. A move would have had a big impact on my family, with Jack about to start school. Also both of our families are in Shrewsbury, within a couple of miles of our house which has always been a big help, and we were getting married that summer as well. There were plenty of personal considerations, it wasn't about an increase in pay.

It was all happening fast, as I was heading off to my stag weekend in Ibiza in a few days, before getting married the following Saturday. I promised Steve I'd make my mind up before the wedding and let him know either way. I'd enjoyed some great times at Wolves, yet there was an attraction to Bristol City and the exciting new challenge it offered, but moving to Bristol would have meant uprooting my family, and I really felt I had unfinished business at Molineux – I wanted to prove myself and show them what I could do.

Steve rang me as soon as I got back from my stag weekend to check what my decision was, but I asked him to wait until I had heard back from Wolves. Understandably he needed to know soon because there were other players in their sights if I decided not to go. He was going on holiday the same weekend of my wedding so, if I wasn't going to join, he wanted to get some other options in place.

The day of the wedding was getting closer and, even with all the normal stresses involved, it should have been a time for us to enjoy and savour. By the Thursday, Wolves hadn't been in touch and Steve was relentless in chasing me. I couldn't answer his calls because I just didn't know what was happening.

Kenny had said that Jez was going to ring me but the call hadn't come. So on the Thursday I phoned Kenny and told him I had to know what was happening out of fairness to Steve who was still waiting for my decision. It was now, effectively, the last night before my wedding because I was leaving the house on the Friday to go and stay with my friends. I said I needed to know by 5pm, because I felt morally bound to give Steve my answer.

Time passed quickly that afternoon. 1 o'clock. 2 o'clock. 3 o'clock. Nothing happened. I asked Emma that, if it came to it, would she be happy for us to move to Bristol? She said, "Yes, of course, whatever you want to do." I had already spoken with my family the night before and they'd also said I should go if it was what I wanted, particularly with the security of a three-year contract.

It was now 3.30pm. Still nothing. 'Stuff it,' I thought. 'I'm going to ring Jez.' I was so angry by this point. I rang Jez, heard a foreign ring tone, there was no answer and the call went to voice mail, so I left a message. I then tried Kevin Thelwell, Wolves' head of football development and recruitment. He assured me the matter was being dealt with by Jez, and that Kenny said it was getting sorted. I had no choice by then and gave them an ultimatum – if it got to 5 o'clock and I hadn't heard anything I was phoning Steve Cotterill to sign for Bristol City.

It was now 5.10pm and I'd heard nothing from Wolves. The deadline had passed. It looked like I was on my way to Bristol, then my phone rang. It was Jez. I was fuming by now. I demanded to know what the hell was going on – Kenny had told me two days ago that two years was fine and the deal would be done but, here I am, the day before my wedding and seconds away from calling Bristol City's manager to agree a move.

At this point Jez was still trying to negotiate with me. He said he'd e-mailed my agent with an offer but, I said, that wasn't the deal anymore. It was a flat two years, on the money we had agreed, or I was gone. I made it crystal clear that unless he honoured my verbal agreement with Kenny I'd hang up and sign immediately for Bristol City. I was as angry as I'd ever been with Jez, and probably also the first time I'd ever got him on the back foot – something that doesn't happen to Jez very often! The whole affair had annoyed me and this was now a matter of principle. Financially, my contract was so inconsequential compared to others in terms of the money on offer and the money new players were getting.

"Ok. Gentleman's agreement," Jez finally said. "We'll get it done." However, I asked him to put it all in an email to my agent immediately, and phoned 20 minutes later to check it had been received. It had. All sorted. Apart from one thing. I now had to phone Steve Cotterill and tell him my decision.

So much of me had wanted to sign for Bristol City, but two reasons had kept me from doing it. Firstly, the size and stature of Wolves, how I felt I was clawing my way back up at the club and that didn't want to be remembered as a bit of a failure. I desperately wanted to prove myself to the club and its fans. Second was the geography – my family were happy and my kids were happy. I may have been a professional footballer, but I was also a father and a soon-to-be husband. Everything else was screaming for me to go to Bristol City.

I felt like they really wanted me whereas Wolves were maybe doing me a favour.

It was a very difficult conversation to have with Steve. I had been open with Steve and Bristol City about the situation I had been in and I told him I was so sorry but that Wolves had now given me the two years. He was really disappointed and said he felt I had 'played' them a little bit, using their interest to get a better deal at Wolves, which was understandable, but I told him it just wasn't the case. I was five minutes away from joining, and maybe that would have been the correct footballing decision, but on an overall and personal level I still wanted to be at Wolves. He was annoyed with me but I remember saying to him that I really hoped our paths would cross again one day and that I might be able to work with him in the future. A tough call, but Steve messaged me later that night and wished me all the best for my wedding and that he hoped it all went well.

So, I signed for Wolves for another two years and, despite the drawn-out contract saga, and indeed nearly leaving the club, I was feeling positive. Mentally, I was in a very good place. This had been the season when I'd started to focus on my own personal growth, on being more positive, and being able to block out the setbacks and the injuries which had blighted my career.

It all came about after that Preston game the previous January. I had scored in the game, but then got injured in the week which followed.

Carl Howarth was our first team physio at the time – working with Phil Hayward – and it was Carl who looked after me during my rehab. He told me he'd started reading a lot of personal growth books and felt that the way I spoke, the way I was talking about my body, in fact my whole mindset was very negative. It was almost as if I was waiting to get injured and I didn't have any faith in my body. He commented that every time I did an interview I was talking about how hard I was working to stay fit and that I didn't want to get injured again. I was putting so much energy and so much focus on not being injured that maybe it was almost contributing to those injuries happening!

He suggested I read a particular book – *The Secret* by Rhonda Byrne – about the law of attraction: that what you think and how you think affects what you attract and what can happen to you. He said that a lot of people think the theory is completely ridiculous and nonsensical but, even if I was sceptical, just to give it a try. Carl felt it would change the perception I had of myself.

Don't get me wrong. At first, some of it did sound strange. It was completely different to any other book I'd read, but fairly quickly it got me thinking. More than anything, however, it made me feel that there was no point being unhappy. Regardless of what was happening, whatever I was going through, there is never any point being unhappy. It was about thinking happy thoughts, being more positive, being more aware when I was with my family and about making the most of that time. I would be a happier person and then things would improve.

Guess what? That book, and the theory it promoted, absolutely transformed my life from top to bottom and I've been reading books about personal growth ever since. My car is like a classroom and, every morning on the way in to training, I listen to audio books. It is all about improving as a person.

As a result, I have learned some new techniques which have helped me massively. Previously, I'd always allow my mind to get carried away, and very quickly head to a negative place – maybe obsessing about getting injured – to the point, to be honest, where I was approaching depression. Unfortunately, that is the natural way of thinking, perhaps it is even the fairly standard human way of thinking. The natural fear mentality in the human body going back to the day when people had to fear danger.

I took steps to change my mentality by becoming aware of what I was thinking. If I started daydreaming, and on the cusp of thinking negative thoughts, I'd challenge myself and ask, 'What are you thinking about that for?' I introduced a few simple triggers to halt any negativity such as changing the screensaver on my phone to a collage of pictures of Emma and the kids, and of the good times I'd experienced in football. I began to focus on all the aspects of my life I was really grateful for. Gratitude plays a big part in positivity. Every morning when I woke up I'd think about all those things in my life which I appreciated and was grateful for.

I loaded videos on my phone that made me smile. Videos of the kids which made it impossible for me to be unhappy when I watched them. The first one I used was one of Jack laughing uncontrollably. Isn't it great when kids do that? I would watch it over and over again and it would never fail to make me smile.

THE WOLVES REVIVAL

Hand on heart, I can honestly say that discovering this outlook and learning these techniques was the best thing that has ever happened to me – and it's really played a difference on the pitch. From that point, when I returned from injury with my new mindset, I got back in the team and the impact was powerful - goal after goal after goal. I felt I could get a goal every game and everything I did in training was about, 'right – how can I score goals?' With every possible scenario, I'd challenge myself – 'how could I score a goal from here?'

A lot of my goals came from crosses, so if the ball went out wide, what was the optimum position to take up to get a goal. If it worked in training, do it in a game as well. The success I had on the pitch in the final stages of that season reinforced my belief in everything I was doing in terms of my mentality off the pitch. It carried on into the next season as well, and ever since. I have scored a lot of goals in recent seasons, more goals than I was scoring before.

The positivity makes such a difference. There is nothing in my skillset that justifies me from giving an eight or nine out of ten performance on a Saturday, and then being rubbish and dropping to a three out of ten on a Tuesday. A professional footballer's skillset doesn't change from game to game, but their confidence levels and mindset can. Heightened levels of anxiety and mental stress can adversely impact the performance of us all, whatever the situation. For me, it's about what's going on in my mind. If I can keep my positivity and confidence as high as possible, and everything else nice and level, then I should be able to perform to a good standard. Over the last few seasons, since making this life-changing discovery, I think I've played the best and most consistent football of my career.

It's helped me with the fans as well. At the time, I'd been getting a lot of stick from the supporters, certainly after the two successive relegations. When the fans started to call me 'Dangerous Dave', in all honesty, I was certain they were taking the mickey! There was a photo of a group of fans wearing masks of my face at the end-of-season game against Coventry. To me, they were probably saying, 'Well, he is scoring goals, but he's still crap!'

Then it seemed to grow into a bit of a fondness. Well, I hope so anyway! It's certainly stuck with the Wolves fans over the last few years, and not just at the games. A few months ago, I'd taken the kids to the Snow Park at the Chill Factore in Manchester and afterwards, when we went to the Trafford Centre for a meal, a chap walked past and said: "Hey, it's Dangerous!" Jack was intrigued and asked me why the man had called his daddy, Dangerous? From then on he started calling me Dangerous around the house. Not long after, Evie told me I was called Dangerous because I once left the lid off the jam and it squirted everywhere. Kids eh?! It was a bizarre nickname. At the time it felt a little bit strange, maybe a sort of back-handed compliment, but I'd like to think it has grown into a term of endearment. Only the Wolves fans can tell you that!

One aspect of my personality that was a source of negative thoughts when I was younger, was caring too much about what people thought of me, whether as a person or a footballer. I used to hate the thought of people believing I wasn't a nice person, or that I was crap at football. The way I handle this now is to know that every single time I go on to a football pitch, I give my absolute all and, likewise, away from football, I will go out of my way to make sure I am nice to people. If there is anything out there that is negative towards me, then it doesn't bother me. There is a lot more positivity out there than negativity, and if the negativity is beyond your control, then don't let it get you down.

I know if I've had a bad game. I don't need anyone else to tell me. If I have a bad game, I won't look on my Twitter feed to see what other people thought. I don't put myself in a scenario where I can read it or I can see it. If anyone ever mentions anything to me, or looks like they're about to tell me what people are saying, I tell them to stop. Genuinely, I don't want to know. There have been times when I've taken the Twitter app off my phone, as it cuts out the temptation to have a look.

My brother is a big Wolves fan, and he'd go on forums to see what supporters were posting on social media. I'd sometimes get a message from him saying, 'They're hammering you today,' but I'd respond with, 'I don't want to know!' It's not that I disrespect the fans, it's because, for me, if I've had a bad game, I'm already thinking about how I can improve and how I can get back on track for the next match. Negativity doesn't even enter my head. Why should it? There is absolutely nothing to gain in life from being negative.

After our promotion from League One, this new outlook helped me look forward to playing in the Championship. Mentally, I felt like I was in a really good place and found a way to be fit, healthy and happy. I was adamant that this was going to be a big season for me and I would show I was a good Championship footballer, whereas a year earlier I'd been wondering where my future was going to lie. I was feeling good, and determined to make it a good campaign.

I was involved at the start of pre-season, and although I was a bit in and out when it came to the starting line-up for the friendlies, I got the nod to start the first League game of the season against Norwich. It was a TV game on the Sunday, and had a big profile to it with Norwich having just come down from the Premier League. It was a tense encounter and very tight, like most games are on the opening day. Rajiv van La Parra was making his Wolves debut and was having a great game on the right wing – so much so that the Norwich left back Martin Olsson had been sent off around the hour mark for two yellow cards.

Just a few minutes later, Rajiv picked up the ball again, and as soon as he pushed it past his man I knew he was going to get the cross in so I made my move and managed to dart across the front of Russell Martin. Those sort of headers are my trademark – I much prefer heading it from the right hand side across the goal – a cushioned glance into the top corner! What a start to the season and a great afternoon, as we won the game 1-0.

That great start continued when we went to Rotherham the following weekend and, although we lost 1-0, we absolutely battered them. Under Kenny we had suddenly become a really possession-based football team, knocking the ball around. I wouldn't say it was something we'd particularly worked on, but it was a sign of everyone's confidence from the previous season. We had good quality players, were passing the ball out from the back and it wasn't a way I think I'd played at Wolves before. We did everything but score and, from a corner late in the game, the ball bounced in the box, I tried to hook it clear but hit the guy closing me down and went in. While we were really disappointed to lose the game, we knew we had played well, and we still felt confident.

We then went to Fulham, put in a terrific performance to win 1-0, and the run gathered pace, beating Cardiff, Blackburn, and drawing at Blackpool. However, in training, I sensed that the gaffer was desperate to get his new signing from Chelsea, George Saville, into the team and, like a lot of times in my early career, that I'd be the one to make way.

I could see it coming, but I was still furious when I was left out for the game at Charlton. We didn't play well in that game, but we came from behind to draw 1-1, with me coming on as a late substitute. I was back in the team for the next game against Bolton, before being dropped to the bench for the next game at Reading. I came on and scored, but it was given as an own goal. These were frustrating times but I came back in against Wigan, and got a goal – perfect timing for the upcoming international break, when I returned to the Wales squad for the games against Bosnia and Cyprus.

Our first match back was away to Millwall, where we were brilliant for two thirds of the game, going into a 3-0 lead, but somehow we were pegged back to 3-3. I stayed in the team from there, but we had an awful run of five successive defeats, including 4-0 away at Brentford. We next faced Bournemouth, and started very well with Danny Graham putting us ahead before Rajiv got sent off for an innocuous challenge which was later rescinded. Bournemouth were in really good form at the time and were an excellent possession-based team, moving us from side to side. They hit back with two goals and won the game.

We couldn't buy a win at that stage so the gaffer changed the way we played to a narrower formation – to make us harder to break down. We got a great win at Sheffield Wednesday, with Leon Clarke scoring the winner late on, and then a draw at home to Brighton thanks to Danny Batth's late goal, which took us into the Boxing Day fixture at Watford – a televised evening game meaning we could travel on the day and spend Christmas Day at home. We passed the ball really well at Vicarage Road and Nouha Dicko got the only goal of the game to give us the three points.

Our fortunes had changed and we went on a winning run, beating Brentford and drawing away at Fulham in the FA Cup. I also had one of my most prolific goal scoring spells. I got the winner at Blackburn, cutting in and shooting from outside the box, which was a collector's item for me. I was on the bench for the Fulham game as the gaffer had said he was going to rest me, but we were 1-0 down at half-time and not really playing too well, so I came on. I managed to get a goal from a Dominic Iorfa cutback and then Rajiv scored to take us 2-1 up before they equalised. At that point it started snowing and, as the game went into extra time, it turned into a blizzard. Very quickly,

There was always a football around! Trying to tackle my brother Chris as Dad looks on during a camping holiday.

I look pretty pleased with Cup Winners' medal and League Runners-up medal with Worthen Juniors under-10s in 1994.

With Chris again...and a couple of sheep. I wasn't really cut out for life on the farm!

With my sister Sarah in our Newcastle kits!

Top: The world is my football pitch! Though the goalposts probably need a bit of work.

Left: Proud as punch again, with the Chronicle Cup and other awards in 1997.

Bottom: Me and Chris at home in 1996.

With Marco Adaggio, Gavin Cadwallader and Joe Hart at the 2005-06 Shrewsbury Town photocall.

Top: Watching Shrewsbury with Nigel Vaughan, who was a huge influence on my early career.

Right: Semi-final play-off success against MK Dons, and so I decided to turn captain Richard Hope into Shrewsbury mascot Lenny the Lion for his post match interview!

Celebrating a goal for Luton against Swindon with Darren Currie, one of my boyhood Shrewsbury heroes.

Bottom: Helping to force a Liverpool own goal in the big FA Cup tie which turned out to be my last appearance for Luton.

Battling against Stockport and The Gay Meadow pitch.

A rarity - playing at home in our away kit - when Bristol Rovers turned up with only their away kit.

Celebrating my goal in a 3-0 win in the 'A49 Derby' against Hereford.

Winning the Championship with Wolves in 2008-09 – what a squad and management team that was.

Every Premier League goal was a big one! No idea what Jamie O'Hara was doing here after I scored against Wigan.

Left: The Welsh Wolves! Enjoying the Championship title celebrations with Wayne and Vokesey.

The minute's applause for Gary Speed. He was my hero growing up and his loss was such a tragedy for everyone who loved him.

Scoring a Premier League winner against Manchester City past my former housemate. Sorry Joe!

How do you get past this little lot then? It was great to test myself against some really top players in the Premier League.

Putting Wolves 2-1 ahead against Aston Villa. Eventually losing that game 3-2 was a massive blow and a few weeks later Mick McCarthy was gone.

With a very young Jack! I love that he has been able to watch me play and that we share a love of football.

Celebrating with a fan after scoring against Crewe to clinch my second Wolves promotion. Another great season with a great group of lads.

Having almost left the club in the League One title-winning season, I ended up in the best scoring form of my life and with another medal!

My favourite photo, taken when we were crowned champions of League One.

Two great shots from Wolves photographer Sam Bagnall. It was an emotional night in the FA Cup against Fulham after the passing of Sir Jack Hayward. I came off the bench to score twice in the snow.

Top: Wolves physio Phil Hayward treating me at Preston. I suffered a lot with injury but have managed to avoid too many serious problems in more recent years.

Left: Handing my shirt to a young fan.

Bottom: A proud moment. Leading the team out at Anfield as Wolves captain - and we won!

Celebrating the end of the
2016-17 season with Jack,
Evie and my nephew Tom.

My final game for Wolves, against
Southampton.

I know I have divided opinion among Wolves supporters, but I hope I
managed to win a few over during my time!

My new life as a Royal. It's a great club with fabulous fans and they know I'll give everything to bring Premier League football back to the Madejski.

New club, familiar colours. Thanking the fans after a win at Derby.

Another home victory, this time against Nottingham Forest.

What a feeling! It's always a thrill to score your first goal for a new club and this one, against Millwall at The New Den, was no exception.

At the launch of the Little Rascals Foundation with TV presenter Jacqui Oatley and my best friend, fellow trustee and business partner Ben Wootton.

Family is massive for me. This is the day after Evie was born, as Jack met his little sister for the first time.

A different type of boots on a family break in Pembrokeshire.

The Edwards family enjoying a summer holiday in Dubai.

the pitch was completely white and it was incredibly difficult to see anything. I thought I'd scored the winner, with a backheel from Danny Batth's cross, and celebrated with a 'Klinsmann' dive, which I instantly regretted because it was so cold, but – in the last minute – we gave away a free kick. Ross McCormack scored and the game went to a penalty shootout. I scored the first penalty – a sort of hat trick for the game – but we eventually lost. The winning run had come to an end.

Sadly, our club president and former owner, Sir Jack Hayward, had died on the day of that Fulham game, so the following match – at home to Blackpool a few days later – was his memorial game. Blackpool were going through a rough patch at the time so we were expected to win but they played really well and it proved tough for us. I had a great chance before half-time, running through in the 'keeper with Nouha square of me, but I was caught in two minds – whether to shoot or pass – and ended up putting the ball wide. I took full responsibility for that mistake – I should have put us in front – and vowed to put things right. Fortunately, I managed to do that, not long from full-time. It was a tap-in, in front of the South Bank, and Benik Afobe had came off the bench for his first appearance to add the second, minutes later to seal the victory. It was such a relief, not only to get the three points, but for the team to win on the day the club paid tribute to Sir Jack. We were all wearing black armbands in his memory and I held mine aloft in recognition of a man who'd done so much, not just for Wolves but Wolverhampton as a whole.

That emotional victory helped us generate some real momentum towards the end of the season. However, because Benik and Nouha were playing so well together up front, I was in and out of the team during the run-in. I started, and scored, in a 5-0 win against Rotherham and, even if I didn't start, I was still coming on in most of the games, including a very memorable one against Leeds. We'd been on the brink of the play-offs for a while, and there had always been the feeling that something special might happen that season. It was Easter weekend, and having beaten Nottingham Forest on the Friday, I came off the bench on the Monday against Leeds when we were 3-1 up. We were pegged back to 3-3 but then, with a couple of minutes to go, I managed to head home the winner in front of the South Bank. With the atmosphere, the way the game had gone, and what was at stake, I think that has to be the most memorable goal of my Wolves career. The stadium was rocking and the whole place just went berserk.

That win took us into the top six, with just a few games remaining. Having finished so strongly against Leeds I thought I'd have a chance of starting the next game at Birmingham, but no. In fact I didn't even come on. We went 1-0 up but then found ourselves 2-1 down in the closing stages. The gaffer only made one substitution that game, which was a bit frustrating because I always felt I could go on and grab a goal. That defeat proved to be the pivotal blow to our promotion hopes. We needed a result to keep ourselves in the top six but when we didn't get it we lost our momentum and never got back into the play-off places again.

Over the final three games we took seven points, but it wasn't quite enough and we missed out on the play-offs on goal difference, despite a really good tally of 78 points. One of the highest totals not to make it into the Championship play-offs. Still, it had been a positive season and we felt everything was finally moving in the right direction after the promotion from League One. The atmosphere on the final day against Millwall was terrific and I think the fans thought we were going to give it a right good go the following season.

On a personal note, I made 45 appearances and I was only unavailable through injury for one game – at Derby – after I'd been on the end of a heavy tackle at Ipswich, which was annoying as I'd been determined to go through a season injury-free. I felt I was still making a good contribution to the team and things were looking good. Unfortunately, that isn't how things turned out.

Bakary left, and the club signed Conor Coady, Nathan Byrne and Jed Wallace, as well as Emi Martinez, Adam Le Fondre and Sheyi Ojo on loan. We went to Clairefontaine in France for pre-season, and it was here I had a few good chats with Kenny Jackett about his plans for the new season. The gaffer explained that he was looking to play Benik Afobe and Nouha Dicko up front and, having brought Conor in, as well as having Kevin McDonald in the squad, I was again uncertain of my position. I assured him that I was still desperate to be in the team, wanted to play a part, and didn't really mind where that was. I'd played a lot on the right or left of midfield during my career, so if there wasn't a role in the centre, I'd be more than happy to go wide.

THE WOLVES REVIVAL

So, I was asked to play on the left hand side, but what a hiding to nothing that was – following in the footsteps of a player like Bakary, who was fast, exciting and a real fans' favourite. I was probably going to get some stick and some fans would be on my back but, to be honest, that didn't bother me at all. I was now at a stage where I knew what I could do, and I wasn't really listening to stuff on the outside or being influenced by what other people might say. It did appear to bother Kenny, though. Perhaps the fans would compare what we had previously with Sako, to what they had with me. Being exposed to that was no problem for me. I've taken stick all my career. I was concentrating on trying to offer something completely different to Sako, but also something that was effective.

We played Aston Villa in the last pre-season friendly and I was tucked in on the left with James Henry on the right. Benik was roaming around, as he did when at his most dangerous, and then we had Nouha stretching the pitch. It worked really well. I then started on the left in the first game of the season at Blackburn. Even though the fans hated it, it was from me being on the inside that helped get the first goal as I headed it through to Benik to score. The second goal also came from me being tucked in and meeting a cross from Nouha who had run the channel down the left hand side. That was the infamous handball goal. The ball flew across the goal, instinctively I tried to get something on it, but it ended up being my hand. I don't know why I did it. I had never done it before, and never have since, and it isn't something I was proud of. As I wheeled away, caught up in the adrenalin, I was feeling very sheepish and remember telling Benik and the lads that it was handball. I felt very guilty.

I was considering fronting it up to the referee, but the general consensus was 'shut up, don't say anything!' It was a really difficult moment. I felt bad, because I pride myself on my integrity and base my whole character on that. I remember Blackburn's manager at the time, Gary Bowyer, coming over and telling me he thought I was better than that. I tried to reason that teams end up on the wrong end of many decisions, and that one had actually gone for us. Had I owned up and we'd ended up drawing the game, or worse, I don't think I would have been particularly popular inside the dressing room. It didn't stop the guilt, however, and I remember staying off social media for a good few days afterwards. I don't think the Blackburn fans have ever forgotten it, which is totally understandable.

As for the game itself, I thought we played well, and I'd enjoyed that left hand side position. I was getting so much of the ball in that pocket of space. As a central midfielder, I hate it when the winger comes inside because the full back can't come all the way across to cover as it opens up the channel. You can get some decent space to try and make things happen.

We then welcomed Hull for our first home game. They had just come down from the Premier League and were among the favourites for an immediate return. Once again, we played very well, and got a 1-1 draw from a fairly even game. So, four points out of those two tough games was a good start.

Although we'd enjoyed a decent start to the season at Blackburn, the gaffer had made a change to the goalkeeping position, bringing in Emi Martinez on loan from Arsenal. He was an excellent young 'keeper and had plenty of potential, but it felt a strange decision to drop Carl Ikeme after the Blackburn game, as he was such a top 'keeper who had really made the position his own. The players could have understood Emi coming in to push Carl and battle for the position – but not to go straight in at number one. Particularly as Carl hadn't done anything wrong, apart from one mistake with the Blackburn goal. Carl was such an integral part of the dressing room, was still a good goalkeeper and dropping him affected the team. The general view among the players was that there were plenty of positions across the pitch which needed strengthening so why change one – the goalkeeper – where we were already very strong. Once Kenny got something in his mind, he very rarely shifted from it, and that seemed to be the case with the goalkeeping department.

Next up was QPR at home on a Wednesday night and, for the first 35 minutes, it was arguably the best football we had played under Kenny. It was all free-flowing with James Henry out wide right, I was tucked in on the left, and Benik was in the hole with the freedom to roam. We seemed to have options everywhere and were playing some really good stuff. We went 2-0 up and then, just before half-time and against the run of play, Charlie Austin scored from a header. Emi couldn't do anything about the QPR equaliser but the two he conceded in the second half were very soft and he would have been disappointed to have let them in. From there we couldn't get back into it and, having played such fantastic football for 35 minutes, it was difficult to believe we'd ended up on the losing side.

Kenny was now starting to get some stick, in particular for me being on the left wing. He had brought in Sheyi Ojo – another great, young talent – from Liverpool just before the start of the season, but for him to go straight in and impress in the hustle and bustle of the Championship was going to be a big challenge, especially following Sako into that left wing position. Sheyi had come off the bench in a few of the early games before making his first start away at Cardiff. The gaffer changed our shape that day and I reverted to the number ten position, playing in behind Benik.

By this point, with a few days of the window remaining, there was also plenty of speculation about Benik's future. In the end, he didn't actually go anywhere – not until the following January anyway – but I do think his head had been turned. Benik is a great lad, and a top player, and he was brilliant at Wolves – his goals-to-game ratio was fantastic. I got on really well with him, but he just seemed to lose a bit of intensity. After the Cardiff the game the gaffer was particularly furious with Benik although, to be honest, we were all poor in that one.

Those back-to-back league defeats increased the pressure ahead of the final game – at home to Charlton – before the first international break. By this point it had become clear Richard Stearman was being sold to Fulham, and he sat out the game. Again, this felt like a really strange decision. Stears was in the form of his career, having come off the back of a really good season when he cleaned up at the Player of the Year awards. I know for a fact he didn't want to leave and was pushed out of the door. He was into his last year, and would happily have signed a new contract at Wolves, but Fulham came in and must have offered a good deal, which the club accepted. I couldn't understand footballing reasons for selling one of your best players, a view shared in the dressing room.

Suddenly, our solid start was becoming fragmented. We'd lost Sako in the summer, Kemes had lost his place, Benik was unhappy, Stears was being sold, and then we were to lose Nouha to a serious cruciate ligament injury in the Charlton game two days before the transfer window closed. On top of that, there was a lot of speculation around

Kevin McDonald's future, and he had been a big player for us. We were experiencing some turmoil.

I was handed the captain's armband for the Charlton game, which was special for me, but I also felt a lot of responsibility and expectation to try and carry the team through when there was so much other stuff going on. I think it was a time when the gaffer wanted to know he had people on the pitch who he could really trust. I was back on the left hand side and, although we'd been doing ok, we went 1-0 down, which didn't help the uneasy atmosphere. The gaffer made a double change, moved me into the centre of midfield, and I equalised shortly afterwards.

Dicko had picked up that horrible injury but, with five minutes to go, Alfie (Adam Le Fondre) tucked home a cross from Sheyi for one of his typical goals. It was a big win going into the international break, given everything else going on off the pitch, and at a pivotal time when the team could have kicked-on or, just as easily, imploded with unhappy players not wanting to be there. It was up to the players to stay committed and keep the team going.

After the international break we lost 2-1 at Bolton, with Jed Wallace – who'd arrived with such optimism as a summer signing before picking up an injury – unfortunate to miss a couple of good chances. We then struggled against Brighton at Molineux and I got a really nasty tackle in the first half. Coming just a few weeks after what had happened to Nouha, I feared the worst. My knee buckled at a ridiculously bad angle and I had a shooting pains. Phil Hayward came on and checked me out. Due to my numerous injuries, I've often spoken to the physios about identifying symptoms and possible preventative measures, including showing me the specific test for checking whether the anterior cruciate ligament (ACL) had been damaged. So, when he came on to treat me, I knew that I could be in trouble if he did the test. He did do the test but, luckily, I was ok and had just over-stretched. It was certainly sore for a few minutes but I was able to carry on. Conor Coady got sent off at the start of the second half, but we managed to grind out a 0-0 for a crucial point. The next morning my knee was really sore and a scan revealed a little tear in my lateral ligament on the outside of my knee. I worked really hard to recover and only missed a fortnight – one game – when it could have been a lot worse.

The international window saw me with Wales securing qualification for the Euros, but I picked up a slight groin injury which kept me out for a couple of Wolves games. I came back for the Middlesbrough game and scored with header to finish a good move, but Kortney Hause got injured so Conor had to move back into defence and we ran out of steam a little bit, going from a goal up to losing 3-1.

We'd now lost three on the bounce and were heading to Birmingham for another big derby. I love playing at St Andrew's and the atmosphere was brilliant. Mike Williamson was playing his first game for us, really steadied the ship alongside Danny Batth and I managed to get a goal early on. Sheyi Ojo added a second late on and we came away with the points. That took us on to Bristol City on the Tuesday and what was a very different performance. A goal down at half-time, the gaffer surprised us by bringing on Grant Holt and Adam Le Fondre for Benik Afobe and Nathan Byrne and going 3-5-2, a system we hadn't really done much work on. We didn't improve in the second half and it was a really disappointing result.

Three successive draws followed before we won at Rotherham, and then hit a disappointing run, which included defeats at home to Leeds and 4-1 away at Sheffield Wednesday. I was an unused substitute at Hillsborough that day but there were a few strong words at half-time and full-time. 'Lenny' (James) Henry came in at the break and started a bit of a rant by saying: "I don't want to blame anyone but..." and then followed it up with "what are our centre halves doing?" He was having a pop at Danny Batth, one of his mates – they got on really well. A few people had to step in and it was quickly all fine again but it is just one of those things that you remember. Everyone was blaming each other and sometimes, especially after the game, getting a few things off your chest can actually help. Very often you find people who are good mates off the pitch having a go at each other. Then, on the bus on the way home, it's all fine again.

Having had some bad results, we were in danger of being dragged into trouble. Whenever we were in that sort of situation, Kenny was excellent in getting us to 'win ugly'. If we didn't have the confidence to play open, expansive football then he would change things and make us a lot harder to break down. We'd switch to a 4-3-3 and, instead of me playing as a number ten, I'd be more of a holding midfielder alongside two other central midfielders. The fans probably wouldn't say it worked well in terms of the performances, but it certainly did with the results. We got battered by Reading at Molineux on Boxing Day – but won 1-0. Then we went to Charlton, played better, and won 2-0. On New Year's Day we were at Brighton, and I'm not even sure we had a shot on target but we won 1-0 with an own goal. Winning three games on the bounce was massive for us. It was just what we needed and steered us away from trouble a little bit.

The highlight of this period was the introduction and the form of Jordan Graham. He was always the one who could make something happen. Myself, Kevin McDonald and Conor Coady needed to work our absolute socks off in midfield and do all the legwork, so we could keep the wingers fresh and get them up against their full backs. Jordan was producing chance after chance by taking people on. We played well at West Ham in the FA Cup, only to lose to a late goal – a special day as we knew it would be our last time at Upton Park. Then, against Fulham at home, we started really well, going 2-0 up thanks to two goals from Michal Zyro, and while Fulham came back into it we ended up winning 3-2. Cardiff was a disappointing game and a disappointing way for the winning league run to end, especially with losing Jordan to a cruciate knee ligament injury. A really bad day at the office.

That took us on to the away game at Queens Park Rangers, where I suffered my metatarsal injury and started my race to recover in time for the Euros. Wolves stuttered through to the end of the season, winning only four further games and finishing in a disappointing 14th position, miles off a play-off place. There was still work to do at Molineux, but I knew I had to focus everything on my recovery, and get fit for France.

13

Euro 2016, Here we Come!

'If everyone is moving forward together, then success takes care of itself'
Henry Ford

After Wolves' season finished with a win over Sheffield Wednesday at Molineux, it was all about whether I could make the squad for the Euros. There was no way I was a shoo-in for the squad, far from it. It had been a disappointing season at Wolves, but I'd managed to get myself fit and playing again after my injury which was what I needed.

Because that recovery had been so intense, I wanted to try and get some time away with the family, especially if, as I was desperately hoping, I was going to be away for a few weeks in the summer. So we went on holiday to Dubai for a week which was amazing – just what the doctor ordered – enjoying some family time, some good weather, and all in the knowledge that as soon as I got back it was very much a case of getting down to work. I was in the hotel gym most days, just to keep myself ticking over. A little bit of boxing and so on, just to keep the weight off, but without doing too much loading on my foot, given I had come back from a broken metatarsal.

We got back on the Saturday morning and then it was time to meet up with Wales. I had been named in the provisional squad of 30 for a training camp in Portugal, which would then be whittled down to 23. The various squad scenarios were playing heavily on my mind and looking at the midfielder options, trying to second guess what the gaffer might do and how many he might take. It's a strange situation because everyone in the squad gets on really well and you're up against your mates for a place at the tournament. It was like going back to being a kid again, and on trial. It was just about getting away for the week and making sure I did everything right – and then, what will be will be.

We met up on the Monday night and flew out to Portugal early on the Tuesday morning, to the Vale Do Lobo complex which was absolutely fantastic. We were split into different apartments and in ours was myself, Sam Vokes, Andy King, Hal Robson-Kanu and Simon Church. There was a little pool out the back and a golf course nearby and it was all very relaxed, albeit with some tough training sessions thrown in. Most nights we'd go out on to the putting green at the back and have little competitions, with a bit of money on it to make it interesting.

I felt really good in the training sessions. I'd had the break from February to April so my mind was really fresh, perhaps different to how it sometimes is at the end of a long, hard season. We also had a game of golf, my first for about three years. I love golf, but had knocked it on the head after my back problems and injuries, so I dug the clubs out again for a round with Kingy, Vokesey and Chris Gunter. The course out there was amazing.

Knowing that if I did make it into the squad, I'd be away from the family for a long time, I felt lucky to have had that week's holiday in Dubai because not everyone in the squad had managed to get that time with their family. I was FaceTiming the kids during the week and was a bit gutted to have missed Jack's first football game for his school. I also FaceTimed Tom, my nephew, on his ninth birthday. He was proudly showing off his new Pogba Juventus shirt, unaware that his hero would soon be wearing the red of Manchester United.

Although I was really enjoying it, by the end of the week I just wanted the camp to be over and know who was going to be in that final squad of 23. Once that squad was named, whichever way it went, I knew I'd be able to deal with it and the pressure would be off. There hadn't been any clues during the week at all. No hints from the gaffer or the staff, and no real team shape or specific sessions which might have pointed to who was going to be in. Then, on the Friday, there was a bit of shape work with what looked like it could have been a starting

XI, but with a lot of rotation. I was the last of the central midfielders to go into what looked like the strongest team, so that got my mind working overtime. Was that a signal of my place in the pecking order?

That left me feeling a little bit subdued, and I was speaking to Vokesey and Kingy who I knew were nailed-on for the squad. They were telling me not to be so stupid and that I would make it, but I still couldn't take anything for granted. I was still trying to stay positive and using the positivity techniques I'd adopted. Focusing on doing everything in my power over those few days to make it in but, if not, preparing myself to make the best of it and know I would have a great summer with my family. There was that nagging feeling of not making the Belgium squad the previous summer, but as long as I gave my all at the training camp, I had to remind myself that anything else was beyond my control.

On the Friday evening we went out to a restaurant down by the sea, followed by a really light session on the Saturday. That evening we all gathered to watch the Championship play-off final, as Hull beat Sheffield Wednesday, and then the Champions League final – Gareth Bale and Real Madrid against Atletico Madrid – with some nervousness as we watched. Everyone wanted Gaz to come through unscathed and ready to join up with the squad. It's fair to say we knew he was going to make the cut.

He actually went down with his calf before the end of the game, cramping up. He took a penalty in the shootout, and scored, but he was really hobbling. Thankfully we got a message soon after the end of the game that he was fine. The gaffer must have been watching through his fingers, but with that news at least he could sleep well that night. All the boys had cheered Gaz on to a second Champions League title, an amazing achievement.

The next day we had a practice match within the squad. It was treated the same as a proper match in terms of all the preparation, but you just didn't get a cap at the end of it! I felt I'd done quite well and I knew I had put everything into it. The pitch was quite soft in places, without as much 'give' as a normal pitch, so I didn't want to be too aggressive and end up picking up a niggle. Unfortunately two of the boys did pick up injuries in the game. Tom Lawrence went over on his ankle and ended up being out for eight weeks, ruling him out of what I thought would be a definite place in the squad. Hal also went off early on in the game, but fortunately he was ok.

I was pleased to get the game out of the way. There was nothing more now that I could do to change the gaffer's mind either way – I had given everything out there – but assumed he must have known his squad irrespective of what had happened during the week. He was quite loyal, so part of me was being positive, knowing I'd been involved in most of the qualifying campaign and him knowing exactly what I had to offer, but then I'd look around the other midfielders and recognise the quality they had to offer, and couldn't really see anyone who would be left out.

Joe Ledley was out there but hadn't trained properly as he was still recovering from his broken leg – he was a definite choice if fit. David Vaughan had been involved, as a holding midfielder, in the shape work in Joe's absence, so I knew he would probably be going. Kingy had come off the back of a Premier League winning season with Leicester and was also a definite, and, to me, Emyr Huws was one of the most gifted players we had – a really good footballer. I was just hoping the gaffer might take all of us, and compensate in other positions.

As we were getting off the bus that Sunday before going home, a few of the boys said the gaffer had spoken to Adam Matthews and told him he wasn't going to make the squad. That had happened to a few others as well, but not any midfielders. That was it for me, I just wanted to stay away from the gaffer at all costs. Not get in his eye line, completely avoid him! If he was to say, "Dave, can I have a word?" I knew that would be it. Game over. So I was head down, probably being quite rude, hoping not to get that shout.

I got back to the airport, and managed to get on the plane without any interruptions. So far so good! I'd got the kids some presents – a Portugal kit for Jack because he really likes Ronaldo, and a rucksack and some ballet stuff for Evie – and I was really looking forward to seeing them, although by the time I got back on the Sunday night they'd be in bed.

The squad announcement was due on Monday, and then whoever was in it would join up on the Tuesday. I contacted Mark Evans, the Welsh FA's head of international affairs on Sunday night, asking when we might hear. He said he didn't know. Despite every effort to stay positive, my anxiety levels were now on warp-drive. 'He must know!' I thought.

As Monday dawned, the Edwards clan were having a day at home. Emma nipped out to the supermarket and I was with the kids, constantly checking my phone. This was nerve-racking stuff. To be fair to Mark, he'd told me we'd be notified via email, so I was clicking the refresh button every few seconds.

Then it came through. Like all the emails you get when squads are announced, but obviously this one was slightly more special! 'Squad for Euro 2016' was the title header. Scrolling down I soon saw my name, but I quickly started to count the names, just in case the FAW had included standby players. Luckily, I noticed that the players were all numbered through the positions, and it went down to 23, and then the list stopped.

I was buzzing, but was just at home with the kids. Emma was out, and I didn't really want to tell anyone else until I'd spoken to her. I told the kids though. Jack was just as excited as me, if not even more so. Evie didn't really have a clue what was going on. Never mind! I was still chatting to Jack, when he started drawing a picture, so I left him to it. Then he came to show it to me. It was me in a Wales kit, getting ready for Euro 2016. He'd got my green boots on it and everything. What a wonderful little man he is.

When Emma came back she asked if I had heard anything. I said, "No". Naughty! But I told her that Jack had drawn a picture for her. When he showed her she clicked. It was quite bitter-sweet for Emma. She was absolutely delighted for me, and really proud, but she also knew that this news meant I would not be at home for at least a month, maybe more.

After that I phoned all my family - mum, dad, brother and sister - with the news, and it quickly turned into a celebratory day. We went to Emma's dad's for a barbecue in the afternoon and my brother's in the evening. He's got some goals in his garden so the kids love it down there. It was great spending some time with the family before heading out the following day. The best bit of the day had been seeing Jack's face when he knew I was in the squad – utterly priceless.

Emma and the kids were quite upset when I left – this was the longest time I'd ever spent away from them. I knew it was going to be hard work for Emma, keeping the kids occupied for a month, and juggling it all with her own work as a personal trainer. Organising everything was going to be a challenge for her.

As I headed to Cardiff, I had to have some blood tests at a hospital, something everyone at the Euros needed to get done, then a quick haircut in the city centre as I wasn't sure when the next chance would come. We had some integrity and commercial meetings in the evening, which was a talk from an FAW official covering UEFA's tournament guidance – what we should and shouldn't do during the tournament, and what we should and shouldn't say. We were going to need to do everything by the book. It included details like having to use Adidas-branded washbags when you go into the stadium, and only using officially branded headphones with your personal gadgets. Some of the lads disputed that, saying that Cristiano Ronaldo would – 100% – be getting off the Portugal bus with his Louis Vuitton bag or his Beats headphones or whatever it was he normally had.

I remember watching the first game and seeing everyone going in with their own gear, completely ignoring the protocols we'd been given. It even extended to social media and which hashtags we were supposed to use on Twitter and Instagram and so on. An extraordinary amount of detail, and quite a boring meeting to be honest, but the FAW had to get this right and make sure we avoided any unwanted fines or sanctions.

It was now June 1st, a Wednesday, and were back in training, a really hard session in which we were out on the pitch for two-and-a-half hours. In the evening came the official send-off dinner which started at 6.00 and finished at 11.30. It was amazing to see all the support for us, and loads of money was raised for the Prince's Gate Trust and Tenovus Cancer Care. There was a lovely atmosphere and the best bit of the evening was the Manic Street Preachers playing the official *Together Stronger* song for Euro 2016. I'd always remembered England having some good World Cup songs including *Three Lions* and it was great that Wales had got such a good one for the tournament.

A tactical session followed in Cardiff the next morning and then an event at JD Sports in the city centre that evening, which was the start of us receiving a lot of free stuff: trainers, PS4 games, headphones, and other bits and bobs. I sent the PS4 game home to Jack who was delighted. The Friday was a lighter day with some training and a bit of down time in the afternoon which was good after all the events. Then came the Saturday departure, which was quite special, even though we weren't yet going to France as we had a friendly in Sweden. We were all suited and booted, and had a photo taken on the plane of all the boys together which went on social media.

We arrived in Sweden on the Saturday night, ready for a friendly on the Sunday. It's a lovely place but we weren't there for a city break. I was hoping for some game time and to try and show the gaffer what I could do if called upon. It wasn't our best performance, that's for sure. Our form since qualifying for the Euros hadn't been great and there was a feeling of edginess ahead of the tournament. We lost 3-0. I came on at 60 minutes and had quite a lot of the ball but it wasn't a good game.

The gaffer was raging after the game but he didn't say too much. You could tell he was really thinking about what he was going to say. Looking back, maybe the defeat was a blessing in disguise – a bit of a wake-up call – and a reminder to not get ahead of ourselves. We needed to rediscover that spark and spirit that had got us to the tournament in the first place. With the game over, we flew straight to the Breton town of Dinard, our base in France, arriving in the early hours of the morning. Very quickly we re-focused on what we needed to do and how we needed to perform. The first game against Slovakia was now less than a week away, and we needed to be ready.

14

Slovakia for Starters

'He never realised that people are capable, at any time in their lives, of doing what they dream of'
Paulo Coelho in The Alchemist

I headed out to France just delighted to be in the squad and hoping to be involved in maybe one of the games at least. It hadn't really crossed my mind that I might start the opening fixture in Bordeaux. I was just going to give my best in training and see what happened.

The build-up in that first week in Dinard went really well. The facilities were amazing and the hotel was perfect, with branding throughout that just oozed the 'Together Stronger' motto. It was even emblazoned all over the training facilities, which were equally impressive.

It was nice to be able to get out as well, and on the Monday a few of the lads – complete with our security guys Les and Grant – walked along the coastal path into the centre of Dinard – a quiet town, but beautifully picturesque – and to a typical Breton *crêperie*. It was a standard sugar and lemon *crêpe* for me, with a green tea. Very nice! In the evening I relaxed with a game of cards with Sam Vokes, Andy King and Ben Davies.

The next day we also managed to fit in a game of golf, which was perfect after all the training and travelling we'd been doing. Me and Vokesey took on Simon Church and the Doc, Jonathan Houghton. We lost on the 17th hole! Alongside the training it is always good to try and relax, whether it's on pre-season with your club or here, in my first experience of a major tournament, with Wales.

We also had a quiz on one of the first few nights and, after dinner, the whole team and staff watched a Joe Calzaghe documentary film. I'd seen it before but I loved it as I'm a huge boxing fan. It certainly inspired us as we moved towards such a massive first game of the tournament.

During that first week, we were called to a meeting with our analysts Esther Wills and James Turner. Esther led the meeting and started by giving everyone an iPad Pro to use during the tournament, loaded with analysis details so we could get as much information as we needed about training, opponents and our individual clips. The lads were excited because we thought we were getting a free iPad. That hope was quickly extinguished as Esther said they needed to be returned at the end of the trip. If not, there'd be a fine, as there'd be if any of the lads visited any inappropriate websites – as the junior age groups at the FAW would also use the iPads afterwards.

The meeting was then abruptly halted in complete pandemonium, when Les, the head security guy, burst through the doors shouting, "Get out of here now, follow me and don't look back!" Wow. Panic time. Everyone surged to the door, led by the gaffer. It was chaos. We ran down the corridors, heading towards the basement, all the time with Les shouting: "Keep moving, keep moving!" I immediately assumed this was a terror attack, and you could tell by the panic and look on the other lads' faces that they were equally scared! I was towards the back and we had Grant, the other security guy, bringing up the rear and also giving instructions. I turned to Grant and asked, "What's going on?" To which he replied, "Don't worry it's just a drill."

This gave me some relief, but by the pace the boys in front were moving they definitely didn't realise. As I got to the basement we moved into an underground car park. The front of the group were 20 yards or so ahead and there were some tall railed gates to the right. I could see the gaffer going past them and, all of a sudden, someone on the other side started shaking and rattling the gates. Everyone was petrified and in pure panic mode!

Les stopped at the far wall and started speaking. "Relax now boys, that was a drill ... we needed to show you where we would go if there was any sort of emergency." The lads didn't know whether to laugh or cry as we all trudged back up to the meeting room. As we walked in, it was obvious that everyone had thought it was the real deal because the chairs were everywhere – strewn all over the room – and poor Esther's iPads had just been thrown all over the place. It was remarkable how none of them had been damaged. As we all put the room back together and sat down, an air of calm came over the group and the gaffer broke the silence: "Who the bloody hell was shaking them gates then?" Once again, laughter broke out and the mood was lightened.

Even though I was having the time of my life, I was already missing Emma and the kids. We were celebrating our second wedding anniversary during that first week and, although I'd organised for some flowers to be delivered, I was gutted not to be able to spend the day with my family. It was tough, but I knew it had to be worth it for this experience. Then, on Wednesday, only 48 hours before the game, came the news which certainly made me feel it was worth it.

I think I'd decided that Kingy was going to be playing against Slovakia. The manager had said he wasn't going to risk playing both Joe Allen and Joe Ledley because they had both been injured for a period of time, and Andy – a terrific player – had come off a fantastic season with Leicester. Having been part of a team that had won the Premier League, he would be full of confidence.

Wednesday was an important training session at our Dinard base where we were going to nail a lot down in terms of the tactics, set pieces and so on. It was Andy who came to me on the bus on the way to training, and said, "I think you might play on Saturday". In disbelief, I responded with a "No chance."

Andy, who I know very well and trust totally, then explained his thoughts. It turned out the manager had spoken to Andy, saying he knew he'd be disappointed but he wasn't going to start. The talk was along the lines of Joe Allen, Jonny Williams and Aaron Ramsey – playing in behind Gareth up front – all being terrific ball players who'd want to come and look for the ball. Andy is another one who is good on the ball and can do that. The reasoning was, therefore, that the gaffer was looking for someone else – and this sounds daft – who wasn't actually going to be too interested in going to look for the ball too much all the time. Instead, he wanted someone he could sit in there, think defensively, stay in the middle of the pitch and make sure that everything was organised. It didn't look like he was going to risk Joe Ledley at this stage of the tournament either.

SLOVAKIA FOR STARTERS

As Andy was telling me this, I was thinking, 'Wow, I might be playing in the Euros.' An incredible feeling! It was a shame because I could tell Kingy was disappointed, and he's such a great lad as well. It was as if he was telling me to make sure I was ready. If I was happy and bouncing around inside, I wasn't going to show it – out of respect to him, and still not wanting to get too carried away.

At the Thursday training session the media were there at the start, so the gaffer mixed it all up, and changed things around so as not to give anything away. We couldn't risk anything getting out that might give Slovakia an advantage. Then, after the media had left, we did the set pieces and, sure enough, I was involved in the shape of what looked like being the starting XI. The manager didn't officially name the team but I dared to dream just a little bit – I was just so excited at the prospect of playing in the European Championships!

Previously, I'd thought that even if I'd got one minute coming off the bench it would have been so amazing, but here I was, possibly starting the first game of a tournament which was so huge for Wales. I can genuinely say there were no nerves. I was too excited. I think that's down to the mentality that I've developed. Had I been 21, I think I would have been petrified, but at 30, and with so much experience behind me, I just wanted to embrace every moment of it.

So, from that Wednesday, leading up to the game, I made sure I took in every last drop of the experience: the flight, the hotel, the fans, everything. The flight itself was worth remembering. We had loads of room, it was business class throughout and I remember feeling very lucky, apart from being delayed after landing because the pilot had turned off at the wrong exit on the runway. We were stuck on the plane for about 45 minutes, at a complete halt, before we could find a slot in the landing schedule to get back on the runway and to where we supposed to be. Once we were off, we had a police escort all the way to the team hotel. We were treated like kings, with all the traffic stopping to try and take a look at the branded Wales Euro 2016 team bus.

I have really distinct memories of that game, and even as everything was happening I was conscious of embedding as much of it as possible in my mind so I'd never forget it. On the Friday night we trained in the stadium, and then I had a massage from Dave Rowe whilst watching the opening game between France and Romania. Dimitri

Payet grabbed the last-minute winner for France and I dared myself to think – imagine if that was me tomorrow.

The entire build-up to the game was just brilliant. The hotel was situated in quite an industrial place not far from the stadium. There was a pub-type restaurant literally just across the road from the hotel and, from the evening before the game, it was very full. At this stage it was mainly the locals looking for the likes of Gareth Bale and Aaron Ramsey, and trying to get photos but, when we woke up the next day, it was just a sea of red everywhere – it was incredible.

The game wasn't until 5pm but if you looked over to the pub you could see and hear the Welsh fans singing *Don't Take Me Home*. Every time we went for a meal we had to walk down a long glass corridor at the front of the hotel, about 50 metres long – where the fans could see us! It was really hot so all the windows were open and, as we walked down and the fans noticed, we could hear all the cheering and the singing. All the lads were leaning out of the windows taking videos and things like that – it was great. I've got a load of pictures and videos just from those meal time walks.

In the afternoon we had a team walk. It's was regular thing, both at Wolves and with Wales, just to loosen the legs off and get a bit of fresh air. Usually with Wales, it's fairly relaxed and we do it somewhere quiet, but of course here we were, at the start of the Euros, in the middle of Bordeaux, in amongst fans who had been drinking all day! We had security guards with us, mainly for Gareth Bale, and some volunteer stewards from Wales who were out there helping with the fan parks, so off we went. We came out of the hotel and walked down the main road next to a tram line which ran down the middle of the road. Every time a tram came past, full of Wales fans, you could see them doing a double take when they realised it was the Wales squad. Fans followed us in their thousands the whole way around the walk – it was amazing.

Not one negative thing happened as we made our way around the route. It was just a fantastic moment to share with the fans. The Wolves Academy manager Gareth Prosser was there too, with his son. Gareth is another very proud Welshman. I can't imagine many countries would have done that, a team walk surrounded by fans and interacting with fans. The security guards were there just in case there were any problems but there really weren't. Yes, a few were merry – this was a once-in-a-lifetime trip after all – but mainly they was just singing songs and wishing us all the best. The lads loved it – a treasured memory. It was a really nice experience and a great build-up to the game.

After that it was back to the hotel. Kick-off was at 5pm, and sometimes before an evening game I might have a nap in the afternoon. There was no chance of that today – not with that atmosphere. I was in the room, on my own, and I just wanted some normality, so I made a few phone calls. Well, lots of phone calls. I spoke to my mum who – like most mums – is a bit of a worrier. She asked me if I was nervous? "No," I replied. "I'm absolutely fine." She was back home preparing to watch on the television and reminding me to make the most of it and to enjoy it. My dad and my step mum were due at the game as they'd been cycling in the south of France and, of course, I spoke to Emma as well.

After the pre-match meal there was maybe an hour to have a shower and get ready before going back for the team meeting. I'd already showered and was ready, so that hour was just spent waiting around, reading a bit of my book, and relaxing. I must have phoned Emma three or four times and told her she just had to listen to everything that was going on outside the window. I stood there, holding the phone out of the window so that she could hear. I felt almost guilty that I couldn't share this experience with everyone I knew. It was so surreal and I wanted to share it with family and friends as much as I could. All the people that had played such a big part in my football career – I felt selfish that I was there enjoying it, but they weren't. I was also incredibly excited, in a positive way. I was visualising how the game would go, what my roles in the team were and what the manager was asking me to do. Even visualising myself scoring a goal – only positive thoughts.

Then we all made our to the team meeting. The previous week, Suzanne, one of the FAW staff had asked us all for the names of our next of kin, be it partner or parents, and their phone number. She said they needed it for their records, so none of us thought anything of it. We just handed over the details. As we sat down for that team meeting, we were told the manager had something to show us, and the room went dark.

All of a sudden Maddy, Sam Vokes' girlfriend, appeared on the screen. I was sat next to Sam at the time and he jolted forward, totally stunned to see her. No one knew what was going on. The FAW had arranged for every single player in the squad to have good luck messages from their loved ones. As the beaming faces of each player's nearest and dearest appeared, you could just see all the lads welling up. Having their parents or partners or children saying how proud they were of them, and telling the players to enjoy it was an incredibly emotional experience for us all.

Emma had filmed the kids saying, "Good luck Daddy, we love you." It was amazing. Here I was a few hours from the biggest game of my life and I was close to breaking down and crying. I just about managed to hold it together, although Jack – right at the end of the message – shouted, "Score a goal, Bale!" Not me! That put a smile on my face.

The message for George Williams, from his father, was particularly memorable. George's dad said how proud he was of him, what he'd achieved in his life and what a great young man he had become. That one made a big impact on us all.

It was such a great touch by the FAW and really helped with the preparations before the manager started to speak. Chris is such a passionate guy and really gets his players fired up. It was now, full with passion and determination, we went straight to the bus and off the to the game. From the hotel to the stadium, there were fans everywhere, such an amazing sight. It was incredible. People sometimes talk about trying to treat every game as a normal game but in those sort of circumstances you can't, and I didn't want to either. I wanted it to be special, right from the outset.

The *Stade de Bordeaux* was a beautiful stadium, with quite a different look to it. There was maybe a quarter of a mile of straight road leading up to it and, as we approached, the Wales fans dominated – it looked, and sounded, like we had 90% of the support. Then the bus went underneath the stadium to the team entrance and it went a lot quieter.

I was determined to enjoy the moment and not let anything pass me by. When I think back, I definitely did manage to take it all in and have so many wonderful memories from this game. I knew I was playing from the training sessions and the set piece work which we had done during the build-up but, getting into the dressing room and seeing my kit laid out was something particularly special. That is when it all became real – I am about to start a game in the European Championships. Wow. Time for another photo.

There was still about an hour and 40 minutes before kick-off and we went out onto the pitch to have a look. Having trained there the night before we knew how good it was – the playing surface was immaculate. As we all walked out, there was a big roar. I couldn't believe that, with so long until kick-off, there were already maybe 3,000 Wales fans inside the stadium – more incredible memories. This was the first time I got a view of the Spider Cam, which is used in the big games and at the big tournaments. It's such a strange thing, a camera on metal wires suspended from the corners of the stadium. The guy controlling it must have some skills.

As we walked out the camera quickly dropped down and swung towards us. You see it coming in towards you, then you look up and it's your face on the big screen, with the fans cheering. It might seem so innocuous mentioning it now, but that was another aspect of the day that seemed very special at the time. I hadn't played in a game involving the Spider Cam before!

We were on the pitch for a couple of minutes before Gareth came out. The camera immediately swooped towards him. He must be used to it now – nothing fazes him – and all the fans start cheering again.

As I was watching Gareth on the big screen, the Slovakian team appeared. Cameras were filming them coming off their team bus and it followed Marek Hamšík walking towards the dressing room wearing his small round glasses and with his famous Mohican hairstyle. This was the player we were most worried about, and I knew I would be coming up against him quite a lot. As I watched, my initial thought was, "Damn, he looks fit ... I was hoping he might not turn up!" No such luck.

Back in the changing room there was a really relaxed atmosphere. Like most players, I have my own pre-match routine. I had a bit of treatment from the therapists, and some work on my feet. The dressing room was large, with lots of space, so then I did my stretching exercises, then got changed and ready to go out again for the warm-up. By this point the stadium was half to three quarters full and you could see the TV cameras down at the side of the pitch. Jason Mohammad was presenting pitchside, with John Hartson. I had done a bit of media work with Jason while I was injured in the pre-Euros build-up so we exchanged a quick hello. I felt really relaxed by this point and couldn't wait to get the game started.

The Slovakian team then appeared for their warm-up and I got my first face-to-face glimpse of our opposition. There was a big sense of excitement, and we got another big roar from the fans as we went back into the dressing room. I always warm-up with my pads on. I'm not sure many others players do, but I find that when I put the shin pads on, it completely changes how I feel. It's a reminder that the game is coming and I'm about to go to work, so I always put them on before the warm-up and keep them on. Then, pretty much all I need to do when I go back in after the warm-up is to put my shirt on.

Those final few minutes waiting for kick-off are always a little bit strange. I just want to sit down and have a quiet moment to myself, but everyone is different. There are so many different personalities in any dressing room with many different routines. Some players just want to be left alone to concentrate on their own routines of psyching themselves up. Others need to be in that group environment and go around high-fiving and getting each other going. Then there are the leaders in the dressing room who are talking and giving out instructions. All this is going on and everyone was wishing each other luck. There is a real close bond and close-knit squad at Wales. We all shared one goal, to win the game. We were in this together.

Then, just as it all went quiet ahead of the manager's team-talk, there was another incredible moment which I'd never previously experienced. We were sat in the dressing room, in total silence, apart from a thudding noise from the stadium. It was the Welsh fans singing. It was all we could hear. This was a new stadium and usually, with the insulation, you just don't hear anything from the crowd. You might hear a little bit of a rumbling-type noise without making out what they are singing, but the Wales fans that afternoon were deafening. It was another reminder of how special this day was, and how privileged I was to be there. Then the manager spoke. In those final minutes he gave us the final talk before we went out.

Chris Coleman is one of the best I've worked for in terms of his team talks, the passion he shows and how he can get you going. By this point you don't necessarily need the motivation. It's there already.

He'd already gone through the tactical side so we all knew our jobs, but he has an ability to feed off our motivation and add that bit of extra spice to it. His talk ahead of this game was based on telling us to relax, and take it all in. He told us we had done our country proud, and gone further than Wales could ever have dreamt in the last 58 years. Regardless of what happened in the match, he told us we were heroes, we were the squad that got Wales to a major tournament. "Be proud of what you have done, and don't get lost in the moment." It was almost backing up exactly what I had been thinking.

This was such a special occasion, he was telling us not to let it pass us by. "Don't go out there and try too hard." He said he'd played in big games which had been a blur to him and he didn't want any of us to feel that way after this one. The talk finished with applause and a massive 'come on', and then Ashley Williams was the one who really rallied us and got us going. Nothing really specific, just adding to the gaffer's words and making sure we were all ready.

Then it was out to the tunnel where the teams lined-up on either side and the cameras were going down the line. I met the mascot and tried to speak in French as I knew it was a special moment for him as well, but I'm not sure how good my French was to be honest and whether he understood me!

It was quite a low tunnel so, as we walked out I could see the bottom few rows of the opposite stand. It was a brilliant hot day with bright sunshine, and I could feel the excitement outside. As I walked onto the pitch I made a point of taking it all in, making sure I looked around, felt the atmosphere and embraced it. I knew this was going to be amazing.

Lining up, I was thinking that here I was, in a major tournament, about to play for Wales. It was all hitting home to me. It was something you always dream about as a kid but, with Wales not having qualified for so long, and my personal position with the injury leading up to the tournament, I was just so thankful and grateful that I was there. I knew that this was a moment that I would be able to tell people about for the rest of my life. One of those huge highs of my professional career, knowing how fortunate I was to be playing in a major championships. Then came the anthems.

Everyone knows how stirring the Welsh anthem is, but on that day in Bordeaux it was stirring beyond words. I learned the anthem a long time ago, but when I first started playing for Wales I wasn't too confident in being able to sing it very well. In more recent years I've made sure I can sing it with confidence. It is such a patriotic anthem and means so much. I think even people who aren't Welsh will enjoy the anthem, in the same way as when you listen to the French or the Italian national anthems. There is so much passion in it.

We were singing it, with the Welsh fans away to our right and behind us. We could hear the roar from them belting it out with so much emotion, and we could see all the lads on the bench in front of us, with the manager and the backroom staff, all with their arms around each other. The atmosphere was out of this world.

Towards the end of the anthem, I looked up to the big screen and there was a Welsh fan screaming it out with tears streaming down his face. We knew how much it meant to those fans, how much it had cost them to get to games, the time they'd taken off work and the personal sacrifices they'd made. Seeing that fan on the big screen just brought it all home to me about just how much it meant for Wales to be at a major tournament after so many years.

Then came the team photo. Wales have become known as having an alternative attitude to the team photo with players taking irregular positions. Initially, it wasn't something that happened on purpose – it was just a bit sloppy – but leading up to the game it was something the lads discussed, and we decided that it seemed to be a lucky thing – so we'd just keep doing it. The team photo against Slovakia wasn't too bad, actually quite regular, but for the rest of the tournament you could generally see one player left out on the end of a row. It's not necessarily done deliberately. Just that when it happens no one corrects it. Footballers can be a superstitious bunch.

The team huddle was next, with Ash in the middle just trying to calm everyone down. We'd now come to the point where it was time to take the emotion out of it. It was now a game of football – XI v XI. We all knew our tactics. Let's get on with it. The Spider Cam came flying down and was spinning around. That was the moment when it filmed me before kick-off taking a very deep breath. Let's take it all in, and let's go. Game on.

There was a fairly slow start and I just wanted to get that first touch. Not to do anything spectacular. Just to get a touch. When it came, James Chester passed me the ball and I just set it back to him. I probably could have turned but I just wanted to get that first pass away without any problems. Then the game started to get a bit more frantic. Slovakia broke away and Hamšík, was on the ball. Part of my job was to try and watch his runs, but he was away with the ball down the right hand side. Ashley Williams came over and Hamšík shaped to shoot. I was so fired up for the game I threw myself towards the ball and Ash did the same – we were about to collide – but Hamšík, at full pace, just chopped inside, faced up to 'keeper Danny Ward and knocked the ball past him. With only three or four minutes gone, Hamšík was going to score. What a start that would have been.

Then, with the goal gaping and from absolutely nowhere, Ben Davies came flying across and produced a goal-line clearance which probably saved mine and Ash's blushes. The manager always tells us to try and stay on our feet – "no big shapes" – and don't go flying in to challenges unless there's no other option. Through the qualifying campaign we had earned a reputation for making blocks and throwing our bodies on the line, but it had to be at the right time. We got it wrong in Bordeaux, probably with the emotion of it all. Ben dug us out with his unbelievable clearance, and it settled us down, setting us up for the rest of the game. It helped me massively as well, a huge warning: 'Don't do that again!' It was the one moment in the game where emotion got the better of me. Hamšík looked like he was going to pull the trigger, so I went for the block. It would probably have been better to trust the goalkeeper rather than sell yourself.

The game settled after that and we were keeping the ball and switching play really well, which is something we had worked on with the wing backs. For me, playing alongside Joe Allen was fantastic, watching how comfortable he was on the ball in such a high pressure game. I'm steady enough on the ball and don't give it away too much, but I am more conservative in my passing than someone like Joe, and I try and do a lot of my work off the ball with making runs or tracking back. Joe can go and get the ball in dangerous areas and be so composed in bringing it out or switching play. He is a joy to play alongside in midfield. When the ball is being brought out by the back three, you see Joe and think, 'stay out of the way and free it up' for him to have it, because he is that good on the ball. I was playing in a different role to the one I was more used to at Wolves, being more disciplined rather than the number ten role or as an attacking midfielder, but it is also a role I enjoy, especially with players like Joe around.

Jonny Williams is another player who carries a threat. We all joke to Jonny that he is the sort of player who should be shooting more and scoring more goals, but he is very good at running with the ball. In the final away friendly that the lads played in Ukraine when I was injured, Jonny must have been fouled ten to 15 times in that game but Gareth wasn't playing to be able to take advantage with the free kicks. In Bordeaux Gareth just told him to keep getting those fouls, and he would do the rest, and so it proved, ten minutes into the game. Jonny got the ball in the final third, jinked past a Slovak, and was then brought down. The ball was 25 yards out, on the right hand side. We knew Baley was going to hit it. It was the first real chance he'd had to get into the game.

His free kicks are so consistent. I have never seen anyone else like him. He hits 40 or 50 every day after training, and must hit the target with 95% of them. The amount of movement on the ball is frightening. In my opinion he is the best free kick taker in the world and more consistent than Ronaldo. We'd worked on set pieces and I was going to be on the right hand side of the wall, running in towards goal. With the amount of movement he gets on the ball, I was planning ahead – Baley will shoot, the 'keeper will parry, and I'll get on the end of it. 1-0, Edwards! I'm off celebrating and it's going to be amazing. That is what I had in my head as we waited for the free kick.

Baley assumed his stance. Straight legs. Puffs out his chest. This was the moment for a superstar to seize his moment. The stadium was expectant and you could almost reach out and touch the energy. He ran up and hit it, and I knew straightaway he had hit it well, with power and plenty of movement. It was fairly central but then, at the end, it shifted over to the left. The 'keeper seemed wrong footed and ... GOAL! I was sprinting towards the goal as the ball hit the net. What followed was pure emotion. I felt as if I'd scored the goal myself. I turned and sprinted for my life to try and catch up with Gareth and Chrissy Gunter as they headed towards the dugout to celebrate.

I think that shows what a close-knit group we are. That Gareth ran for the bench so everyone could join the celebrations. Everyone was jumping on each other and I've got a great photo at home of me jumping on the back of three or four other players. In that melee there are arms coming across your face, and everyone is screaming and shouting. If you could bottle up the emotion of that melee it would be so powerful. It was almost like a blur. I came out of the throng saying 'well done' to Jonny and then going over to Gareth and telling him he was incredible. Or words to that effect.

Ten minutes in we were 1-0 up against Slovakia and for the rest of the half we were the better team. We had taken advantage of Ben's brilliant defensive work to get our noses in front. We were moving the ball really well, across the back three, in midfield, and were very patient. We could even have had another goal. Jonny should have had a penalty when he broke down the right and Martin Škrtel came across and caught him with an elbow. Somehow it wasn't given, but it was a nasty one, that's for sure.

I had one potential opportunity when Chris Gunter had gone down the right and hung the cross over towards the back post. Neil Taylor was climbing for it about ten yards outside the back post. It was one of my only forward breaks but I'd read it as a third man run, and if Tayls could knock it down, I was arriving in the penalty spot area. He saw me and knew what was needed, but unfortunately it just skidded off him and fell about five yards to my left. That was probably my only real chance of getting a goal, but the team played really well in the first half. We were good value for the lead.

When we went in at the break, all the talk was about keeping calm and relaxed. We'd been the better team and just needed to do exactly the same in the second half, but as we'd all burned off so much energy and emotion during the pre-match build-up and first half, we were drained and needed to calm down. I changed my shirt, which was drenched, took on more fluids and then just relaxed. I spoke to the gaffer and he mentioned the Hamšík run. He told me I was doing well but just to guard against throwing myself in. I put his mind at rest pretty quickly, and told him I wasn't going to make that same mistake again!

The second half started and we had a couple of good chances with Rambo breaking down the right and heading for goal, only for the referee – 40 yards away – to blow for a foul on the defender. The fifth official, who was right on the spot, gave nothing. Then a cross was hung up for Baley at the back post, who got in a decent downward header only for the 'keeper to make a really good save.

Slovakia then picked up the pace and our domination of the midfield was being put under pressure. I challenged for the ball against a couple of Slovakia players and, as it bobbled about, I felt a sharp pain in my knee where I'd been caught by a stud and began to hobble around. I tried to carry on but it was no use, I had to go down. I had a quick look and saw a gash, maybe only an inch long, but it was really deep and gushing with blood. The ref asked if I was ok. I wasn't, but I didn't want the physio coming on as I'd have had to go off, just when they were getting on top, so I pulled my sock up over my knee and struggled on.

The next five minutes were a bit of a blur. I was trying to manage the pain whilst running it off, but then disaster struck. Slovakia made a break down the right. Róbert Mak had gone past one player so I came across to try and block him. He played a cutback to the edge of the box and it ran through to Duda who slotted it home – 1-1. After all our hard work, we hadn't taken our chances and now we'd been pegged back. Our energy was drained, and my knee was in bits.

For the next five to ten minutes we were under the cosh as they grew in confidence, and we had to hang on to regain a foothold in the game. The gaffer knew a change was needed and took me off in a double substitution, with Joe Ledley replacing me and Hal Robson-Kanu coming on for Jonny Williams, which quickly made an impact. We didn't concede and started to get back into the game, as I watched from the bench getting some ice on my knee which had started to stiffen up.

With about ten minutes to go, Joe put a great through pass into Rambo on the half turn, who stumbled towards the edge of the box, looking like he was going to fall over but, just at the last moment, he got the ball out of his feet and it ran to Hal Robson-Kanu. Then came the best scuffed finish ever! The ball rolled past the 'keeper and just about over the line. I was sat there with the ice on my knee but as the bench erupted I ripped off the tapes and celebrated with the boys. We were back in front and the relief was clear to see, for us and the fans – who went wild. I can't remember much of the last ten minutes but we kept the ball well and saw the game out, surviving a final chance when they hit the post very late on.

SLOVAKIA FOR STARTERS

Overall, that 90 minutes was just the best feeling ever on a football pitch. It was such a big win for us – 58 years in the making – and set us up perfectly for the tournament. It took the pressure off going into the England game, which was always going to be huge.

The celebrations on the pitch went on for a long time – it felt like we had won the Euros already! We went over to the Wales fans in the corner to thank them for their support and to share the moment, something we did after every match. In our post-match huddle, Ash stressed how big an achievement it was to get the three points, but that the job wasn't done. One more win would get us through – even another point might be enough – but the relief on top of the ecstasy of the game was something else. We had three points in the bag, and wouldn't be playing catch-up in the group. It was a great buzz.

As I came off the pitch, Mark Evans from the FAW approached me. "Dave," he began. "You've been picked for the drug testing, you have to go in this room," and I was ushered into a small room alongside the tunnel. Two players from each team had been selected. Wayne Hennessey, who had missed the game due a back spasm in training the previous day, was already there in his tracksuit alongside two poor Slovakian players. I was annoyed about being unable to go and celebrate with the lads in the changing rooms but these Slovakian boys must have been furious. After all, they'd lost the game. I don't think the small TV on the wall playing the match highlights helped either.

Drug tests aren't easy at the best of times but after such a hard game, when so much fluid would have been lost through sweat, I knew it was going to take some time. I did my bloods straightaway and started guzzling water so I could produce a sample. It's not just the dehydration which is difficult at these times, it's also the fact that the drug tester has to physically watch the urine come out. It's not a time for any stage fright!

I was in there about an hour before I managed to get everything done and dusted, then I headed back to the dressing room, and it quickly hit home that we had another massive game in a few days time. It was all about the recovery, with the ice baths and the masseurs getting to work. There was that short period of time to enjoy the result, which was a bit of a blur, then it was on to the next one. I showered.

the doctor had a look at my knee and put three or four stitches in the wound. He said the knee would be stiff for a couple of days, which quickly focused my mind on doing everything I could to be available for the England game.

It had been an unbelievable start, and by the end of the evening we would still be top of the group after England drew with Russia, but of course, there was another fairly big game lurking just around the corner in Lens.

On you go! John Toshack hands me my senior Wales debut against the Republic of Ireland.

Celebrating my first Wales goal in the World Cup qualifier against Liechtenstein.

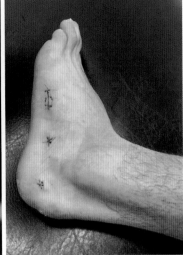

A night of celebration as we beat Andorra in Cardiff having already booked our place at Euro 2016.

My dream of playing at Euro 2016 was now turning into a nightmare following an injury to my 5th metatarsal. I vowed to do everything I could to get myself fit for France.

It was an emotional day when my selection for the Wales Euro 2016 squad was announced, and when I saw Jack and Evie's message.

We're on our way! The squad leaves for Sweden for the friendly prior to heading to Dinard for our European adventure.

Training in Bordeaux the day before the Euro 2016 opener. My dream of playing in a major tournament was less than 24 hours away.

The team's schedule for the big day!

A proud moment. In the starting XI for Wales' first game of the Euros, the anthem being sung like it's never been sung before, and the Red Wall's friendly invasion of Bordeaux. Brilliant memories.

Gareth Bale got us off to a flyer with an early goal. What a player. What a celebration! Wales' first tournament goal in 58 years meant so much to us all, and we were determined to enjoy it

Huddle time after kicking off the tournament with a 2-1 win.

The perfect start with victory over Slovakia. I was so pleased to have played my part in a huge team effort.

Cooling down - very literally - in the Cryotherapy Chamber the day after Slovakia. It is freezing in those things!

The FAW's excellent use of our downtime kept us relaxed and played a crucial part in the team's success. We genuinely enjoyed each other's company and had a lot of fun.

Quiz time! There was plenty to keep us entertained away from the football during the tournament.

The Red Wall moved on to Lens for the game against England. The French fell in love with *Les supporters le Pays de Galle,* **whose passion and good humour was infectious.**

Coming away with the ball after tackling Dele Alli.

Top: Devastated to lose in the final seconds after being ahead for most of the game. It was hard to take.

Left: Joe Hart, a true friend.

Bottom: Back into training in Dinard, with Ben Davies.

What a night that was in Toulouse. Top of the group and through to the next round.

After the superb win against Russia. Chris Coleman did such a fantastic job for Wales and we all had total respect for him.

Even the Eiffel Tower got in on the act after that sensational Russia victory, choosing Wales as the most talked about team on that day of the tournament.

With Jack and Evie after the Northern Ireland game. Precious moments.

Jack's left foot is far better than mine, and he got a big cheer from the Wales fans after finding the net in Paris.

Left: In the Parc des Princes dressing room with Kingy and Vokesey. The three of us are good mates.

Bottom: More of us getting involved in the post-game celebrations, with Ashley Williams nursing his injured shoulder. Our team spirit was unbreakable.

A relaxing round of golf, and I won the 'Head2Head' challenge against Vokesey!

Life's a beach! Enjoying an ice cream in Dinard with Sam.

We're into the last four! The scenes of elation with the fans after a magnificent night in Lille.

Top: The celebrations after Ashley Williams had equalised. We really were #TogetherStronger.

Left: On the plane back to Dinard with Wales' head kitman Dai Griffiths. I would sit next to him after every trip and we'd send photos to our mutual friend Simon Shakeshaft, my physio at Shrewsbury.

All good things must come to an end, unfortunately! Thanking our fantastic supporters following the semi-final exit to Portugal.

None of us wanted it to end. Those fans were immense throughout the tournament and played a huge part in our run to the last four.

 **Dave Edwards** ✔
@_DaveEdwards

What an amazing day!! The support has been incredible. Thank you Wales!! #TogetherStronger

`0:03`

12:26 PM - 8 Jul 2016

We'd heard there were lots of people waiting for us outside Cardiff Castle but when the doors opened and we walked out to huge cheers, the size of the crowds was beyond anything we could have imagined. It was breathtaking. To the tens of thousands who followed us to Bordeaux, Lens, Toulouse, Paris, Lille and Lyon, and the millions who supported back at home - *Diolch,* **you were brilliant.**

The scenes when we returned to Cardiff after reaching the semi-finals were just something else. An experience that none of us will ever forget.

Even in my wildest dreams I couldn't have wished for a more enjoyable month, shared with a truly inspirational squad of players, management and backroom staff. We will all treasure those memories forever.

15

England Calling

'Hardships often prepare ordinary people for an extraordinary destiny'
C.S. Lewis

The Slovakia game gave us the perfect start to the tournament, and a renewed sense of determination and motivation in the days that followed.

The next day back in Dinard was pretty much a day of recovery. My knee was still quite sore and I was also very tired as I hadn't had the best night's sleep after the game. That was mainly down to adrenalin, going back over everything that had happened. We did a recovery session and then another in the cryo chamber where the temperature drops to -150 degrees. Other than that it was back to the hotel, catching up with the messages from the day before and playing darts with the lads. There was also plenty of football to keep up to date with. Northern Ireland drew, meaning we were now the only 'home nation' to win their first game at the Euros – a nice stat. Then followed an early night to catch up with the sleep I'd missed out on the night before.

By Monday my legs felt a lot better and we did some shape work in training. It looked like we were going for a different shape for the England game, and a system which suggested I wasn't going to be in the team, but at that early stage you couldn't be sure.

Away from the football, we also held our first court session where I was issued with a forfeit. We'd had been split into teams at the pre-tournament camp in Portugal but, as a couple of our lads hadn't made the final squad, our team was a man down. It was serious stuff and we were convinced our depleted numbers would play against us. There were quizzes and competitions going on through the week where teams could win points and, conversely, if anyone was spotted doing something wrong – being late for a meeting, or not putting their kit in the laundry – another team could report you and have your points deducted. Each week the results would be tallied up and a member of the losing team would be nominated for a forfeit by the team captain but, as we progressed further through the tournament those forfeits became more and more bizarre. Our team had lost out in the overall challenge so Neil Taylor, as our captain, had to nominate someone to do the forfeit. He nominated me – cheers Neil!

Once nominated, you had to roll a massive dice with its numbers representing a particular forfeit such as singing, dancing, serving dinner, cleaning the changing rooms, being able to pass the nomination on to someone else, or making a phone call – the one everyone wanted to avoid. Even when I'm watching others singing in those situations I get nervous – for them. Unless you are super confident or really enjoy getting up and singing, I don't think it is ever easy.

I rolled the dice and had to sing. I chose *Sitting on the Dock of the Bay* by Otis Redding and absolutely hated it. Some of the boys can really get on your case when you're doing things like that but, because they know I'm a fairly quiet lad, they took it easy on me. I had to stand on a chair and say my name, age and position. I was supposed to sing for 30 seconds but I'm not sure if I even made it that far – it felt like a lifetime – and everyone else seemed as keen as me to see me get down off the chair. Once it was over I had the consolation of knowing, I couldn't be nominated again by Tayls if our team was bottom, until everyone else had taken a turn.

Training continued through the week and I was still enjoying that, even though it was looking likely I wasn't going to start the game. Joe Ledley had come on for me against Slovakia, proved his fitness, and played a part in the winning goal. All in all, I felt he and Joe Allen would be the first choice midfielders, and that was how the manager was going to go.

Even so, after the knock in Bordeaux, I wanted to train well and my knee right. As the game got closer and the feeling I wouldn't start grew stronger, there was more than a feeling of disappointment because, after all, this was England.

ENGLAND CALLING

Whenever Wales play England you want to be involved. It's as simple as that. There is always so much more interest, and that goes for my friends and family as well. I was sure some of them had watched the Slovakia game, but I knew all of them be watching the England game. The majority of my friends are England fans, so I knew that when we were playing Slovakia in the late afternoon quite a lot of them were out drinking ahead of the England v Russia game, and I'm not sure how much notice they took of ours!

Whilst I was disappointed when it looked like I might not play, I was still delighted to have already started a game in the Euros. I also tried to stay positive, thinking that – given the manager hadn't yet named the team – if I was on the bench, there'd be a good chance of coming on. He'd said on the Tuesday night that he wasn't going to name the team because the line-up for the Slovakia game had been quite well-known in the press. Somehow that team had got out, whether it be via some pictures from training or people speaking to their families, so this time he wanted to keep it completely under wraps. Both teams knew pretty much everything there was about each other's players, so it was important to try and keep those line-ups as confidential as possible.

The press were constantly looking for news, or gossip, so we enjoyed the press conferences when we could have a bit of fun with them. We all looked forward to media day, which were usually two days before the match and when, not surprisingly, Gareth was the one player all the media wanted to speak to. As the media day approached, we would discuss - at dinner and at training - if there was anything in particular that might be quite fun to say, maybe slipping different planned words into the press conference, with rest of the world oblivious to our own little jokes.

Before the England game Gareth replied, "None," to the question, "How many England players would get into the Wales team?" It caused uproar. He then said that whilst the English players clearly had passion, he believed the Welsh players had more. The media loved it, and so did we - all gathered in the team room, with the lads getting treatment, watching it all unfold. All of us - staff and players - would be giggling away at some of the storms Gareth would be starting.

Once it was finished we would all wait patiently for Gaz to return with a box of goodies from the media room, the best of which were the toffee muffins. We would all tuck-in, making sure we weren't spotted by our head of performance Ryland Morgans. The media days had their serious purpose, of course, but we also saw them as a way to have fun and keep relaxed.

The day before the game we took a short flight to Lens before and had an evening training session in the stadium. Lens is a fairly small place but the stadium was better than I might have imagined and the session in the stadium was good. It also proved to be our final stadium session of the tournament. Training at 6pm with an early kick-off the following day probably wasn't ideal and why, I think, we didn't do that again. I quite enjoyed it, getting my boots on, being out on the pitch and getting my bearings, especially after flying, but there was still no news of the team. We were all still waiting. Waiting, and hoping.

We were staying just outside of Lens, in Lille. These, pre-match, hotels were all picked by FIFA, not by the FAW. Some were really nice and some were fairly basic – not hotels you'd have expect to be staying at in at such a major tournament. I'm fairly low maintenance so it was never a problem for me, more just a bit of a surprise.

On the day of the game we were given a bit of a lie-in, before having breakfast and a wander to our treatment room. Jonny Williams popped in. Like me, he'd started the Slovakia game but told me the gaffer had pulled him, he wasn't starting against England. Jonny asked if the gaffer had spoken to me yet. At that stage he hadn't. Not long afterwards the doctor appeared and told me the gaffer was looking for me. It's fair to say I knew what was coming.

It wasn't long before Chris found me, and asked me to pop to his room for a chat. He said I wasn't starting and all the reasons why. He was very complimentary and very impressed with how I'd played in the Slovakia game. and he said he knew he could always count on me. He also told me to make sure I was ready as it was very likely I would be coming on in the game because Joe Ledley was unlikely to last the 90 minutes.

It wasn't down to anything I had done wrong, just that the two Joes had worked really well in the qualifying campaign and the gaffer felt he had to go with them in the England game. I had no qualms with that – after all, I was being told that I was very likely to be coming off the bench to figure against England at a major championships.

Would I have taken that if it had been offered to me at the start of the tournament? Too right I would.

There is nothing worse than a team being named just before kick-off, and you're not in it. There isn't time then, not so much to get your anger out, but to get over the disappointment. It has happened to me and to other players and you end up on the bus on your way to the game solely thinking about not playing and feeling disappointed. For me, you should be on your way to every game thinking what an amazing experience this is and planning how you can make a positive impression. At least I knew early in the day and, after the conversation with the gaffer, I'd heard his reasoning and felt positive. Although I knew what the reasons were going to be, it was nice to hear them from the gaffer himself and to know it was pretty much identical to what I'd been thinking.

It never really comes as a complete surprise when you are dropped or not involved. You get a sense that it is coming – if you are going to get left out, then generally you will know. Once I know I am going to be left out, and if I don't feel it is completely fair, then I prepare what I am going to say in my defence. That might involve quoting some statistics, or just reasoning, in order to get my points across. In those situations – when I'm told I'm not playing – I do stick up for myself. There have been times during my career when I've felt I'm the easy one to leave out of the team. When I was younger that definitely used to happen to me a lot. More recently I've responded firmly but positively to managers and it's got through, perhaps giving them something to think about. No player should be able to talk their way into a team but, on the right occasion, you do have to try and stake your claim and make sure they understand what you believe your value is to the team. I'm not sure that's always been noticed during my career.

There is a time and place for those conversations but, this game was certainly not one of them. I absolutely understood everything Chris Coleman was saying. Another thing to remember was that team spirit was so important to us. We were all so desperate for Wales to do well that we would happily sacrifice ourselves if it meant the team getting a result. I was so grateful to be there in the first place, and just to be in the mix. Ten minutes after the conversation with the gaffer I phoned Emma and then told my mum, dad, brother and sister. They could then spread the word and avoid having friends and family switching on the TV in expectation, only to be surprised that I wasn't starting.

From there it was all about the preparation for the game. As we drove into Lens, a small town which reminded me of my village back home, and whilst a lot – especially those without tickets – were staying away because there were very few pubs or places to go, we noticed how the numbers of supporters had switched – plenty of Wales fans but so many more England fans.

There were white shirts and big St George's flags everywhere. There was also a bit of grief coming our way. You get that everywhere when travelling to an away match, but this was on a far bigger scale. Obviously with all the branding on the team coach, we weren't exactly inconspicuous. I think a few of the lads saw their parents and family members, just keeping themselves in the background and staying quiet.

When we arrived, the England coach was already there and their players were all getting off, so we had to wait – for some reason the two sets of players weren't allowed to see each other, even though a lot of the guys knew each other anyway. A lot of the guys wished we'd arrived first so it was them having to wait! We finally went in and it was a long walk from the car park, down a thin corridor to the changing rooms. Even though, on the TV, it looked a fantastic stadium, behind the scenes it was a different story and was very out-dated. Bordeaux had the 'wow' factor, whilst Lens felt more like a past-its-best Football League stadium.

We went out onto the pitch for a quick walk – with the Spider Cam flying down again – and there were a lot of boos. Initially it felt like an England home game but as we emerged, the Wales fans, who were away in the right hand corner behind the goal, and around the corner flag into the other stand, let out a massive roar as, once again, there were so many of them already inside the stadium an hour and a half before kick-off. That was one of my favourite moments of the tournament – hearing the noise from the Welsh fans, pre-match at Lens. It was amazing.

We went back in and started preparing for the warm-ups, which was a bit different for me, knowing I wasn't going to be starting the game. However, I did all my preparation exactly the same because, if there's an injury, you could come on very early but, at the same time, your mindset is more relaxed than if you knew you were starting. The warm-up isn't as intense because, as a substitute, you don't want to do too much work and then go and sit on the bench for a while. There were different warm-ups for the substitutes and we did that over in front of our fans. My sister and her boyfriend, and four guys I am in business with outside of football, had all come to the game and I could see them in the Wales end. Two of them – Ryan and Stu – were definitely supporting England but the other two – Mitch and Gary – were out-and-out Wales fans by the end of the tournament! I managed a quick hello to them which was lovely.

When we came back out for the match I was a bit disappointed with how many England fans there were compared to Wales. It was probably 75-25 in England's favour. Why wasn't there an equal amount for each team with the rest going to neutral fans? I know there were so many Wales fans who hadn't been able to get a ticket. It did feel a bit unfair, but the Welsh fans who were inside the stadium were still making plenty of noise and the atmosphere was amazing. I was on the bench for the anthem this time, but there was still that strong sense of togetherness as we all linked arms and belted it out.

When it came to the anthems, both sets of fans were really well behaved. There was no booing of either anthem, with each set of fans applauding the others' after each one had been sung. They were two really passionate anthems from two passionate countries and that level of mutual respect was very refreshing to see.

The sun was beaming down and it was very hot and humid. The pitch may have looked beautifully green but it was very dry, meaning that when the ball came to you it was going to be slow and sticky and could get caught under your feet. In those conditions a split second delay could result in a player getting caught on the ball and the team losing possession in dangerous areas. The tempo was going to be absolutely manic and no place for the faint-hearted. It's in games like these when you really appreciate the ability of world class players who can do it at the top level, week-in week-out.

I'd seen Joe Hart – in the tunnel busy getting the England lads fired-up – as I was walking out and we exchanged a quick 'hello' and high fives. We may have been on different teams but Joe and I are good friends from our time at Shrewsbury Town and both having grown up in Shropshire. There was quite a big deal made of Joe doing that afterwards, but having known him for so long, that is just the kind of guy he is. He was shouting like that, firing everyone up, in the tunnel at Gay Meadow. He'd always be the loudest one before a game. Just because it was England, and because he made one or two mistakes in the tournament, it was all magnified out of proportion. It is never a bad thing to be passionate, and Joe has always been like that. It certainly wasn't for 'show'.

Even in that second or two when speaking to Joe, I took a moment to think just how mad this all was. I have lined up with Joe in Shrewsbury's first team but not only that – also at youth team level, county level, and I remember an epic penalty shootout in a school game against him.

He always played a year above his age group at school so was in my year in that respect, him at Meole Brace and me at Mary Webb – Shrewsbury's arch rivals.

We played in a semi-final of the District Cup one year when we were about 14 or 15 years old. The match had finished 0-0, and Joe had made a great save off one of my shots – the first time I noticed what an incredible 'keeper he was. I struck a shot really well, one of those shots in schools football that you just don't expect the 'keeper to get near, yet Joe just caught it! Plucked it out of the air. Nice and easy. So, the game went to penalties. I took the first one and sent him the wrong way. Everyone else scored as well, including Joe, all the way through to 10-10. Then a poor lad called Michael Holland missed his spot kick and we lost the semi-final. Sorry to bring that up again, Michael. Hope you are over it now!

That was the first battle I had with Joe, at Shrewsbury College of Arts & Technology, in front of about 30 parents. From that, we'd gone to playing for our countries in a European Championships group fixture, in front of 35,000 passionate fans in the stadium, and watched by a TV audience of hundreds of millions all around the world. Watching Joe singing his national anthem at the top of his voice, and thinking back to that schools semi-final. Here we were, about to do battle again.

The game began and, as I'd expected, the tempo was incredibly fast. Straightaway, Joe Allen was fighting for possession of the ball to set our rhythm. Some observers think footballers are brave when they go hard into a tackle, but that is nothing compared to watching

Joe or Aaron Ramsey go and get the ball in such tight areas and have the courage to look for the right pass rather than just smash the ball forward. It's incredible to see how confident they are in their own ability and in what they want to do with the ball.

Raheem Sterling had a really good early chance for England, when the ball was cut back and he hit it over the bar. Apart from that it was a really cagey game. Then, towards the end of the first half, we got a free kick. Immediately, all of us on the bench shared one thought – Baley!

We had seen his goal from a free kick against Slovakia, and we knew what he was like in training with 95% of his free kicks ending up in the back of the net. This one was a long way out, though, so we were all thinking the same thing. 'He's never going to try it from there is he?' He just put the ball down, walked back, and you could tell from the way he was standing that he was going to have a go. Go on, Baley!

The anticipation grew. The guys on the bench linked our arms around each other. "He's going to score. He's going to do it." We had that much confidence in him it was almost the equivalent of someone taking a penalty. We all knew that as soon as he hit it we would be able to tell by the trajectory whether it had a chance. We could sense the expectation amongst the Wales fans at the other end of the ground – that feeling that something special was about to happen.

Baley stepped up, hit the ball and, straightaway, we all gripped each other a little more tightly – we knew this had got a chance. The ball dipped before it reached the goal, and there was a split second lull when we couldn't really see what was going on, and then we saw the net ripple and Gareth running off.

The bench just erupted, the biggest release of energy you can imagine. He'd done it again. The substitutes and the coaching staff were hugging each other and Gareth ran off to the corner. This felt even better than the opening goal against Slovakia. We were turning to each other on the bench and asking how on earth he'd done it. This Welsh superhero could do almost anything with a ball.

From then, for us, the game settled and it was all about getting through to half-time and keep it at 1-0. If we could win the game, we'd be top of the group and through to the knockout stages. Of course, there was so much work still to be done, and you should never get carried away, but you can't help some of these things starting to go through your head.

Did I stop and think about Joe, my mate, who had just conceded the goal? In all honesty, no, not straightaway anyway. We needed to win the game, however we could but, a few seconds later, as things settled down, we saw a replay on the big screen. I'd initially thought it was an amazing free kick but, I then turned to Sam Vokes and we both asked the same thing – should Joe have saved it? As I watched it again I knew that Joe would be disappointed. A goal's a goal and I'd have taken it all day long – 1-0 up, just before half-time – but there was that little pang, that 1% maybe, feeling for my mate Joe. I remember wishing that Baley had just stuck it in the top corner and given Joe no chance. I know what the English media can be like with the national team. The pressure and the scrutiny put on those players is immense. I don't want to be too critical of the media because they have a job to do and they have to sell papers or get people listening to radio stations and TV programmes, but you can see what it does to young players. It can destroy them. You can see it in them and sense their tension.

When a Wales player goes on the pitch for a game like that, they know they could be a hero, but an England player steps on the pitch and knows they could be the villain. That is the difference for me, and I genuinely believe it. It wouldn't necessarily apply to the biggest characters such as Wayne Rooney, who has been through everything but, for Raheem Sterling and other talented young players like him, expectation levels with England seem to be magnified and are unjustified. The fans were on him so much at that game. Just one bad touch and you could hear it. Surely those fans want their team to do well, they want to be supporting them and giving them as much backing as possible.

You could sense it. When Sterling had that chance, I don't believe he was thinking, 'Wow! I could score here and end up being a hero.' I'm certain he was thinking, 'Don't miss, please don't miss.' I genuinely believe that is the way it is. It's a different mindset. That tension could be seen in all the games England played at Euro 2016. I know they went on to beat us, but they didn't really play as well as they should have done, given they have so much quality in their team. England played well in possession but, at times, looked like a bag of nerves, which comes from the pressure they're under.

So, we went in at half-time a goal ahead. Don't get me wrong, I don't think we had played particularly well. Compared to the Slovakia game we hadn't passed the ball as well and were getting into the habit of going long a bit early and giving possession back to England. The manager told the lads to relax, even though he knew it was hard to do in this type of game. They'd got so 'up' for this contest and, with that atmosphere, it was hard to be calculating. After a disappointing result, some fans comment that players didn't 'want it' enough or show enough passion. There is such a fine line between building yourself up for a game, and over doing it to the point that you lose control.

In sports that rely on power, such as rugby, players need that physical edge and being over-hyped is not necessarily a bad thing but, if a snooker player gets themselves really fired up for a game, it's likely to be counterproductive. Footballers have to be in the middle. We need that drive, and to be able to get ourselves up for a game, but you have to be in control. Chris Coleman had a great saying: "You need fire in your belly, and ice in your veins." We need to be up for the game, but also calm and calculated and ready to play our part in the team's gameplan. We can't do that if we're over-hyped for it. So, at half-time in Lens, the manager was just trying to calm everyone down.

I went out to warm up at half-time knowing I had to get myself as prepared as I could. I was sprinting around just trying to get myself going and get myself ready for the possibility of going into such an important and high-tempo game. It's always good to come on when you're a substitute, but it's a lot harder than when you start a game. Some people think players should be able to come on and automatically make a difference with that fresh energy, but it doesn't necessarily work like that. It can be very hard to get your 'second wind' when you come on.

When coming into a game where the tempo is already so high, it can be tricky to get up to that level straightaway, as it takes a while for your heart and for your legs to adapt. I wanted to give myself the best possible chance of being able to settle quickly if I went on, giving myself plenty of touches of the ball, just so I felt confident and ready for the opportunity. The manager had told me to be ready once the second half was underway, so I was getting myself fired up and prepared, including heavy breathing and panting – yes, I know! – just to make sure the pace of the game and the conditions wouldn't be a shock when I came on.

At the start of the second half we were really starting to come under some pressure. It felt like we were already into the final ten minutes of the game and hanging on for a win. I was warming-up down the touchline where England took the corner from which Jamie Vardy scored. We heard shouts of, "It's offside, it has to be offside," and that was our thought, but we hadn't seen that the ball had diverted back to Vardy off Ashley Williams. Vardy wheeled away, and the goal was given. All the England fans behind us were screaming, effing and blinding at us, just the usual stuff. We felt quite low at that point, momentum had changed. I had to be completely prepared when I came on as it was going to be even tougher now.

I got the shout at about 60 minutes and wanted to get into the game straightaway, whether it be an early touch or go crunching into a challenge. I wanted to make sure, like when I knew I was playing in the Slovakia game, that I didn't get too nervous. Embrace it. Enjoy it.

Luckily enough, when I came on Neil Taylor had a throw-in down the left hand side – just in our own half – quite close to where my family were sitting. It was a difficult one to go and show for as your first touch of the ball, but I wanted to do it. I wanted to get going. So, I checked to my left and came back to the right to get the ball. Neil threw it into me, I felt someone coming at me from the right, so I just set it back to him and we were off and playing. It felt good.

I was playing down the left hand side of the midfield three and I got a few touches in the early minutes. I was really in the game, and was winning a few headers as well. The ball was bouncing in the midfield, just in my favour, and this was the time when I wanted to leave something on someone. I knew I was getting the ball, and so I pushed my arm into Dele Alli to make sure I was winning the ball and he went down, and I charged off with the ball towards the edge of the box, but there was no one in there. I laid it into Jonny Williams and ran in, looking to get it back, but Jonny went on a little run and had a shot instead. Fair play, it wasn't too far over the crossbar.

ENGLAND CALLING

Shortly afterwards, the ball was cleared from their defence towards the halfway line. I thought I could really clean Daniel Sturridge out going for the header so I went in and won the challenge, leaving him on the ground. I felt really good that I was imposing myself on the game. All fair challenges but strong challenges too. I was involved.

By now England were starting to pile on some pressure. We were dropping deeper and I we needed to keep our shape. Sturridge is so tricky in possession, and I was thinking, 'Don't sell yourself, keep your eye on the ball when he does his stepovers.' It was about trying to make him pass, make him pass sideways and my job was done. We were defending the box and defending corners. The onslaught continued.

Heading towards the 90-minute mark we were just wanting to see the game out. A draw would be a good result and put the pressure on the other teams going into the last game. A ball got played over to Marcus Rashford on the left, about 40 yards from goal. I was sure I could get in and nail him with a challenge but, to be honest, I didn't realise just how good he was. I knew he'd made a great start to his career but I just wondered if it had been a good run at the right time. I went in to try and nick the ball from him but he just dropped his shoulder and went the other way. Such really good feet. That showed me. He got away from me, but luckily nothing came of it.

Then came the moment. The decisive moment. The horrible moment. In the 92nd minute Sturridge was again on the edge of the box and I was facing him. He was jinking his feet and I'm shouting to myself, 'Make him pass! Don't let him go past you!' A second later he's flicked it past my right hand side and gone the other side of me. Chris Coleman always said to never let a 'give and go' happen. Take a foul if you need to but don't let them past. I was turning with Sturridge and running back a few yards with him, then saw two or three Wales players ahead of us so decided not to run into the melee.

With the benefit of hindsight, I should have carried on running and gripped him and put in a challenge – 100%, without a doubt – but in that split second I thought he was running into our numbers. I assumed we had him covered so I'd keep our shape on the edge of the box. Then, almost in slow motion, there was a ricochet, I could see Sturridge's run, and I just knew it was going to pop out to him. It just fell into his path and he took a really early shot, before Wayne Hennessey could even react, and it was in the bottom corner.

I sensed it was my fault. I should have put in a challenge, even taken a foul, anything to stop him. I was so dejected. Could I have done anything different? I was so sure he was running into a Welsh wall of bodies and that we would have been able to deal with it. At that moment, Joe came tearing down the pitch and my guilt pang from earlier vanished. "You can **** right off, Joe!"

We still had a minute left. Could we get one more chance? You never give up. Even though the England fans in the stadium were going crazy, and we were all devastated. To have put so much effort in, and this to happen in the 92nd minute, against England. It's impossible not to think those things even with the clock still ticking. We actually got the ball forward and into the England box, and Baley had a header which went wide. The final whistle. Absolutely gutted.

It was disappointing enough to lose the game but my head was spinning, thinking I was partly responsible for the winning goal. When something like that happens, you never really know what has actually gone on until you watch it back. There have been goals conceded where I've thought I was at fault and then, after watching it back, you can see that wasn't the case. I wanted to see this one again to see what I could have done. Could I have done more?

Joe came over. We shook hands and said we would swap shirts and have a chat after. He was really consoling me, saying he was so sorry and that we had deserved something out of the game. A true friend. It was a low moment, but I appreciated it.

We went over to the Wales fans where Chris Gunter did his iconic 'chin up' – we're still in this. The fans were brilliant, like they'd been all afternoon, and they lifted us at the end. Despite the defeat the atmosphere was still positive, still one of togetherness. We got into our team huddle again, and agreed that it was still in our hands. A draw might be enough to qualify, but a win against Russia and we would definitely be through.

We left the pitch, went down the tunnel and into the dressing room. The manager came in and said he was absolutely devastated – not for himself, but for us. He said he was so gutted for us after playing with so much heart, so much desire and so much passion. We hadn't played particularly well, we all knew that, but we had certainly deserved to take something out of the game. It was a very quiet dressing room.

People not really knowing what to do with themselves. So much energy had gone into the performance on the pitch.

After the Slovakia game, our dressing room had an incredible buzz. It was now the opposite, in the space of just four days – from a huge high to a bottomless low. That's football. I'd been so excited about the Euros, and being involved, that I'd assumed that even though we'd lost a game, we would still feel positive. Well, I soon discovered a big 'no' to that assumption. This was the ultimate low. Down there with a relegation season. You're not going home, yet, but you are going back to the hotel knowing there's one massive game coming up which will decide your fate.

We needed to lift ourselves quickly, which happened that evening and the next day. There was still so much to play for. Joe Hart helped me as well. I had five minutes with him after the game, and I remember him saying how relieved he was that England got back into it, otherwise he would have got even more pelters for Baley's free kick. He felt he should have saved it.

The good thing about the conversation was the advice that came from Joe. He said that we had to keep our spirits up, we were still on three points and England were only on four. He told me that we were better than the Russians – 100% – and that England should have beaten them. That we had more than enough to go and get the result. He said we had to stay together, and couldn't afford to let anyone get too down. Get rid of the disappointment straightaway, and keep upbeat. It was a stirring talk from Joe, good advice from a mate, and it was nice to hear.

From there it was just a case of getting back on the coach and leaving the stadium. In a far less happy mood than when we'd arrived a few hours earlier. It had been a gut-wrenching finish to the game. Against England as well, but this was the Euros, and there was still one more game left for us to make the most of this opportunity. A potentially all-or-nothing meeting with Russia. It couldn't come quickly enough.

16

From Russia With Love

'Fear is a reaction. Courage is a decision.'
Sir Winston Churchill

Trying to sleep after the England game was difficult. We had flown straight back to the base in Dinard after the game, had a light meal and checked the itinerary for the next day. I was speaking to family, watching a few things on my iPad, but still feeling absolutely gutted about the game.

The following morning the focus completely switched. We were all down after the England result. Everyone was, but we quickly started to look forward to the Russia game and to think about achieving something momentous. One game, one win, and we would be into the knockout stages. The chance to be heroes all over again.

We hadn't had any real time off or downtime in the tournament so far, but the manager said we were getting out of the hotel for a while and going for some lunch nearby. We all got on the bus and headed out to the *Restaurant Du Décollé*, about ten minutes away, on the cliffs overlooking the sea – an absolutely beautiful setting.

Chris told us we could order whatever we wanted, probably contrary to the views of the sports scientists, as long as we weren't stupid. Happy days! In contrast to what we'd been eating in camp – vegetables, pasta, rice and fish – the players mostly plumped for the cheeseburgers, chips and ice cream for dessert. The planning and nutrition throughout the tournament was spot on, but the manager had realised we had been away for a long time and hadn't really had much time to ourselves, away from the controlled environment of the hotel, not to mention suffering a really gut-wrenching defeat. This was purely a one-off, and a nice pick-me-up.

It still felt similar to being at the hotel in the sense that we were all together, and ate together, but the surroundings were very different and it made a pleasant change. After the meal we spent about half an hour just chilling on a grassy area nearby, overlooking this beautiful beach. Just chatting away before heading back to the hotel.

You learn a lot more about people when you are away. The relaxed and completely random conversations, when you pick up more about their personalities and personal lives, come from moments like that. The England game certainly wasn't mentioned. This was just a chance to relax. In my case, I was looking forward to getting back on the training pitch the next day and I am sure all the lads felt the same.

With just over 48 hours until the Russia game, we had a tough session that Saturday, and then nothing really during the afternoon until the meal in the evening, which turned into something absolutely hilarious. It was time for the court again, and there were loads of nominations. Joe Ledley and Owain Fôn Williams were the men in the dock for something that had gone on a few days previously. The three judges, as usual, were the gaffer, Osian Roberts and Paul Trollope. The evidence was presented and, at the end of it, the lads had to do their nominations, the dice was rolled and the forfeit was the dreaded phone call.

We were all sat there at dinner, the phone is put on speaker, and Joe had to phone 'IG' (FAW head of public affairs Ian Gwyn Hughes) and say there was a story coming out in the national newspapers on Monday about him having an affair. Yes, on Monday, the day of one of the biggest games in Wales' history. Picture the scene. All the squad and staff are there listening, stifling the giggles, as Joe phones IG, who is only a short distance away in his room.

"I'm sorry IG," he said. "I've got something I need to tell you. I'm ashamed, especially with the game coming up on Monday, but this story is going to come out in the national newspapers about me having an affair." Joe then began alluding to the graphic details, laying it on thick. He is just unbelievable at things like this. IG kept asking if he was joking, but Ledds managed to convince him he wasn't. After a minute or so of explaining the situation IG asked: "Have you told your parents, Joe?" To which Joe replied, "No, how can I?" Then the line went silent for about five seconds before IG's reply of, "Bloody 'ell Joe, what have you done?!" That was it, we couldn't hold back the sniggering anymore, the roar of laughter was deafening as we collapsed about the place in hysterics. It was absolutely hilarious. Joe is such a funny guy, and delivered to a T.

I think Owain had to do his a few days later because the first attempt went to answerphone. He had to phone Suzanne, who looked after a lot of the behind the scenes stuff with the squad with various arrangements such as ticket allocations. Owain phoned to tell her he had ordered some tickets for the Russia game, and had sold them to a group of Russians, who were now going to be able to sit in the Wales end. He said he was offered so much money for them that he couldn't turn it down. He told Suzanne he now realised he'd made a huge mistake and it had only just dawned on him what was going to happen. Similar to IG, Suzanne was asking if he was having her on and then: "What on earth were you doing?" Once again, much laughter when all was revealed.

Joe and Owain's court sessions and forfeits both played a massive part in lifting everyone's spirits. Those two lads are so comfortable in front of the boys, taking the mickey out of each other and playing the fool. They are both great lads, and it was hilarious. I think it was one of the funniest nights I've ever had.

On Sunday, the day before the game, it was all a little bit more rushed than normal. We were flying in the afternoon, and instead of heading to Toulouse and training on the pitch in the evening as we had done before, it was decided to have a morning training session at Dinard instead. It was a change in approach but I think the staff just wanted to get everything done at our base rather than in the stadium the night before the game. We still went to the stadium in the evening, as it was part of the media requirements to have an open session for 15 minutes but, like a lot of the other teams, we just went out there in our tracksuits and had a walk around for 15 minutes while the media got their footage and photographs.

The Sunday was also Father's Day. I'd been missing the kids and Emma a lot anyway but it was particularly difficult on Father's Day. The first one I had missed since becoming a dad. I FaceTimed the kids and they had both made me cards. We had said all along that if we got through the group stages, Emma and the kids were going to come out for the next game, which added to the motivation to go out and get the job done against Russia on Monday night.

Monday dawned and the countdown to the 9pm kick-off in Toulouse began. An evening kick-off always means a long day, but even in a normal domestic season you don't have to wait until 9pm for a match. You can't escape the waiting and feel like you eat loads of food. Breakfast, dinner, then pre-match. It's all about taking enough food on board, but not over-doing it. We were allocated a block of free time in the afternoon when some of the lads popped to their rooms for a sleep, but I find pre-match sleeping difficult, so I made some calls, did some reading, watched a couple of programmes on the iPad, and had a bit of treatment – anything to while away the hours.

Then came the team meeting before leaving for the stadium. The gaffer was once again totally inspiring but, at the same time, relaxed and not getting too carried away. He said a lot about how we hadn't played well against England. "That isn't how we play," he said. "It wasn't how we played in qualifying and wasn't the identity we had given ourselves." He told us we had to get back to that identity, and we had to play our football. He said he trusted every single one of us, and that all of us could handle the ball. We had done a lot of work in training the day before where the centre halves were giving the ball to the two central midfielders. "Just give it them," the gaffer would say. "Even if they had a man right behind them trust them to handle it and bounce it off and then we're out."

He was re-iterating that he didn't want us to go long too quickly, and how he wanted us to get the build-up right, going through the different zones. "Keep passing it," he said. "Even if it is tight and, if you give it away, it is my fault. I've asked you to do it, so don't worry about it. I will take the blame if it goes wrong, so just stay relaxed out there and play your football."

His talk helped everyone relax. He didn't want people wound up too much or caught up in the occasion as had happened before the England game. Just stick to the gameplan, he said, and he would take responsibility for whatever happened.

Everyone knew it was going to be the same team apart from Sam Vokes coming in to start. Hal Robson-Kanu had been great but I was pleased for Vokesey, who hadn't played in either of the first two games. I am really close to Sam, we'd been friendly since he was at Wolves, so I was pleased that he was going to get his opportunity in such a massive game for Wales.

The players, like the fans, had been through all the different qualification scenarios around that night's possible results. We could have lost, and still gone through, and we were also trying to second guess the England v Slovakia game. We knew Slovakia were a decent side, and England needed to get something – they couldn't risk a defeat. A draw would probably be enough for us, but if we got through and finished third that would mean a more difficult tie in the last 16. The key was to just go out there and win the game. If we did that, we'd finish first or second in the group. There was no discussion about being defensive and certainly not going for a draw – we were going all-out for the win.

This was the game that felt the most normal of the fixtures so far. It is difficult to describe why that was, given there was so much at stake. I suspect the first game of any tournament is huge, especially with Wales having not been there for so long. Then came England, our arch rivals, and now Russia who we'd played a fair few times. Another factor was the stadium in Toulouse. As lovely as it was – and the atmosphere on the night was terrific – it wasn't the biggest and perhaps felt more familiar. Also Russian football at the time wasn't where it wanted to be either, with an ageing team as well, especially at the back. Approaching the game we felt confident, and didn't feel the pressure. It felt like it was just another game of football. Nothing more. We knew what he had to do, and were going to go out there and do it. That was the message right the way through.

In the first few minutes of the game the lads were just incredible. Watching from the bench, I remember the ball going out wide to Ben Davies a few times. Ben is a great footballer with a lovely left foot and his passing is just so crisp. In those few minutes he was rattling the ball in to Joe Allen, and Joe would just kill it stone dead with one touch, pass back to Ashley Williams and then out to the other side. Russia were trying to press high but we were just breaking through them time after time, creating chance after chance. Vokesey had a really good chance early on when he tried to give their goalie the eyes, but he read it. I was gutted for Sam, I was so keen for him to get a goal.

The whole team was playing so well and a goal seemed inevitable. After 11 minutes the breakthrough came when Joe Allen got the ball, broke from midfield and played a world class pass through for Aaron Ramsey, who was through on the 'keeper one-on-one. From the bench, I was expecting Rambo to go round the 'keeper or place it, but he did neither. Calm as you like, in a massive game for Welsh football, he waited for the 'keeper to commit, then dinked it over him, into the net and wheeled away in celebration – 1-0. What a finish. What a pass.

We had started the game so well, but goals change games, so it was important we had broken the deadlock. It was total domination from the lads and now we were in front. Not long after it was two thanks to Neil Taylor, who never scores! He'd scored a wondergoal at the training camp in Portugal before the tournament. We could hardly believe it, and now he was doing it in the Euros as well.

Our formation was perfect for Tayls and Chris Gunter to play as attacking wing backs and Tayls was pushing forward when the ball broke to him in the box. It took two efforts but he fired the ball home, and then looked totally bemused that he'd scored. His previous goal? For Wrexham against Grays Athletic in the Conference in 2010! We were all in absolute dreamland. Two-nil up after 20 minutes and creating chances almost at will. The gaffer had got the gameplan spot-on. Play your football, don't get caught up in the emotion. That first half was just magical.

Half-time came and the gaffer was delighted as you might imagine, but also keeping everyone focused. We just needed to do the same again in the second half, but the next goal was going to be crucial. Score – and we had a foot in the next round. Concede – and Russia were right back in it. Chris wanted the lads to keep dominating possession and to kill the game. They couldn't score if we had the ball, and if we had the ball we'd keep getting chances.

Of course Gareth had to get a goal, and it came midway through the second half. Aaron picked the ball up on the right from Chris Gunter and ran across the pitch. The back four tried to squeeze and leave Vokesey offside, but he just stood there motionless as Baley came flying in to produce a lovely outside-of-the-foot finish into the bottom corner – 3-0, game over and the Welsh fans singing *Don't Take Me Home* on that warm summer night. What a scene.

We were on our way into the last 16. The lads on the bench were all amazed at how the team had dealt with the situation and how well we were playing considering the enormity of the game. Wales usually made things a lot harder than this! When you are on the bench, at 3-0 up, you're desperate to come on and be involved. I was warming up and the gaffer had told me to get ready as soon as that third goal went in. It was on 74 minutes that I replaced Joe Allen, who had played two consecutive 90 minute games. I was delighted – it meant I'd played a part in all three of the group games.

I had an awful lot of the ball in the closing stages as well. Probably almost as much in the final 20 minutes against Russia as in the first 60 I'd played against Slovakia. We were keeping the ball, knocking it from side to side. Andy King came on as well and that was nice for me. I'm close to Kingy and we were also on the pitch with Vokesey as well. I would say they are my two closest mates in what is a very tight-knit Wales squad. We spent a lot of time together during the tournament and we literally didn't want that game to end. I even fancied nicking a goal if I could. I was still doing the defensive midfield job but we had a few breakaways when I tried to get up the pitch. It just wasn't to be, but we controlled the game so well and saw it out for the 3-0 win.

The final whistle went and we went over to the Wales fans in the far left corner.

My dad and step mum Mary had come to the game, having stayed down in the South of France after seeing the Slovakia game. They are very keen cyclists and were riding in the Pyrenees. Also Mitch and Gary, the two guys who had come to the England game, had the Wales bug and wanted to come to this one as well. I hadn't managed to see any of them before the game or during the warm-up so was trying to spot them at this point, but I couldn't work it out from where I thought their tickets were.

The atmosphere was unreal, and was about to get better. There was a big screen in the corner and, all of a sudden, the Wales fans started cheering wildly. I looked up and the England result was up there. A 0-0 draw with Slovakia. We knew they were drawing during the game but this was confirmation that we'd won the group, and the fans starting singing *We are top of the League*. What an amazing achievement to go into a tournament and to top a group containing two footballing heavyweights such as England and Russia – and Slovakia are no mugs either.

Such memorable times. We just didn't want to leave the pitch, and I don't think the fans wanted to leave either! *Don't Take Me Home* was in full flow once again, and how perfect those words fitted this particular moment. We formed another post-match huddle, this time with the staff, and just enjoyed the moment which reinforced that sense of togetherness.

At the end of the game the gaffer walked onto the pitch. I was shaking everyone's hands and offer him a high five, but he just pulled me in for a big hug and said "F****** brilliant, Dave." It was a great moment.

The way Chris talked, and interacted with the lads, was brilliant, and his man management skills were right up there alongside the best of the managers I have ever worked with. He made every player feel they were such a massive part of everything that was going on. Whether it be starting the game, coming off the bench, not even coming on, or the chef, kitman, everyone – he made people feel that they were an integral cog of the whole thing all the time.

We got back in the dressing room and there were cans of lager in there. We allowed ourselves one each to celebrate and mark the occasion! A Carlsberg if I remember right. We knew there was another big game coming up but we had a bit of a longer break having topped the group and it was just another really nice moment to share the success of how far we had already come. It had been my most amazing experience on a football field ever, and I just wanted time to stop so I could soak every last drop of it in. If Carlsberg did Mondays, eh? I was buzzing, and would be needing a sleeping tablet that night before my head hit the pillow.

I got out my phone, started reading some of the messages and then saw I'd had some missed calls off my dad. He had messaged to say that Sam had gone out to see his family in the stand and that he and my step mum were still in the ground. I went out to a near deserted stadium with maybe 200 or so fans in there and went over to see my dad and Mary, still in my kit! We had a quick photo and then again with Mitch and Gary from Q Financial Services, the business I am involved with, and that photo is now on their office wall. It was great to have that bit of normality as I hadn't seen my dad since being in France, even though he was at the Slovakia game.

We now knew we were going on to play at *Parc de Princes* in Paris the following Saturday in the round of 16, and the result also meant another development which I'd been particularly waiting for. The chance to see Emma, Jack and Evie. The gaffer had got us all together at the start of the tournament to talk about our families. He said he understood that other teams would be able to see their families whenever they liked away from training, but he just wanted us to give him this ten days of our time, from the Slovakia game to Russia, and not see our families and focus everything on our football. We all accepted that – this was a huge time for Wales and we completely understood the sacrifices involved. The fact we topped the group suggests it worked.

With that promise and the sacrifice in mind, the gaffer and the staff organised an event for the players and their families and friends in Toulouse the following day. My dad and Mary couldn't stay as they had to head home, but Gary and Mitch came along. There was a big courtyard in the middle of our hotel and we had a barbecue. Gary and Mitch were very hung-over, having been out late the night before. Still England fans, they were becoming more Welsh by the day, but were too delicate to touch any of the free drinks on show. It must have been a good one the night before.

Emma and the kids weren't there, but now I knew we were definitely involved on the following Saturday – even though we didn't yet know our opponents – I could start the arrangements to get things sorted. Playing in Paris made a massive difference and it would be so much easier for them to get over on the Eurostar. I had been in touch with Emma to get her to book the tickets as soon as we got through – before the prices went up! I said the same to my mum, dad and my brother. "Get it booked up as soon as possible." We were off to Paris!

17

Sudden Death in Paris

'I became an overachiever to get approval from the world'
Madonna

After the barbecue in Toulouse we all said our farewells to friends and family and headed back to base at Dinard. After dinner, I went off to bed watching some of the final group games – I think it was Spain against Croatia. We had done our job, booked our place in the last 16, and could now watch the other teams face a bit of pressure instead.

It was also a time to take stock and think about what we'd achieved so far in the tournament: six points from the three group games, finishing top, and all whilst playing good football. We had a game plan and it worked for pretty much all the games, although there was a disappointing end against England yet, ultimately, it may have proved something of a blessing in disguise. It was a reminder for us to go back to doing what we do best against Russia. The lads passed the ball well, played through the lines, and got our key players on the ball in dangerous areas.

For me, it had been an unbelievable experience. From the moment I got injured with Wolves in January, I had been keeping a checklist, ticking each achievement off as it happened: making sure I was fit and available for selection, making the provisional squad, making the final squad, and then just trying to get on the pitch. I had been so proud when the manager picked me for the first game and was really enjoying the position I was playing, whether starting against Slovakia or coming off the bench against England and Russia. I was in the team to be disciplined, get around the pitch, close down the space, win the ball back and give it to our attacking players.

At Wolves, I'd been able to get into the box at the right time to get on the end of things, but that wasn't possible with the more defensive role with Wales, even though the same qualities of anticipation and timing were required. The important thing for me was that the gaffer trusted me in that role. He showed faith and I always tried to reward him by working as hard as I could both in training and the matches. The main thing, however, and what every player agreed with, was that it was all about the team. Everyone in the squad was made to feel a part of it whatever their role and everyone was fully behind the eleven players on the pitch. Because no one wanted this journey to end.

The training session on Wednesday was really tough for me and the other boys who'd been on the bench against Russia. The lads who'd started the game had a recovery session but for us it was full-on, in sweltering heat. The FAW's fitness gurus, Ryland Morgans and Adam Owen worked us really hard on the training pitch. followed by a conditioning session in the gym to keep us ticking over.

Whilst we were preparing for the game, the identity of our opponents in Paris had become clearer. Mark Evans, the head of international affairs with the FAW, had been showing us all the permutations about who we could face. It was complicated. We had won our group, but because some of the third placed teams could qualify we still knew we could end up playing a number of different teams. Immediately after our win in Toulouse, Turkey were the favourites to face us but, within a couple of days, we knew we'd be playing Northern Ireland.

At that time we didn't really fancy facing Northern Ireland. As a small country that had exceeded expectations and were growing in confidence they were quite similar to us. Player for player we thought we shaded it, even though they had some very good and experienced players like Jonny Evans, Gareth McAuley and Steven Davis, but they were all good, honest professionals with an impressive team spirit. We had seen all their matches, and knew they were a team that could stay in the game.

We also knew there'd be a different atmosphere surrounding this game. For the first time in the tournament, here was a fixture we'd be expected to win. They would sit deeper, and we would have to break them down. Historically, that's where we struggled, doing better when teams attacked us and we could counter with blistering pace. As soon as we knew it was Northern Ireland, the focus really started. It would be tough, but we were being very positive. We knew that if we played to the level we were capable of, we should be able to win the game and reach the quarter-finals. Dreamland! You don't want to think too far ahead, but equally, that opportunity was now within our grasp.

I had organised for Emma and the kids, my mum, my dad and step mum, my brother Chris and his wife Amy, all to come to the game. Sharing this amazing experience with all of them was something I was really looking forward to. I also knew I wouldn't be starting the game unless there was an injury, and I certainly wasn't wishing that on anyone. I wanted our strongest XI to be fit, firing and ready for the match. The level of the performance against Russia was so high, it was going to take something special to break into that team.

My preparations focused on making sure I was physically right for Saturday, so while that Wednesday training session was tough, it was just what I needed. Then it was a relaxed evening before another light session on Thursday. More a tactical day to prepare for Saturday, to look at our own game and also the threats posed by Northern Ireland.

Video analysis has become a major part of the Welsh national team in recent years and throughout the tournament we spent time looking at aspects of our own performances and also the opposition. Most days we would have video meetings with our analysts James and Esther alongside the coaching staff – before breakfast, after training, and then sometimes in the evenings as well. During the early part of the week, we would recap the Russia game, and look at how we did in and out of possession. We'd revisit the key points we took into the Russia game, and see how well we'd carried them out.

As the week progressed, we'd start the analysis on the opposition – their strengths, their weaknesses and our best chance of getting some goals. Although we would often play a very similar shape from match to match, there would sometimes be very subtle tweaks, maybe in positioning or where we had to be in defensive situations, and that would all come out at these analysis sessions. They were short – ten minutes – but incredibly focused, just enough to get the key points across and keep it manageable for the lads. I'm a huge believer in match analysis and I'd be happy to sit there for 45 minutes to make sure I've grasped all the relevant information. Rather than having to watch a full match again, the analysts helpfully clip all your bits from a game and all the phases you are involved in. I do know there are some players who are not so keen and who just want to go out and play football, which is why the ten minute chunks work best for everyone by getting the key points across which can be revisited later, in more depth, if necessary.

I had a sleep on the Thursday afternoon, which is very unlike me. Usually I try to avoid daytime sleeping as it can affect my body clock, but I must have drifted off. The impact was predictable and I was completely knocked out of kilter, which wasn't great as I was up in court at dinner in the evening, for the second time in the tournament. On this occasion I'd been nominated by another team, and this is why....

I am an absolute stickler for timekeeping and being punctual – an obsessive. It probably stems from my younger days when my mum and dad were always late, especially when taking my brother and me to football. We were always the last to arrive to get ready for a game, rushing and flustered. As a result I am always really early for things, something I'll probably be passing on to my little ones as well. I hate being late or racing against the clock so, during the Euros, I always made sure I was well on time and one of the first in the room for all the team meetings.

Well, apart from once. On the Wednesday. Before tea. At a quarter to seven. There was a TV screen on the ground floor of the hotel by the lift and, every day, I'd take a picture of it on my phone, because it displayed the day's itinerary. I wanted to know exactly what was going on. On that morning there were no details of any meetings – just dinner at 7pm. However, by the afternoon, the display had changed and now showed the details for the rest of the day. Coming back from training I didn't look at the screen, assuming, like every other day, it hadn't changed since breakfast. You can guess what's coming.

There I was, at a quarter to seven, lying on the bed in my room, just thinking about heading down for dinner when my phone rang. It's Sam Vokes. As soon as his name flashed up on the phone my heart sank. He had no need to ring me – his room is only three or four down the corridor from mine. I knew I was in trouble.

"Where are you?" he asked.

"In my room –why?" I replied.

"Because there is a meeting."

"No there's not, I checked the screen."

"Yes there is – everyone is down here, waiting."

Oh dear! I knew it wasn't a joke. Vokesey wouldn't do that to me. So, I made the walk of shame down to the meeting room knowing that everyone was going to be in there, waiting.

As I arrived I saw Danny Ward coming in, also late, so at least I wasn't the only one – the safety in numbers scenario. He didn't know there was a meeting either, so in we go in together to the anticipated round of applause and the gaffer shouting "nomination!" It was inevitable. Being late for something was always going to result in a nomination and I was going to have to face the music 24 hours later.

Me being me, I prepared and was ready to put forward my defence. Rest assured, I've seen all those law programmes on the TV and I was adamant that, with the phone picture as evidence, I had a solid case. Wardy went up before me and pleaded not guilty, with the most bizarre excuse that he didn't have a phone picture, or any evidence to support him. He pleaded ignorance. Unsurprisingly, he was quickly found guilty.

Up I went. Pleaded not guilty. Presented all my evidence and explained what I did with the phone pictures every day, but the panel said everyone else knew there was a meeting. They had all turned up. In my defence, I claimed that had been the only occasion I'd walked past the television that day and that all the other times coming back from dinner I would have come from the other direction and taken the stairs.

I was getting into this lawyer stuff by now and started going on the offensive, which was a bad move. "Our team is built around organisation," I said. "And you're telling me you are changing things around at the last minute?" I think that played against me, especially when the gaffer and his staff are on the judging panel – guilty! They said they could understand my case and my reasoning – but everyone else had made the meeting. So there was no escape.

I was given the dice, ready to roll to decide my forfeit. As before, the options were singing, dancing, serving tea, cleaning the dressing rooms, making a phone call, or escaping scot-free. Serving tea, cleaning the dressing rooms or escaping were the ones I was after.

I had already sung, and that was bad enough. The phone call was to be avoided at all costs, whilst singing and dancing is ok for some players, but not for me. I rolled a four and looked at the forfeit chart – dancing. Oh no, 30 seconds dancing in front of 22 players and 15 or so staff. Fair play, you do get a choice of music, but I have to confess this wasn't something I had ever really prepared for. You can't, can you? I thought quickly, and spoke to James the analyst. "Can you get *Hey Macarena* through the speakers?" That was a track I remembered from school discos and play dancing with my kids. Thanks to modern technology and very keen members of the FAW staff, the track was found in seconds and blasted through the speaker.

Off I went, arms everywhere, trying to do the Macarena. I remember looking desperately at Mitch, the psychologist, who was in charge of the challenges and was timing me. The seconds passed like minutes. "Is that me done, Mitch?" "No, 15 seconds left." Really? You could see from the lads' faces they were already getting bored of me hopping around trying to dance. I got it done but was so embarrassed. Job done.

Friday was a strange day. Another great day for football, but not away from it. The EU referendum result left me feeling very underwhelmed. I couldn't personally see how that decision was going to be good for the country. Going to bed on the Thursday night, I knew the vote was going to be close, but there was no way that we would vote out of the EU. Yes, it was a public vote but, usually, when big companies and the people with influence want something to happen, it just seems to happen and the views of the public very rarely seem to go against it, so I was still confident we would remain in the EU.

So, the next morning, we went down for breakfast and were watching the big screen when the result came up – 52% to 48% – in favour of Leave. I was baffled and it knocked me for six. With my business interests I speak a lot with people involved in commerce and they are people whose opinions I value. On this issue they were all on the same wavelength. They said it wouldn't be disastrous to leave, but that it would be far better to remain. The jury's out on that one.

We trained in the morning and then travelled to Paris in the afternoon. Arriving at the hotel the day before a game was something all the lads looked forward to, especially when it came to the food. There would be pizzas, chicken goujons, and plenty of the stuff that the boys loved. You eat so healthily for most of the tournament that treats like that are what you really look forward to. We then went off to have a look around *Parc de Princes* stadium, passing Roland Garros – where they play the French Open tennis – on the way in. I do like my tennis, so it was nice to see, both as a tourist and sports enthusiast. Paris looked beautiful, we could see the Eiffel Tower and just to be in the capital was a great feeling.

I was so impressed with the stadium. We were in the home dressing room and I'd never seen anything like it before. It was huge, with a massive warm-up area, medical area and showers. The seats were those posh big seats you see in dugouts, and all the branding was there with inspirational quotes in French and, with Zlatan Ibrahimović still at PSG at the time, a lot was linked to him. It was a magnificent arena with top drawer facilities.

To wake up in Paris, ahead of a last 16 tie in the European Championships, can't fail to produce a buzz. We had our pre-match walk around Paris in the morning, and saw a fair few Welsh fans dotted around. A car drove past us before braking to a sudden halt – on yellow lines – as a dad and son in their Welsh shirts jumped out to say hello and take a photo. Driving around Paris I am sure they didn't expect to suddenly stumble upon Gareth Bale walking around with the Wales squad ahead of such an important game! It was another memorable moment.

The excitement of the game was building but I was also really looking forward to seeing my family and friends. They'd all been allocated tickets just behind the dugouts in some great seats. Mitch and Gary had come back as well, with their wives this time. It may have been a big ask to have another trip to France, but with it being in Paris, and maybe the offer of a shopping trip or two, they had managed to persuade their better halves that it was worth joining up for a weekend away. Good thinking, lads!

I saw them all sat there before the game but not to speak to. Just a wave. It was difficult seeing your wife and children a few yards away but being unable to give them a hug. As a professional you just have to block it all out until after the game. I think my little girl Evie was really keen to see me, whereas Jack was probably thinking, 'I'm at PSG's ground – I'm about to watch Gareth Bale play!' He'd got his priorities sorted.

It was a boiling hot day and the pitch was immaculate, albeit firm and bouncy, and it was quite hard for the lads to get the ball under control. We played quite well but it was a scrappy game, just as we had anticipated. We knew they were going to try and frustrate us, and we knew they had a very good organisation and spirit about them. There were hardly any chances in the game for either team and, as the match went on with the score 0-0, the more I felt I was probably not going to get on. If we needed a goal it was more likely the gaffer would send a striker on, or a winger, or someone more likely to be able to get one. I know I'm always capable of popping up on the end of something, but there were perhaps more attacking players on the bench whom the gaffer would turn to.

The gaffer had made a couple of changes as the second half went on, bringing on two attacking players – Hal Robson-Kanu for Vokesey and Jonny Williams for Joe Ledley – as we chased a goal. Vokesey had sent a good header just wide before he went off and then Baley had a free kick saved by the 'keeper. On the bench we were all waiting for a bit of magic from someone and, with 15 minutes left, the breakthrough finally arrived.

Baley had the ball on the left and produced an amazing cross, with pace and whip, right across the face of goal in the six yard box. It had taken the 'keeper out of the game – he was at the near post – and Gareth McAuley, in trying to clear, turned it into his own net. In fairness, McAuley had to go for it, he had no other option because Hal was waiting behind him, eyeing up an easy tap-in. It was unfortunate for McAuley that he got the own goal, and unfortunate for Hal it didn't come through for him so he could score.

We were 1-0 up with just 15 minutes to go. Hold on to this and we were in the quarter-finals of a major competition. There was still work to be done, though, and for the remainder of the game they were piling on the pressure, forcing us deeper and deeper. As we chased everything there was a collision when the two Williams, Ashley and Jonny, smashed into each other. Surprisingly, it was Ashley who came off worse taking a nasty knock to his shoulder. He was clearly in pain and looked odds-on to come off. We all assumed that Big Ginge, James Collins, would come on as Ash was holding his shoulder and looked like he could hardly jump. Ginge hadn't played a game as yet but he was one of the best in the squad in the air and was perfect to see the game out. Ash, being the leader he is and a Welsh warrior, refused to come off and insisted he was "Ok". He wanted to see the job through.

In those final few minutes the lads coped well with the pressure. I can't remember Northern Ireland having a real clear-cut chance despite pressing forward and dominating possession. Then came the final whistle. What a feeling. For all of us, whether we'd been involved in the game or not, we were in the quarter-finals of the European Championships. What an achievement. Absolutely incredible.

The guys on the bench went berserk, running on the pitch and hugging each other. I went around everyone individually saying well done, without even a hint of disappointment that I hadn't got on. It was a team effort, and we were through. We headed over again to the Welsh fans who were to the left behind the goal we'd been attacking in the second half. They were understandably ecstatic and it was hard to pull ourselves away from that mass of singing, dancing, and crying fans.

Then I went back towards the dugouts where I knew my family were. I saw some of the lads grabbing their kids so I thought this would be a great opportunity. I saw Emma, and gave her a hug, then my parents and my brother, who was really emotional. He had tears in his eyes. Emma handed Jack and Evie over to me. Evie has always been a mummy's girl, but since the Euros, when she didn't see me for weeks, she doesn't like me going out or spending any time away from her. Jack just wanted to get on the pitch. He saw the green grass, and he was off.

We went on the pitch and Dai Griffiths, the kitman, asked if we wanted a ball for the kids to kick about. What a great idea! Gareth was doing an interview in front of one of those glass sponsors' boards and, unbeknown to us, Jack was running around behind the glass display and was seen by millions watching on the telly. Then, all of a sudden, Jack asked: "Can I go and score a goal?" "Of course you can," I replied. Evie had been following him but now he started tearing towards the goal from the halfway line so she came back to me.

Jack must have been 30 to 40 yards away from the goal when the Welsh fans clocked what was happening and started cheering. It was one of those cheers which grew in volume as they urged Jack on, as he got closer and closer to the goal in front of them. With his Wales top and Edwards 14 on the back I realised they had spotted him, although he was blissfully unaware as he ran into the penalty box. As a dad, my first thought was, 'Oh! No!' He was wearing pumps and I thought he was going to slip where the grass had been watered – 'Please don't slip over' Jack. 'Please don't miss!'

Jack wasn't bothered about placing the ball into the back of the net. He was just going to hit it as hard as he could and, from around 12 to 15 yards out, he just smashed it into the middle of the goal. The whole of the Welsh end cheered. They'd cheered my boy. As a dad, it was a very emotional moment. I looked at Jack and he had the biggest grin I'd ever seen. He'll never forget scoring at the *Parc de Princes*, aged six, in front of thousands of Welsh fans – and neither will I.

Luckily Emma has a video of it at home. It was lovely to spend some time with my kids, that just happened to be in a football stadium in Paris – something to truly savour. Jack and Evie were at the perfect age for that magical experience, young enough not to be overawed but old enough to take it all in. Jack probably thinks it was normal, just to go on and kick a ball around in front of thousands of people. I'm not sure he realised how lucky he was.

It had already been decided that the following day would be a family day so I knew I'd see them all soon, and it wasn't worth Emma and the kids coming to the hotel on the evening as they were going to be shattered. So we said our goodbyes and headed in different directions.

Back in the changing room, spirits were high and this was when the video of Joe Ledley leaked out, and we still don't know how! Someone played the music from *The Inbetweeners* film, and Joe just jumped onto the table in the middle of the dressing room and performed a mad little dance – better than my Macarena from a few days previously – before sliding through the pizzas at the end. There was such a good buzz in the dressing room and I tried to keep hold of as many memories as I could and stay in the moment.

Our journey was moving on to the next stop, the quarter-finals of Euro 2016. Bring it on!

18

Belgian Fun

'Synergy – the bonus that is achieved when things work together harmoniously'
Mark Twain

On the evening of the Northern Ireland game we had a bit of a drink in the hotel bar. Families and friends of the lads came over and Mitch and Gary were there with their wives.

There were a few Wales fans there and a bit of a sing-song was going on. The famous Will Grigg song was changed to *Gunter's on Fire* – with Chris leading the chanting – as well as *Don't Take Me Home* which had become *the* supporters' anthem while we were out there.

The weather in Paris the next day was lovely, perfect to have our families around and to enjoy each other's company over a relaxing afternoon. Jack and Evie had brought me their Father's Day cards which I kept in my hotel rooms for the rest of the tournament. A lot of planning had gone into making sure everyone was looked after and there was a soft play area for the kids, plus children's entertainment and face painting. It was great to spend time with the children and my family and a few of the lads without children went off with their partners to have a look around Paris.

Jack was completely star struck around Gareth Bale. He had brought his Euro 2016 sticker book and got every player to sign their sticker with Chris Coleman to sign on the front. He even got a photo with Gareth, which he cherishes even now. Jack's knowledge of the players at the Euros was second to none. Even when the tournament was over he was still telling me how much he knew. A couple of months later he still had loads of stickers left and came across one of the double stickers from Belgium – Axel Witsel and Radja Nainggolan.

"Who's that?" I asked him.

"You must know who that is?!" Jack replied.

"You play against so many players in a career," I said, "that you can't remember them all."

"It's Nainggolan," he said. "He scored against you in the Euros!"

Good knowledge! Maybe he's destined for a career in scouting.

It was a lovely day, and a bit of an emotional goodbye when everyone left. I knew they weren't going to come back out again unless we got to the semi-finals. We also knew we had a huge quarter-final to prepare for, so it was time to think ahead, and be ready for what was around the corner.

Monday was another day off. With the game scheduled for that Friday, I think the gaffer wanted a three-day build-up and, with everything we'd done, he gave us the day off. A few of us – maybe 12 to 15 – went off to play golf, out in the beautiful Breton countryside about half an hour from the hotel in Dinard.

It was a rematch, with me and Sam Volkes against Simon Church and the doctor, and we got our revenge by winning on the 18th hole. Then it was back to the hotel for dinner and for all of us to watch the England game against Iceland in the evening. What a game it proved to be, and we all know what followed, with the video getting out of the lads celebrating Iceland's win.

It was absolutely unbelievable watching that game. We were all watching the game because, between us, we knew a lot of the players, and also some of the staff, such as the former Wolves physio Steve Kemp. We were watching the game in the team room, where some of the lads were having treatment and, as the game went on, everyone became more and more engrossed. When England went in front everyone just assumed the game was over and they would go on to win fairly comfortably, but Iceland got back into it and equalised. From there, for whatever reason, we all just started getting behind Iceland.

It certainly wasn't an anti-England thing. Far from it. Most of the lads in that room had teammates and friends on the England team and among its staff. It was more of an underdog thing, and I suppose a selfish thing too, thinking that one of the bigger teams may be going out before the last eight stage, perhaps making it a little bit easier for us to make further progress. There were also a few lads in our squad who knew some of the Iceland players.

There was also a real admiration for Iceland as we had all followed their story. Like us, they were underdogs. Like us, they were making progress in the tournament. Their story was even bigger than ours, given their population is just over 300,000 and having no professional league. So, their story was similar to ours, but with an even smaller pool of players to pick from. As they got back into the game we all sensed this could be amazing for the tournament and could open things right up. They were on the tougher side of the draw and Iceland getting to the quarter-finals would be an unbelievable achievement.

Then they took the lead! For me, that second goal was a tough one, knowing Joe Hart so well, as I felt he would be disappointed with it, and would no doubt be heading for some more criticism after the game. As full-time got ever closer, I think that was when the feeling became so strongly behind Iceland, both for our own hopes in the tournament, and because it was going to be a really special moment. I remember a big ovation when Jón Daði Böðvarsson came off. He had put in such a shift, and had a great game. It was the first I'd really seen of him but when he joined Wolves a few weeks later I certainly remembered his performance and was delighted we had managed to sign him.

So Iceland had won, and then *that* video went viral. We're still not sure how, but maybe it was passed through a chain of people until it reached someone who made it public. For us, it was a celebration of the underdog winning. It certainly wasn't anything anti-English, despite what some might believe. When I was at Shrewsbury we lost 2-0 at Histon, and it was a horrible feeling. Yet we knew that all the neutrals out there would have been willing Histon to win. I am the same now – if there is a non-league team playing Manchester United, I'd want the non-league team to win. It's just how it is with most football fans. You root for the underdog. The video caused a bit of a stir, which is understandable, but there wasn't anything more to it than that.

The last eight teams were now known and we were up against Belgium, the toughest side we could have faced on our side of the draw but we knew they wouldn't want to be facing us. We'd played them twice in the group stages and remained unbeaten, winning one and drawing the other. We'd also faced them in the previous qualifying campaign, drawing with them in Belgium but losing at home, albeit after James Collins had been sent off early on. Belgium would know we had the capability to exploit any weaknesses and the potential to beat them.

Having studied them so closely in the qualifying campaign, we knew their system, and how they played. Belgium had many world stars and top quality players, but we believed that our team ethos and our team spirit made us a more cohesive unit. Our work ethic and how we played for each other could give us that edge.

Going back into training on Tuesday, I knew it was important for me to put in a really good session. I hadn't been involved in the Northern Ireland game, and knew the following two days would be lighter sessions ahead of the quarter-final, so I needed to put in an intense workout. It was certainly a tough session – perfect. I was feeling really good.

Throughout the tournament I made a point of taking every opportunity to improve myself. Even at my age, and with having been in the game for a long time as a player, I always feel I can learn more. During the Euros I studied the coaches' sessions closely to understand how I could improve further. The amount of knowledge and experience amongst the staff and other players in the Wales camp is huge and I knew that picking up new innovative thinking would help me when I got back to club football.

At my age, it is harder to improve technically. It's more difficult to go out and do extra work like I did when I was younger, because it takes that little bit longer to recover, which could be a detriment to what you do on a Saturday. It's more about maintaining your standards and your physical levels, but improving mentally and psychologically which can make a difference as you get older, and can make the most out of all your experience. It's more a case of trying to prolong everything, rather than looking for extra gains, and then using that extra knowledge to keep you a step ahead.

After training on the Tuesday afternoon, we went into Dinard to meet the locals and hand over some gifts and Welsh memorabilia organised by the FAW. It was important that we showed our appreciation and thanked the local people for their hospitality while we had been based there. We also hoped that they would invest emotionally in us as well, and help cheer us on as we tried to go even further into the tournament.

Me and Vokesey went for an ice cream and as we walked on the beach we ended up having a kickabout with some local children on the sand. The trip into Dinard was obviously all organised, but the game of footy wasn't. It is difficult to walk past a game on the beach and not want to get involved, isn't it? It was good fun and nice to get out of the hotel and spend a bit of time in the town.

There was a very important job on the agenda that evening, and it had nothing to do with the Euros. It was a call with two of my mates Will and Richard (Ched), as I was supposed to be best man with them at a wedding the day after the Belgium game. Once we'd got through the Northern Ireland game it was clear there was no way I was going to make the wedding. Even if we were to lose against Belgium, which clearly I wasn't thinking about, I wasn't going to be able to make it back in time. It was just a case of getting together on the phone and having some input into the speech. When I had headed out to France, missing the wedding had crossed my mind but, if that was the case, it meant we'd been successful. I was probably more disappointed about missing the stag do, because the guys had gone to Las Vegas. I've never been to Vegas – it's still on the bucket list.

When Sam and Emily were organising their wedding 18 months earlier, I reminded them to, "Make sure you book it in for June!" May was risky due to the end-of-season play-offs and by July you are usually back for pre-season, so they very kindly booked it in for June. Then Wales qualified for Euro 2016. I have known Sam since school, and Emily is also from Shrewsbury. Emma and I have become really close to them and, as they also have two young children, we spend a lot of time together and regularly go on holiday together, so it was going to be really disappointing to miss their big day.

There was training again on Wednesday, then I took some time off to relax and watch a film – Sacha Baron Cohen's *Grimsby*. It was stupid – but funny. We also had another set of court nominations. Our team, led by Neil Taylor, was a man down from the start and we were a fair few points adrift at the bottom of the table, so it was time for our wild card – the opportunity to do something to impress the judges, pick up some points for the team, and hopefully climb off the bottom.

By this stage of the competition we needed to produce something special and as we'd been watching some international rugby during the tournament – Wales had toured New Zealand in June – and had really enjoyed watching the All Blacks doing their famous *Haka* this got us thinking. David Vaughan had attempted the *Haka* previously after being nominated and – in front of the lads – had given it everything he'd got, so we plumped for an all-out team *Haka* to win some much-needed points.

Stripped to the waist, bandanas round our heads and wearing just training pants, Wayne Hennessey, Neil Taylor, David Vaughan, Jonny Williams and myself stormed into the room making all sorts of random noises and slapping our knees. It wasn't the most technically correct *Haka* you'll ever see, but the place went up and the boys collapsed in fits of laughter. Wayne and Tayls' intensity was awesome as the players filmed us on their phones – another video that went viral.

The judges deliberated then told us it was worth the five points to bring us back into the mix – hooray! – but then someone in our team got nominated and we lost two points – boo! – and back to the bottom we went. The *Haka*, and all the effort involved, had been in vain. Some you win and some you lose.

The training session the day before a game we tend to do set pieces, a possession game and then a small-sided game, and that was the order of the day on Thursday. Unfortunately it proved to be a disaster for me. It was in the small-sided game, when it all gets a bit congested, that I tried to play a pass through to Hal Robson-Kanu. It was a tight gap so I made sure I put a lot on it and really rapped it in to him but, straightaway, I felt a twinge in my groin. Knowing my body as well as I do my immediate thought was mild panic. This was more than muscle tightness – it was a sharp twinge – so I pulled out of training, just hoping it wouldn't be anything serious – nothing a bit of treatment wouldn't put right. I was also furious with myself, in a way that reminded me of the injury at QPR a few months earlier. I began questioning myself for trying such a pass and rapping it in so hard. This wasn't good. It wasn't good at all.

The rest of the day was all about trying to settle it down and thinking about how I could try and get it better quickly. We were travelling over to Lille in the afternoon so I was immediately icing it, getting treatment on it, acupuncture, anything I could. I was still hoping it was wasn't too bad, and wouldn't turn out to be anything serious.

There was a bit of light relief away from my concerns as we headed to the local airport for the flight to Lille. As we approached the small airfield we could see a cluster of reporters had gathered, which was fairly usual stuff but, in the middle of them we saw a cameraman and the very distinguishable and recognisable face of Nick Collins, chief football reporter with Sky Sports.

We'd seen him on TV throughout the tournament, but he'd been based in Chantilly – England's base camp – so what on earth was he doing in Dinard? Well, as England had been knocked out by now, it appeared he'd been re-assigned to report on little old Wales!

When the boys on the bus clocked him, the shout went up from Neil Taylor: "F***** hell, look who it is! England have been knocked out have they?!" There was total uproar on the coach. All the lads were standing up, banging on the windows and shouting general obscenities in Nick's direction to roars of laughter from the staff and the rest of the coach. It felt like another huge moment in our rise to fame to have the fabled Nick Collins covering our journey.

At the same time we weren't massively keen. We liked our own little bubble – no outsiders thank you! Geraint Hughes had been doing a great job covering us for Sky and we didn't want that to change.

The night before the game we did the usual walk around the pitch. The *Stade Pierre-Mauroy* in Lille was an amazing stadium and, with the exception of the semi-final, it was the best we played in during the tournament. The weather was very Welsh – grey and overcast – and the stadium felt like a smaller version of the Millennium Stadium in Cardiff, with a capacity of 50,000. There had been some complaints about the pitch after the Ireland v Italy game so they had actually re-laid it the day before we got there. The forecast was heavy rain which was good news as it would take a bit of the bounce out of the surface, which was not too bobbly as a result.

As I was walking around the pitch my injury situation was creating a few doubts in my mind, but I was still trying to be positive at this point, thinking I'd be fine and available for the game. I knew I wasn't going to start but, if I did everything right over the next 24 hours, I'd be able to declare myself ready and come off the bench if required.

I planned to give myself a really good warm-up, and that would determine how everything was.

The Friday was all about resting up before the game in the evening. Thinking positive, and also being excited about the game. Just because my groin was a bit sore I didn't want it to affect or damage the overall, experience. My mum and her fiancé Dorian were coming to the game, also my dad and step mum, and my brother and his little nine-year-old boy Tom. My brother had promised Tom he could come to the game as I'd used my full allocation for the Northern Ireland game and Tom had missed out.

I remained confident as we arrived at the stadium and went onto the pitch and that amazing Wales matchday feeling was hitting me once again. You could tell by now how much the nation was behind us. It was tangible. We were outnumbered in the city and in the stadium because Lille is so close to the Belgian border, but the Welsh fans were still there in such huge numbers and were so, so loud.

The warm-up came and I was still feeling alright. I did the possession game with the other subs and all seemed well. Just before I went back in I said to the fitness coach that I wanted to strike a few balls. To make sure I was prepared to either make a clearance or have a shot. I had to be completely sure I would be able to handle it. The first three or four strikes felt ok, and then I started to try and whip it a bit more, imagining a ball being played down our right back channel and me having to go over and whip it away. When I did that I cramped up a little bit. Not dreadful, but still sore. That is when I knew that I wasn't quite right, and certainly wasn't right for a nation in the quarter-finals of a major championships.

I had been determined to be fit and, selfishly, I was desperate to be available. Equally, however, I had to be sensible. The last thing I wanted to do was affect the team in a negative way. If I was going to come on, it would probably be at a critical stage of the game so if I then had to go back off and be replaced it would really cause the team a problem, especially if the game went to extra time or I was the third sub and it left us down to ten men. There was no way I could justify saying I was fit, and that is what I told the physio. Anything else would have been unfair on my teammates and the Welsh fans.

We came back in and the gaffer gave his team talk. It couldn't have been any more passionate. We had done our homework on Belgium, and we knew what to expect. It was a wet evening in Lille, and there was so much expectation on Belgium. Our boys were ready. We had played so well against Russia. The Northern Ireland game was more scrappy, but against Belgium we knew there would be more time to play. They were going to come at us more than Northern Ireland did, and we would get the chance to counter attack.

After the team talk the boys got themselves fired up and ready to go out. I was just sitting in my place, coming to terms with the situation. The gaffer came over, put his arm around me and said he felt sorry and gutted I wouldn't be involved. "Don't worry," he added. "We'll win tonight, so make sure you're ready for the semi-final." It was another nice touch. At that stage, with everything that was going on ahead of such a massive game, I couldn't have been the gaffer's priority, but he still came over to have a word.

I put some ice on my groin, kept my kit on and went out. I knew I wasn't going to come on, but was still really excited for the game. My family knew I wasn't going to feature. I'd told them in the build-up what was happening with my groin, and when I came off after the warm-up I had seen them sat behind the dugout. I gave it the hand across the throat signal to show them I wasn't going to be involved. At least they now knew, and could concentrate on the game without wondering whether or not I was going to make an appearance.

The atmosphere inside the stadium was electric, and Belgium started like a house on fire. They were right at us from the first whistle and we had no time on the ball. We were trying to play out from the back and they were pressing very high. It was just wave after wave of Belgian attacks. They had some shots on target early on, and then there was an incident where we made three amazing blocks. Wayne made a save and then Neil Taylor and James Chester popped up with crucial clearances, one of them off the line. That just summed up what we were all about. Team spirit and brave defending. It was getting to the stage where I felt we were riding the storm and could maybe see it out, but then came the Belgium breakthrough.

The ball went up the left wing and, to our detriment, our midfielders were almost too honest. The defence dropped to try and deal with any cross, and the midfielders dropped into the box as well to make sure they could deal with anything that fell in there, or with the runners coming in. The ball was worked out to the edge of the box, and our lads were maybe ten to 15 yards away. Aaron Ramsey went tearing out to try and get a block in, but Nainggolan cut his right foot across the ball and struck it superbly. Wayne did ever so well just to get near it, but it flew into the top corner.

This was the first time we'd been behind since England's injury time winner in Lens, but no one could argue that Belgium didn't deserve their lead. We knew the game was going to be very tough and, all of a sudden, it had become even tougher. They had a few more minutes on the attack after the goal, but we managed to come through that and then, as so often happens, we started to get a foothold in the game.

For the final 20 to 25 minutes of the half we were absolutely incredible. The weather was dire, we were playing against Belgium, and having gone a goal down, yet our response to all of that was fantastic. The lads were knocking the ball around with confidence, and the Belgium players couldn't get near them. Joe Allen and Rambo were on top form, having the games of their lives. Chris Gunter and Neil Taylor were getting forward and causing a threat, and we were getting chances.

Hal started that game and had a header which he was clearly disappointed with. We were playing so well and sucking Belgium out of their shape and then picking them off and getting down the side of them. We were now generating some real momentum. Neil Taylor got himself on to the end of a cut back and caught it perfectly. We were all up on the bench. Goal! Surely! But no, as Courtois had made an unbelievable save. At that point I was starting to think, 'Is this really going to be our day?'

Just to add to that feeling, Ben Davies had picked up a yellow card early on, which meant he would miss the semi-final if we got there. I remember seeing the footage from Gazza at Italia 90 when that happened to him in the semi-final, and it looked like Ben was welling up a bit in the same way. He had been so good and consistent throughout the tournament and was going to be a massive miss if we did get through, but Ben was still going to have to do a job for the team, and do it he did.

We'd had those great chances and were wondering what we had to do to score but then, just before half-time, we won a corner. Rambo took it, and Ashley Williams – Captain Fantastic – burst into the box and powered home a header. He was so brilliant throughout the competition, our leader, and had finished the previous game with his shoulder hanging off! It was great that it was him who got the goal because he has been a key presence for us over the last four or five years.

Ash came tearing up the line towards us for his celebration. To the gaffer and to all of us for a big group huddle. It was a goal we really deserved and half-time came at the wrong time for us, we were so dominant. Belgium were wondering what had hit them and must have been thinking, 'Oh no, not Wales again!' The gaffer was delighted with how it was going and how we had got into the game. After such a difficult start the gameplan had come into effect and the boys had showed such composure on the ball. It was incredible to watch from the bench – this had the potential to become one of Wales' best and most memorable performances.

Into the second half the lads maintained their levels, and then came *that* goal from Hal Robson-Kanu. The turn, once called the Cruyff Turn, is surely now the Robson-Kanu Turn. It's one that my boy has been trying to perfect ever since. The ball broke down the right and Rambo cut it back to Hal. Tayls was motoring up on the left and, from the bench, we were just screaming for Hal to pass it across to him. Then, out of nowhere, came the turn. It was unbelievable. The Belgium defenders thought he was going to pass it too, and he practically sent them out of the stadium. It set him up in the middle of the goal, but even then he had a bit still to do. He made no mistake, and comfortably dispatched the ball past the 'keeper.

On the bench, we all looked at each other wondering what we had just seen. We knew Hal was a skilful player but his tournament performances had been based on his strength and his work rate. It was such a phenomenal moment. For him and for the team. To pull off that piece of skill, in that moment and that situation. If he ever gets near that again in his career it will have to be something special.

Hal wheeled away and was then running back up the line towards us. He went past the subs towards the gaffer and then came back to us. He is really good mates with Simon Church and I remember him and Churchy having a bit of a hug and a bit of a moment. Then we all sat down again, just thinking how amazing this was, 2-1 up, and within touching distance of the semi-finals of Euro 2016. We knew the dynamics of the game would now change and Belgium would really try and come at us, but we had the lead now, something to cling on to. Could we see it through?

This was the point in the game when the gaffer turned to Kingy and told him to make sure he was warmed up and ready. Joe Ledley, still not long back from injury, was not going to be able to last the 90 minutes, and I remember thinking that if my groin had been right then this could have been my opportunity to get on the pitch. What a time to come on as a substitute. It's so nerve-racking when you are a goal ahead in such a big game. I just knew Kingy would go on and make a good impression.

In that situation, and this probably sounds stupid, I don't think anything can really go right for you coming on as a substitute. You are coming on to help protect a lead, and if the team score it's a relief, but if you concede it's a nightmare. Kingy did really well when he came on and put in the battling performance we needed to help see the game out. Vokesey also came on a couple of minutes later, with Hal making way.

By this stage Aaron had been booked, also his second of the tournament, which meant he would also be suspended for the semi-final. Another huge blow. Along with Gareth and Joe Allen he had been among our best players. His bravery on the ball and in making the team tick, is something we miss massively when he's not available.

Like Ben, he was just carrying on, trying to make sure that he may yet get another chance to play in the tournament if we reached the final. We had been under real pressure but Aaron picked up the ball, with a few minutes remaining, and played it down the right for Chris Gunter. Gunts looked up, saw that Vokesey had made a great run in front of the defender, then put in a superb cross. Sam is notorious for his ability in the air and produced a perfect glancing header which gave Courtois no chance and flew into the net. 3-1. It was game over as Vokesey charged across towards the Welsh fans.

He said afterwards he was looking above the big archway which is the route in and out of the stadium, and he saw his dad sprinting down the stairs, with his arms in the air. He spotted him straightaway. What a moment that must have been – and to be able to share – after scoring in the quarter-finals of a major tournament.

I thought I'd seen it all by now, but the celebrations in the dugout were beyond anything I'd experienced. We all went completely nuts and my injury was totally forgotten as we hugged everyone and anyone. What an achievement for the nation. The final whistle went and Wales were in the semi-finals of the European Championships. We all went over to celebrate in the corner with the Welsh fans as normal, and went into our huddle.

This was when our masseur, Chris Senior, went into the middle of the circle with a camera to take some pictures. Somehow, the circle turned into a heart. Nobody planned it. At ground level we couldn't even see it had happened, but it seemed to sum everything up. Gareth had formed a heart with his hands in Bordeaux after our first goal, and we'd formed a heart with our bodies in Lille. It was destiny. I remember seeing the image after the game and it just seemed like it was meant to be.

I went over to see my family, and my nephew Tom was desperate to come onto the pitch. He had seen what Jack had done after the Northern Ireland game, but we'd received an official warning from UEFA about the children going into the pitch after the game. I suppose it was protocol, and they had to be seen to be saying something, but it seemed harsh and a bit silly to me. Not letting the players enjoy such a special moment with their families? These were moments we would never be able to experience again. It's what football is all about. There weren't any more fixtures scheduled for that stadium so it wasn't like there was going to be any damage done to the pitch. It would have been another special end to be able to share it all together.

Despite the celebrations, within minutes my attention turned towards getting my groin right to have a chance of being involved in the semi-final. It was Friday night, and the game was scheduled for the following Wednesday, so there was still time. There was still hope.

Away from the football this had been a very special day back home – Jack's birthday! He was having his party on the night at Little Rascals, an indoor soft play centre I co-own in Shrewsbury, with Crossbar Coaching who do all our kids parties. Crossbar Coaching is run by Gavin Cowan who I played with at Shrewsbury and am really good friends with. He organised some of his coaches to do the party and had the instructions to make sure everything was finished in plenty of time to allow everyone to get home and watch the match. Jack had an amazing time. I had spoken to him earlier in the day and it is never nice to miss your child's birthday. I had already missed my wedding anniversary and Father's Day. Jack was gutted he wasn't out there watching our game but he had his birthday party so managed to get through it.

As it turned out it was probably the best birthday party anyone could have imagined. To beat one of the tournament favourites, and get through to the semi-finals of Euro 2016! I'm not sure Jack will have many more birthdays to top that!

19

Portuguese Men O' War

'In great attempts, it is even glorious to fail'
Vince Lombardi

It was a fairly quiet night after the victory over Belgium. I think one or two of the lads had a couple of drinks in the bar but as there were only five days to the semi-final we all knew what was potentially at stake and, for me, the main focus now was trying to recover from the groin injury. As soon as I got back to the hotel I took a sleeping tablet and went straight to bed.

After a day spent with the family – as lovely as that was – we then flew back to Dinard where I took another sleeping tablet because I wanted to relax my body as much as possible to give it the best chance of healing.

Sunday saw some discussion about my injury with the medical team. To me, the groin felt a lot better, but the staff wanted me to have a scan to check for damage. I was hesitant about that. I didn't really want a scan. Sometimes, if you are looking for something, then more often than not you'll find it. That was a scenario I didn't want to contemplate. My previous experiences suggested that scans can often find a lot more than what is actually wrong, or make the problem seem worse than it actually is. A scan measures the amount of fluid in the muscle, which then defines the size and extent of the tear. I feared that a scan would come back saying 'x' amount of fluid meaning a particular level of tear, and that would be the end of my Euros. I had been really lucky at Wolves and really trusted Phil Hayward, the club's head of medical. We'd had good conversations about this very thing in the past and agreed that we should treat the symptoms and not necessarily the scan.

I felt confident that with the right treatment, and the four days to get it right, I could be available, but the doc and the physio wanted me to press on with the scan, which was understandable from their perspective, so we got it done. The results showed, as I feared, quite a lot of fluid on the adductor, so the doctor and physio confirmed this would rule me out for the semi-final. It was devastating to hear. Having sat out the quarter-final I'd been confident I would be back and available if required. I was still convinced I could be ok and asked them to please not rule me out, just yet.

I spoke to Ronan McCarthy, the guy who'd done wonders for my back problems years previously, who said he would try and shuffle a few things around with his schedule and get out to France, which was great to hear. With that news, and being in constant contact with Phil at Wolves, I was really confident that I could make myself available. I knew it would be the Welsh medical team's call in the end, which is as it should be, but Phil had looked after me for years at Wolves and knew my body better than anyone. It was all about doing everything in the best way possible to make sure I was available for the Wednesday.

Ronan was brilliant, quickly arrived in Dinard and, at about midnight on the Sunday, I had the first treatment from him. It felt better immediately. I then had another session at 7 o'clock the next morning – having had about five hours sleep – and again, I felt really good. I kept the FAW medical team informed of everything I was doing and asked them if we could put the scan results to one side and go with how I felt and what my own instincts were telling me. I explained to them that I was a 30-year-old man and not a naïve youngster, that I knew my body and how it would be by Wednesday evening. I would never put the team at any risk by declaring myself fit if I wasn't – like I'd done on Friday in Lille – it was all about the team and there was no way I would put our overall chances in jeopardy.

Their view was that if we'd got to the final, but my rush to play in the semi-final caused more damage and ruled me out of playing at the *Stade de France*, I'd be even more gutted than I was feeling at this particular time. Eventually we came to the agreement that I could do a little bit of work on the Monday and we could take it from there. So, I did some straight line running, which had been a little bit sore previously, and then got to the stage where I was full out, sprinting. I felt really good but we all knew that the groin would be put under more pressure with the multi-directional work, the cutting and the turning. I was adamant that I wanted to do more but the medical guys were saying I should take it steady, see how the groin reacted, and go from there.

I was so desperate to get myself sorted I was even prepared to come back later in the day and do some more work, anything to put the groin to the test. I had a meeting that lunchtime with the doctor Jonathan Houghton, physio Sean Connolly and head of performance Ryland Morgans. They were all on the same page, not wanting me to do any more work on that Monday. It was a real *Catch 22* situation. They said if I did the session in the afternoon I would be too overloaded to go into the full session on the Tuesday, the day before the game. Yet the only chance I had to be involved, or at least available, on the Wednesday was to train on that Tuesday. At this point my head was all over the place. I was adamant I was fit. Ronan had weaved his magic and I'd been speaking to Phil back in Wolverhampton.

I believed I could do that extra session *and* then train on the Tuesday. This was the semi-final of the European Championships – just give me a chance to be out there! It sounds bad in hindsight, but I was saying I was happy to go into that Tuesday session and risk getting a big tear in my groin that might rule me out for eight weeks. Knowing my body better than anyone else, I was confident and more than willing to take the risk. This was a once in a lifetime situation.

At the same time, the FAW guys were being very open and honest with me, and I completely understood their views. They were saying they had to advise the manager that they didn't believe I was ready and fit to train properly. The scan was suggesting it was a ten day injury, and there was me trying to train after three! I know they really felt for me, they could see how much it meant, and how frustrated I was, and we had some really good and honest conversations. For them – and this is a reason why they are as professional as they are – they have to make big decisions based on what they believe, regardless of sentiment. If I'd been selected on the bench, then sent on – in good faith – by the gaffer only to break down, it would have been their heads on the block just as much as mine. Perhaps even more so.

Yet it was massively frustrating. I know for a fact that if I'd been back at Wolves, I would probably have played, and Phil would have backed me and trusted what I was saying. There are many occasions where I've played without being 100%. That goes for every player. There isn't too often, from the first day of the season, that you aren't playing with some minor problem or niggle. It's what you expect over a long and tough campaign, but this wasn't a run-of-the-mill Championship fixture or even a Premier League game. This was a knockout game – the semi final of the European Championships. Whether or not to be a calculated risk was always going to a huge call.

I asked Sean if I could do an extensive, yet controlled, rehab session on Tuesday. A really tough session which he would put together. At least then, if we did get to the final, I'd be confident of being able to train on the Thursday and be in the frame for Paris. I was also still thinking: 'Do the session, come through it, show them I'm fit and maybe, just maybe, they might reconsider me for the semi-final.' I was just hoping, probably against hope, that they might then tell the gaffer I would be ok to come off the bench if needed.

Sean agreed, so I had my bespoke session on Tuesday. It was a fitness test, to be honest, apart from some really explosive striking of a ball. The last rehab session before you go back into full training. I felt completely fine. I was alongside the lads who were in training. "Any chance of me joining in?" I asked in hope.

I was now coming to terms with the situation, and was just praying we could get to the final. I didn't want my tournament to end here, but at least I had come through a hard session and, if – just if – we could beat Portugal, I should be ready to join in again on Thursday. It was frustrating that I wasn't going to be able to play, but I had a conversation with the manager and the physio who said we could do exactly the same as the Belgium game. I could still get changed and be on the bench, even though it was 99% sure that I wouldn't be coming on. It's not like I was taking someone else's places on the bench because we could all be named among the substitutes. That was important – it meant I still felt part of everything and could maybe contribute in terms of being in the dressing room and around the lads.

I was keen to do the warm-up as well, striking a ball again – for my own sanity and to prove I was fully fit. We had done the stadium walk in Lyon the night before as normal. It was superb. Probably the best we'd played in. The weather was fantastic and the pitch was immaculate. I was determined to enjoy the day, even amid my disappointment. I had eaten well, done a little bit of work in the gym, and left no stone unturned that I would be ready for the Thursday. There was just the small matter of beating Portugal. No pressure, boys! I hadn't been as nervous as in previous games because I knew I wasn't going to be involved but, as a player, as a Welshman, I was just looking forward to the game and hoping that the lads could do the business.

Portugal had been fairly unconvincing in the tournament so far. We had reviewed all their games, and they had only just scraped through the group stages. Of course, we knew what their main threat was going to be – the Ronaldo effect! – and the media was hyping the game up as Ronaldo v Bale. In the hotel we had access to *Sky Sports* and could see it being built up as a clash of the two superstars. It was all understandable given their respective abilities and impact on their respective nations' results. Personally, and I am sure some people will feel differently, but at that time, I believed Gareth offered more to his team than Ronaldo did to Portugal. That is not to dilute or play down Ronaldo's influence or not see what an unbelievable player he is and what he is capable of. I could certainly see that.

However, at that time, I just felt Gareth could do everything for the team. He was working hard defensively and getting things done in an attacking sense, proving a real team player. Ronaldo had all those qualities as well but I was convinced – based on their performances in the tournament – that Gareth was slightly edging it. So, for me, that meant we had a really good chance.

The two squads were fairly similar. One player each who was world class, two or three more who were right up there playing top level football, and then the rest who were full of quality and the work ethic needed to make up any team. Unfortunately, we were also missing two quality players in Aaron and Ben. Aaron was going to be a huge absence because of his ability on the ball and the way he could make the team tick and Ben had also enjoyed a fantastic tournament and been a lynchpin at the back. As ever, though, absences gave other players the opportunity, with Andy King coming in for Aaron and

James Collins, who has been such an important player for Wales for many years, replacing Ben.

So yes, I genuinely thought we had a really good chance of getting to the final. It didn't feel like either team was the overwhelming favourite, and it didn't feel like we were the underdogs. Both countries were thinking that this could be their year and, as a one-off game, anything could happen.

My favourite part of all the games was arriving at the stadium and going straight out onto the pitch. Once again, the atmosphere was electric. There were so many Wales fans inside the stadium early, taking it all in, and anticipating a very special night. I was going into the warm-up at full throttle, really testing myself out, and it was probably even more frustrating that I felt so good. Possibly, if I hadn't picked up the groin injury, I might have been starting the semi-final of a major tournament but, I understood the decision, and there was a far bigger picture out there. It was all about the team and I made sure I stayed positive, helping out wherever I could.

I didn't have any family or friends at the game. Emma and Jack had flights booked to Lyon but once they found out I wasn't going to be involved, the tickets were changed to Paris for the weekend. It wasn't a case of my wife being overconfident, more of her not being able to get a refund – so plumping to switch flights instead. Paris for the weekend and maybe the final of Euro 2016? Wishful thinking maybe, but definitely worth a try.

Then came the game. The first half was really scrappy. We knew Portugal were going to make it difficult for us because they often get numbers behind the ball and sit back. We have generally enjoyed more success against teams who push forward onto us, leaving the space to counter-attack and use the pace and the patterns of play that we are capable of. We found it really hard to break them down. Gareth had a shot go just wide from a corner routine with Joe Ledley. We were off the bench thinking it might creep in. He had another great run and shot which was saved and, at the other end, Ronaldo directed a header over the bar. Chances were at a premium and this felt like the Northern Ireland game all over again. The first goal was going to be so vital – and hopefully we were going to get it.

At half-time I caught the team talk, with the gaffer telling the boys to be patient but also try and get their football going a little bit more.

PORTUGUESE MEN O' WAR

A few minutes into the second half, Portugal got a corner out on the left. It was a good delivery, and we got a great view of it from the bench, which was unfortunate given we could see what was about to happen. It was heading for Ronaldo, who seems to be able to hang up there in the air, and then he produced a terrific header. I'm not sure there are many in the world who can leap that high and get that much power on the ball with that quality. It was world class. James Chester was marking him and, even if Chezzy was a foot taller, I'm not sure he would have been able to get anywhere near the level of Ronaldo's leap, that delivered what we feared could be the killer moment.

That is how it proved. Going behind we were hoping to regroup, to try and create some pressure at the other end and just maybe Gareth would be able to get in a position where he could do the same as Ronaldo, and make something happen. It was about staying in the game and then trying to get back into it.

Those plans were unceremoniously dashed a few minutes later when, from a scuffed Ronaldo shot, Nani deflected the ball past Wayne Hennessey and in. On the bench we all thought it was offside. Nani looked as if he was all on his own in there but, looking back at the replays, he was clearly onside. It was 2-0. Seemingly game over and, all of a sudden, everyone felt so deflated. The atmosphere and the mood changed. The fans knew it as well. It felt like the tournament, our incredible journey from the qualification campaign onwards, was now coming to an end. From then on there was lots of huffing and puffing, and the gaffer made changes, but we just couldn't get anything going. We couldn't get ourselves back into the game.

Gareth was trying absolutely everything. He was coming back and getting the ball off Wayne and just taking it up the pitch and trying to make things happen. Portugal were so good at defending and keeping clean sheets that they stopped us playing and killed the game. That defensive organisation was what probably contributed most to them winning the tournament in the end. That ability to stay in the game, keeping things solid, and picking up results even if you're not playing well. Fonte was excellent throughout the tournament, Pepe missed the game against us but otherwise he was impressive too. They had those firm foundations and, if truth be told, we never looked like breaking them down.

As the minutes petered away, we were all starting to think, 'This is it'. This is the end of the fairytale. So near, but yet so far. On the bench we had time to reflect as the game moved into its final minutes. It was different for the lads who were playing. They were still concentrating and focusing, keeping going right to the end to try and get us back into the game, but it just didn't happen. Portugal were slowing the game down, playing it perfectly, doing a really professional job. It was that grey kit again! We don't seem to have much luck in that one, and grey was probably how the mood felt as the game drifted away.

Then came the final whistle. That was it. The end. The end of our story. It was difficult to take in. We made our way onto the pitch to say 'well done' to the boys who'd given everything and were gutted. Then we went over to the fans and had our usual huddle. Ash was again in the middle, and he gave us some really powerful words.

"Don't be disappointed," he began. "Don't be upset. You have to enjoy this moment. This is such a momentous time for Welsh football, and this achievement will inspire the next generation. We are the ones who have created history and none of us should be down or gutted. Even though it is hard to take, we have reached the semi-finals of a major tournament and this isn't a time to sulk. Enjoy the next few days, make the most of it. It is a special time."

It was a stirring speech. In keeping with everything over the previous six weeks. Ash, our captain, had summed it up perfectly yet again. He told us what our achievements could mean for the future of Welsh football and we all turned, linked arms and said thank you to the fans. We just didn't want to leave the pitch, and it looked like the fans didn't want to leave the stadium. Neither wanting this amazing adventure to end. We had gone further than any of us really expected. Our tournament ambitions of playing well, scoring a goal or two, winning a game perhaps and doing ourselves proud was all we could have hoped for. As we'd progressed, our wildest dreams were being surpassed and our magical journey around France seemed never ending, but now it had to. We were out. We were, indeed, going home.

We went into the changing rooms and had to wait for a couple of the lads who were being drug tested. On this occasion, unlike when I was selected after the Slovakia game, we managed to persuade the drug testers to come into the dressing room with us because we didn't want the boys to miss out. Obviously, they have to keep an eye on the players they are testing, but now we were out of the tournament they were more relaxed about coming into the dressing room.

The gaffer spoke. He gave us a mini debrief of the tournament, more from an emotional point of view rather than anything tactical. He said what an amazing experience it all been and that all of us in that room had changed the face of Welsh football. He told us we had made him so proud – one of the proudest moments of his life – and everything we had done in that previous six weeks had helped pave the way for the run we had enjoyed.

Like Ash, he told us to make sure we enjoyed the following few days. Don't let it pass you by. Enjoy all of it, savour it, including the return to Cardiff, which we already sensed would be something of a celebration. "Stay together," he said, wanting us all to share in the achievement and share the moment. Be proud. Each and every one of us.

It was a nice moment, even amid the disappointment of losing such an important game. You could see the gaffer was disappointed as well. We hadn't really performed at our best, a similar performance to the England game, but in no way was it down to any lack of effort. That's football. You cannot play your best in every game and things don't go for you in every game. It was just one of those nights which happen from time to time, especially against opponents who made it very difficult.

There was plenty of emotion as the gaffer spoke. No one was breaking down in tears, but there were a fair few lumps in throats. It was the end of this memorable journey and you could sense it in the gaffer's voice and the atmosphere among the lads. It was pride more than anything else. We all felt so lucky and blessed to have been part of this incredible journey.

Everyone remembers watching their first major tournament. For kids growing up in Wales this was an incredible few weeks. We had all seen the footage of the fan parks and the kids all wearing their Wales shirts with such pride. It might just inspire more youngsters to play football and give a bigger pool for Wales to pick from in the years to come.

By now, my own personal circumstances were forgotten and irrelevant. It was more about the team, and how everyone had played their part in what had happened every day in training and around the place from game to game. I also started to think that I wasn't too far away now from getting home to see my family after such a long time away. That was a pretty special consolation prize to look forward to.

But, to have been part of, and inside the journey, had been incredible. I know every fan had loved it as well. The over-riding emotion that we were the lucky ones to have done it. To have qualified for the tournament and then reached the semi-finals. We knew it was something that we would be telling our grandkids about in 20 or 30 years time. Something really special. Something we would never, *ever* forget.

Yes, there was still disappointment, and that tinge of regret, but as the gaffer and Ash had both said, we had to enjoy it. Reflect on the achievement as we all knew that, within a few days, that disappointment would start to fade and we had to make the most of the overall success that we'd enjoyed. As we headed back to Dinard for one final day in France, that was exactly what we planned to do.

20

Please Don't Take Me Home!

'Welsh is of this soil, this island, the senior language of the men of Britain; and Welsh is beautiful'
J.R.R. Tolkein

We travelled back to Dinard on the Thursday morning, still disappointed but determined to enjoy the achievement, and make the most of what we had achieved. We were back at the hotel around midday, and had a bite to eat. It was a really nice day and we decided it would be good to have a few drinks together and relax, have some food – pizzas! – we could eat what we wanted now!

The hotel was right on the coast, with beautiful scenery, and a great balcony where you could sit and unwind. We met there for a couple of drinks, but ended up staying until about 9 o'clock at night. A fair few beers were consumed – it was quickly turning into something of a real late team-bonding session! We were all just having a really good time, sharing stories of what had happened during the tournament, all the funny stuff and other memories. It was great. It was now getting late, so we thought it was time to head into Dinard, just to finish the trip off.

We knew France were playing that evening, but as it's such a nice and quiet town, we didn't expect it to be too busy. It had certainly been fairly quiet on the previous occasions we had headed down there. We all got changed and then onto the team bus, complete with the Team Wales branding.

It's fair to say that we were all a bit worse for wear by this point, far different to how we normally feel getting on the team bus, and arrived in Dinard, right in the middle of the France v Germany semi-final which was being shown on the television. As the coach turned a corner, we saw people everywhere, enjoying the game and having a great time. It was just wild – we couldn't believe it. They very quickly clocked it was the Wales team bus but, to be fair, with the branding plastered all over it, we weren't exactly hiding away.

The coach driver pulled over and a load of the locals – 300 to 400 people – came sprinting across. Very quickly, and to our surprise, they formed a guard of honour for us into the nearest bar. It was a great gesture and a really nice moment. It wasn't something we'd experienced before, or are ever likely to again. Another amazing memory to treasure.

To be honest, we didn't actually know where we were going. We just wanted to watch the game and have a beer. We'd walked around Dinard in the daylight and it wasn't the biggest of places, with maybe three or four bars. The FAW staff had gone out earlier, for a meal, so we knew they were somewhere in the town. In the end, we wandered into Le Davy's café and bar, where'd we'd been earlier in the tournament, for a milkshake. No one ordered a milkshake this time.

When we got in there, all the media teams who'd been following the Welsh squad during the tournament were there which was great. I remember seeing Alex Gage, the cameraman from Sky who is also a Wolves fan, Bryn Law, Chris Wathan and a few others. It wasn't planned but it was nice to meet up and have a good chat and watch the game with them. It was actually whilst in conversation with Chris over a pint that he encouraged me to write a book about our amazing Euro 2016 fairytale. Chris wrote a great book about our qualification journey to the Euros called Together Stronger, and when I mentioned I would love to write a book one day he said it had to include the inside story of the tournament.

From there, things escalated a bit as we all carried on drinking and it got to midnight, then 1 o'clock. It was turning into a great night, with everyone getting on well and being able to let their hair down without having to worry about our calorie intake, or training the next day. We were a bit wary of flying home early the next day, with the open bus tour to follow, and none of us wanted to be too hungover for that – it was going to be quite an occasion – but still we carried on. We moved on to another bar, where the FAW staff were, for a while, but by this time the boys were splintering off into different groups.

Gareth, Aaron and Wayne had gone off to play golf in the afternoon and arranged meet up with us later on. Gareth doesn't drink at all anyway – he doesn't touch it – but when they arrived and got out of the car, it was mayhem! He just got absolutely mobbed – the downside of being a superstar – and he and Wayne had to get back into the car after about five minutes and head back to the hotel.

By this time we'd been speaking to the media guys about what there was to do in Dinard. Let's just say maybe they weren't as disciplined as us, and had already put the nightlife to the test. We were asking which places were open late, and they suggested a name we didn't recognise. Anyway, we made use of the public transport and got on this old, rickety bus where we were all singing and banging the sides of the bus. I've no idea what the driver made of it all! Twenty four hours earlier these passengers had been out there in a European Championships semi-final and were now on his bus singing and trying to carry on with a night out!

When we turned up it was the place where we had all eaten together a few weeks previously. 'This can't be right,' we thought. 'This was a restaurant, not a late night bar or club?' It looked dead and we couldn't see anyone around. We got off the bus, found a little side entrance by the restaurant, went in and it was packed. We stayed in there until late. It was such a great night, one of the best I have had. You could just see the accumulation of everything we had achieved in the tournament and the team spirit and togetherness we had built up. Everyone was just really enjoying themselves.

At one point there were sing-alongs going on everywhere, and the boys were up sitting on a raised area by the DJ box belting out *Hen Wlad fy Nhadau*. It was quite a 'studenty' sort of place and the locals responded by singing *La Marseillaise* having just seen their team get through to the final. It was a really nice atmosphere and I think the locals appreciated us being there. They loved the fact that we had really taken to being in Dinard, shown respect for their Breton language and culture via our social media, and had enjoyed our stay. It could only have been bettered if we had gone on to play France in the final.

It was now 3 or 4 o'clock in the morning, and any thoughts of taking it easy and not being hungover before the celebrations in Cardiff the next day had gone out of the window. I don't remember getting back to the hotel, but I do remember trying to pack my bags when I got there. Possibly not the best idea after a few beers, but I knew I wouldn't have much time in the morning, and wanted to get as much sleep as I could.

Being away for so long, and travelling to so many places, you end up with a lot of mementoes and gifts, and we'd all been given a wine bottle holder, in the shape of an arc with a wine stopper mechanism shaped like football studs. It was a nice memento, but massive, and I was trying to get it in my bag along with stuffing all the clothes in. Quite a task, which was probably beyond me at that moment in time.

When I have a hangover, I'm usually ok first thing and then it hits me as the day goes on. After getting up a few hours after coming in, I went down to breakfast to get some food inside me and finished off the packing. With the late night and general tiredness we hadn't given a massive amount of thought to the events waiting for us in Cardiff, apart from a sense that they'd be special and quite a few people would be waiting for us. Quite a few! It felt that the whole country had come to meet us.

We landed in Cardiff at about midday, and there were thousands of fans at the airport. It was incredible. It took ages to get through arrivals with so many fans there to greet us and we were signing autographs and having pictures taken. As we left the arrivals building we headed for the coach, then smiled broadly as we saw that our bus had been emblazoned with FAW artwork and the word *Diolch* down the side – which, to those reading who don't know, is 'thank you' in Welsh. It was a great touch and lifted our spirits even higher. The players and manager and coaching staff were on one bus and all the other staff on another bus right behind.

The journey from Cardiff Airport towards Cardiff Castle takes you through a few small villages close to Barry, and as we drove through every little village there were hundreds of fans waiting for us, and all the traffic islands and mini-roundabouts towards the M4 had been named after different players: Joe Ledley, Ashley Williams, the gaffer. How thoughtful. How special. It was a shame that the blacked out windows of the coach meant that the people lining the route couldn't see us, but I can assure them that we could see them all – the flags, the banners, the waving children – and really appreciated their support. It was wonderful to see.

We got to the castle and everyone chilled out with a bite to eat and a drink – a soft drink this time! We had heard it was going to be reasonably busy but south Wales is still traditionally very rugby-orientated and we still didn't fully comprehend how much football had gripped the imagination of the people from Cardiff and other areas who had travelled down there.

The castle gates were shut so we couldn't see anyone. Then the FAW's Ian Gwyn Hughes came across and said we should go up to the castle ramparts and just take a peek over the walls. A few of us did as he had suggested, and I couldn't believe it. It was an absolute sea of red, as far as the eye could see. It was truly amazing. In front of the castle, up every little side street, there were thousands and thousands of fans. I couldn't see any spare space on the roads or the pavements, and we found out later that almost 300,000 people had come out to welcome us home. What phenomenal support.

We also knew that every ticket for the event at the Cardiff City Stadium – where we were heading next – had been snapped up within hours. The huge wooden gates of the castle were slowly opened, and as we walked out into the bright sunshine the roar that greeted us was immense. What an incredible feeling that was, walking through the crowds to the bus and seeing so many happy, smiling faces. I had no friends or family down in Cardiff to share this experience with me so I tried to capture as much as I could on my phone to show them all later. There was one moment when I was looking over the side of the bus and I heard someone shouting "Dave, Dave!" I looked down and it was one of my brother's best mates who was down in Cardiff at the time. Out of all the thousands of people who were there it was great that I managed to see him from the top of the bus.

It probably took an hour to get to the stadium, as the streets – all of them – were lined a minimum of eight or nine deep. The crowd waiting for us outside the stadium was huge, and having a great time, singing *Don't Take Me Home* and doing the Icelandic Viking clap.

Inside the stadium, the Homecoming show got underway and The Manic Street Preachers performed *Together Stronger* which had become a real anthem that all of us knew really well. The Manics are a fantastic band and quite a few of the boys went up into the tunnel to watch the performance. We were then all invited out into the stadium, where TV presenters Gethin Jones and Fran Donovan interviewed the gaffer and some of the players as footage from the games was shown on the big screens. Seeing the montage on the screens and hearing the cheers of the fans when the goals were shown really encapsulated what we'd achieved and how brilliantly the people of Wales had supported us.

Then the whole stadium sang *Hen Wlad fy Nhadau* – another rousing rendition – and we did a lap of the pitch to say thank you – *Diolch* – to the fans, which was yet another special memory, the perfect way to bring this incredible journey to a close, and another day which will stay with me for the rest of my life.

Back inside the dressing room it was time to say goodbye to everyone, a very strange feeling given how long we had all been away and the unforgettable experience we had shared together. We were all aware that David Vaughan was going to retire from international football after the tournament, so I made sure I spoke to him and wished him all the best. We had all been close for seven weeks so it was strange to be saying goodbye, even though many of us would be back in September for the next game.

By now, everyone was starting to drift away. Some of the lads who had family with them went to a reception at the stadium but others, including me, started leaving in the cars provided for us. Even though it had been another incredible day, I was really keen to get back home. It was about 7pm or 8pm and I knew the kids would be in bed, and I was heading back to good old Shrewsbury.

Emma was sitting on the sofa watching the TV as I walked up the drive and turned the key in the front door. From the noise of the European Championships semi-final in Lyon 48 hours earlier, I was now at home, with the ones I love, popping up the stairs to see my wonderful kids, fast asleep, in a beautiful and peaceful silence. In the weeks that followed, a lot of people asked me what it was like trying to get back into normal life after such an incredible experience and, do you know what? It was fine and not really a big deal. I am very content with my life and with my family. I am very fortunate in that respect and I really enjoy it. So, whilst it had been a really special few weeks and an experience I will never, ever forget, normal life was good to get back to as well. It didn't take long to re-adjust.

The next morning, the kids bounded in and jumped on me while

PLEASE DON'T TAKE ME HOME!

I was still asleep. I had never been so happy to be woken up! They both wouldn't stop cuddling me and wouldn't let me go. Because I had missed Jack's birthday he insisted on having another cake and so he and Emma brought me up a piece of cake and a cup of tea. The kids were very clingy – and I wasn't complaining. It went on to being a fairly normal day. They wanted to go to the cinema so we had a Nando's and then went to see *The Amazing Life of Pets*.

I popped in to Little Rascals where they had really bought into the Euro fever, following the tournament, and I had done a competition after every game giving away a Wales shirt. My mum had also been interviewed there by Ian Winter from BBC Midlands Today in a piece which went out on the day of the Portugal game. It was great to go and see them again, and to catch up after such a long time away. Later in the day we biked down to Pontesbury to see my mum and then back home, into the proper routine which families know so well. Baths, stories, and bed. Days don't get any happier than that.

The following day, having missed one wedding during the Euros, there was another one in the diary. This time for a guy called Gavin Cadwallader, who I had been really good friends with since playing football together as kids. He also came through to get a professional contract at Shrewsbury and we played together in the first team for a short while. It was his wedding and, even though I'd only just got back, myself and Emma both wanted to go. After a morning with the kids, we went off to the wedding service and then the reception at Combermere Abbey in Whitchurch. Obviously there were lots of questions about the Euros – but that was all good.

At the reception, there was this one waiter involved in serving the meals, and who was drawing a bit of attention. Everyone thought he was a little bit strange. His service was absolutely terrible. One of the ladies at table asked for a bottle of water and he looked at her as though she had asked for something ridiculous and just barked: "No!" We were all looking at each other and thinking, 'Who is this guy?!'

We later saw him having a big argument with another member of staff and this was being repeated at all the different tables. Then he came over to me and said: "I hear you play football?" What else could I say but, "Yes"? He had this strong accent, said he was Hungarian and then asked if I had played against Hungary. You get into these conversations from time to time and we were chatting about football but he was making some really strange comments. I didn't think too much of it and just thought he was a little bit eccentric.

Later on he came up to me and started talking about how beautiful Emma was. Then he came up to me at the bar asking if I'd got a cleaner at my house. I said we didn't. "Well, do you want one?" he asked. "I can come and clean your house for you." He said he could clean my car as well. This was now happening with quite a few different people and was getting stranger and stranger.

Then the groom came up to me as he'd seen what was going on, and asked if the guy was giving me hassle. I told him it was fine but Gav wasn't having it and said he was going to speak to the wedding co-ordinator and get the waiter sorted. He said a few people had seen him go outside onto the lawn and urinate against the wall. By this point everyone was laughing and really wondering what on earth was going on with this strange bloke.

Then he appeared at the back of the room and was shouting at everyone, asking if anyone had lost their mobile phone. This was getting really bizarre until, all of a sudden, he grabbed a microphone out of his pocket and starting singing a swing number. Then another guy appeared from behind the top table and started singing with him. We all started to click what was going on. It had all been an act. He came over to me, sat on my knee, put his arm around me and said: "Sorry mate, I'm a massive Wolves fan!" He'd been doing all sorts of things as part of the act. He'd even tried it on with the bride's mother! Gav had organised it all, but his wife knew nothing about it, and she'd been getting increasingly furious before, eventually, seeing the funny side.

So yes, that was my Sunday night, supposedly getting back to normality. What a way to end the summer. An absolutely brilliant summer, full of experiences and memories I will keep with me forever, but now it was over, time to move on. I had a fortnight off and then it was back to Wolves and another new season in the Championship. But first of all, on Monday, it was back to the school run...

Postscript

At the end of the summer of 2017, my near ten years at Wolves came to an end. There were so many ups and downs at Molineux, and certainly more downs than any of us would have wanted, but it was certainly never dull.

The arrival of such a huge company as Fosun to take over Wolves in the summer of 2016 was an exciting development. Steve Morgan and Jez Moxey had done a good job down the years in keeping the club stable and also helping to underpin the three Premier League years which hadn't happened at Wolves for a very long time previously, and haven't done since. But the arrival of Fosun promised a new level of investment and backing which would aim to see the club promoted back to the Premier League, and then developing to become established at that level.

As with any big transition, there were always going to be obstacles and challenges along the way and there were plenty of those during their first 12 months at the helm. Deciding immediately to make a change of head coach, Walter Zenga came in to replace Kenny Jackett, not to mention a huge number of signings before the transfer window closed in August. Bringing in Walter, who had no Championship experience, as well as so many players in similar situations, was always going to be something of a gamble.

I for one quite liked Walter, and enjoyed working with him. He is certainly a very lively and enthusiastic personality, and we enjoyed some great days under his short time in charge, especially the away wins at Birmingham City and Newcastle. Unfortunately we weren't able to deliver the sort of consistency which the owners were looking for, and so another change was made, with Paul Lambert coming in to take the head coach's role that November. As with Walter, I felt I got on well with Paul.

He was very different in terms of his experience, and had already achieved success by taking Norwich up from League One to the Premier League, and he was able to come in with that track record and steady the ship. While we weren't able to pick up enough sustained results over the six months to threaten at the right end of the Championship table, there were some fabulous occasions and performances to savour during Paul's time at the helm.

None more so than during that FA Cup run, and particularly winning 2-1 against Liverpool at Anfield. What a day – in front of over 8,000 travelling supporters – and one of the best moments of my career. I didn't know until the day of the game that I was going to be captain, but I knew the gaffer was planning on making changes, so I had thought about what I might say in the huddle before kick-off if I was playing and normal skipper Danny Batth wasn't.

There wasn't any ranting and raving, or trying to get the lads going – it was purely, "Relax, enjoy it, and take it all in."

I had been lucky enough to play at stadiums like Anfield when we were in the Premier League and, to be honest, it had all become something of a blur. I'd been so involved in those games that the experience all passed me by. My mindset changed when I went to the Euros, however, and I made a conscious effort in France to make sure I took it all in and remember it. So, in that huddle at Anfield, I urged the boys to: "Take a moment before kick-off, enjoy it, and play with a smile on your face, and if you match that with the hard work and togetherness then this could be the best day of your life on a football pitch."

That is ultimately what it turned into and, at club level, it remains probably my most special moment. To captain a club of Wolves' size, and upset Liverpool at Anfield is something else. My boy Jack, my dad and my nephew were there along with a lot of friends so it was a great day for me personally as well.

Before the game all we could hear was the Wolves fans, and there was such a special moment for me before kick-off – I really had to pinch myself. We were lining up in the tunnel and I was chatting to our mascot, Fletcher, and of course Steven Fletcher was the last Wolves player to score at Anfield. As I stood there, I could hear the Wolves fans singing the *Super Dave Edwards* song. To hear those 8,000 Wolves fans singing, above the sound of the 45,000 Liverpool fans at Anfield was very special indeed. The Wolves fans were terrific all game, as they had been all season, and we then had the scenes at full-time with Jón Daði Böðvarsson – now also a team-mate at Reading – leading the Icelandic clap. A sensational day, a sensational experience, and certainly one of the standout moments of a mixed season.

POSTSCRIPT

There were also a couple of other landmarks for me to enjoy, which I will look back on fondly in the years to come. My goal in the team's great win at Fulham in March, a crucial victory in the middle of the run which effectively secured our Championship status, was my tenth of the season and the first time I'd reached double figures. I had gone close on several occasions, so to chalk up the ten goals was a great moment, especially as I was the first Wolves central midfielder to hit that target for around 30 years.

It also came during a season when finding the net meant I'd scored in ten successive seasons for Wolves, joining another illustrious club of Wolves legends such as John Richards and Steve Bull. It was an honour to be mentioned in the same breath as players like that.

Then, on the final day of the season against Preston, came another moment of personal history which I will always treasure. I had made my 300th Wolves appearance in the win against Leeds United at Easter, another game when I was captain, having already started to realise that if I could keep my place in the team, that Preston game would mark my 500th appearance in senior football for club and country.

I'd always dreamt of playing football as a professional, and to have made just one appearance for Shrewsbury – that debut when I came off the bench late on against Scunthorpe – was a dream come true in itself, but to go on and chalk up 500? Well, that is beyond a dream, not least when over 300 of those have been for such a huge club as Wolves, and included 38 international caps for Wales.

Little did I know, however, on that final day of the 2016-17 season, that my time at Wolves was very soon going to be at an end. I was really excited coming back for pre-season and I had started for Wales against Serbia in the big World Cup qualifier when we had got a good point. It was exciting to come back and start working under a new head coach in Nuno Espírito Santo, although I was very disappointed that Paul Lambert had gone. I had really enjoyed working with Paul – I liked his way of playing and his approach – and I had felt that if he had been given money to spend to bring his own players in, we would have had a right good chance in the 2017-18 season. As it turned out, he and the owners must have been on a very different page in terms of their plans for recruitment and it was never going to work out.

As a player, you know that managers and head coaches come and go and, once I saw that Nuno had taken over, my attention quickly turned to the anticipation of working with him. He arrived at Molineux with an impressive pedigree having been manager at both Porto and Valencia, and it is always exciting to work with someone with that experience and knowledge. I was really looking forward to it.

Unfortunately, it became obvious within the first couple of weeks that the system he was going to play didn't fully suit my game. It was similar to the system that Wales play, where I'd managed to adapt and stay involved, so I was equally determined to do the same at Wolves and keep myself in Nuno's plans.

Chris Coleman had trusted me to play a deeper role with Wales and had also used me at number ten in that game against Serbia. I was keen to do the same for Wolves and was trying to impress in training and the pre-season friendlies. It was two or three weeks before the start of the season that it became clear what Nuno's starting team was going to be, if everyone was fit. I wasn't going to be in it, but my reaction to that was to bide my time and try and force my way in.

I have to say I thought the way Nuno worked was really positive. Under his guidance and leadership I could see that Wolves were going to be a top, top team. On and off the pitch, things were going really well and I just wanted to do everything I could to be involved.

I came off the bench in the first league game against Middlesbrough and started the first Carabao Cup tie against Yeovil. Nuno changed the system slightly and I was playing more as a number eight, box to box, and I remember being so desperate to score in the game to prove I was worthy of a place in the team. Because of that, I probably tried too hard and got in the box too much and didn't have the best of games. I was brought off after 70 minutes, was really frustrated and the following weekend I wasn't even in the squad. The same thing happened for the following match and it was starting to become very apparent that I was going to have a struggle to break in.

I started speaking to my agent to see what we should do – this was a potential World Cup year for Wales and I needed to be playing. At the same time I also didn't want to carry on just picking up my money at Wolves if I wasn't contributing. That has never been the way that I am. I was certainly not going to kick up a fuss, it was just a matter of letting my agent know in case I may need to leave. I was still more than happy to carry on fighting for my place at Wolves and then re-assess in January if nothing had changed.

Nuno and I then had a chat about the situation. He said he wanted to be completely honest with me and tell me what he was thinking. He said he didn't see a position in the team where I would be first choice and that I wasn't being named on the bench because I wasn't likely to be coming on. He added that he didn't feel it was fair, at this stage of my career, to take me to games when I wasn't going to be involved. I appreciated that honesty – it is always far better to hear news like that, even if it is disappointing, because it lets you know where you stand.

I enjoyed working with Nuno and enjoyed the way he managed and it's just unfortunate for me that I couldn't prove to him that I could play in that system. He asked me if I would be comfortable playing in a deeper role in the Carabao Cup tie against Southampton, and I said I was. At the time I told him I would continue to work as hard as I could to get back in the team and that he would never have a problem with me off the pitch. I did also say, however, that if anything did crop up, where there might be an opportunity to play regular football, I hoped the club wouldn't stand in my way and would let me go. He said that was fine and we would see what happened over the following couple of weeks.

I played in the Southampton game, a great 2-0 win and, even though I didn't know it at the time, the perfect way to round off my Wolves career. The next day, my agent called me and said there were a few clubs interested. He said Reading in particular were really keen and very close to agreeing a fee with Wolves. I spoke to Emma that night and said we needed to be prepared, that a bid might be accepted, and to get our heads around what might happen.

After training on the Friday, the squad list went up for the Brentford game and my name wasn't there. My agent called again, to ask if anyone at Wolves had spoken to me. They hadn't. Wolves had accepted Reading's bid that morning and I was required to head straight down to Berkshire for the medical, but I said I needed to speak to Emma before making my mind up. My agent said Reading understood all that and wouldn't expect me to sign unless I was completely comfortable with everything.

I have to say Reading were brilliant, they left no stone unturned. They suggested I travelled down with Emma and the kids and that they would put us up in a hotel for the night and make sure I had everything I needed to make my decision. I naturally had mixed feelings at that time. I was really excited about the opportunity to sign for Reading and for a manager who really wanted me, but equally, I had been at Wolves for nine-and-a-half years. A huge chunk of any career. With so many memories. I had just come into training on the Friday morning and was now about to leave. To just drive away from Compton for the last time with most of the other lads having already left the training ground.

No one had said a word to me about the deal, and I could literally have walked out of the door and never seen anyone again! It seemed so cold. I went and spoke to Morts, the kitman, to tell him what was happening and get the customary bin bags which players have when they leave to put all their stuff in. Kit, hats, gloves, bits and pieces from my locker like programmes and newspapers, many of which had been in there since the day I signed almost ten years earlier.

I said goodbye to Phil Hayward and Matt Wignall from the medical department who had both done so much for me over the years, and sat and chatted with Danny Batth, Conor Coady and couple of lads from the press office. Then I packed all my stuff in my car, and left. Football is such a strange industry. In most jobs you generally have a bit of time to build up to a career move, often even six months or more. Yet here, after nine-and-a-half years, I had gone into work and was leaving a few hours later for the very last time! I wouldn't say I was disappointed, it was more a case of feeling flat. Off I went, up the drive thinking that this was the route I had travelled for almost ten years and it was no longer going to be routine. Such a strange feeling.

I picked up some stuff from home, we went down to Reading and I have to say I fell in love with the place straight away. There is a real family feel to the club and they were great with the kids, taking them on a tour of the stadium, and made Emma feel really welcome. I did the medical on the Friday and Saturday and then the deal was announced shortly before the Championship games kicked off on that Saturday.

Subsequently, I spoke on the phone to Wolves managing director Laurie Dalrymple, who passed on his best wishes, and I also had a really nice message from the chairman, Jeff Shi. He told me how grateful he was with what I'd done at Wolves and how much he thought of me, which was something I really appreciated. I did actually go back in to Molineux the following Monday, and to the training ground on the way to joining up with Wales, so I could drop a few presents off for people who had helped me down the years. After that, the next time I'd be there I'd probably be wearing a Reading shirt.

I had an unbelievable time at Wolves. It will always be a special club for me. Over the nine-and-a-half years I'd built up some amazing relationships and I'm ever so proud to have played for a club of Wolves' size and stature, for that long, in an era when that sort of thing doesn't really happen.

Hopefully I'll be remembered fondly but I owe a lot to Wolves for what they've done for me and my family. It was a time where my young family were able to watch me play and that was really special. Evie isn't the biggest football fan but my Jack used to come to a lot of the games, and when I left, I was touched to receive so many lovely messages from Wolves fans thanking me for my efforts and everything I had done.

I've always said that I don't have a problem with anybody questioning my footballing ability, that's their prerogative. All I can ask is that they acknowledge that I've genuinely put in my absolute all and given everything that I can in terms of effort and discipline. As good as it is to be loyal, and how much I absolutely loved my time at Wolves, a fresh challenge does re-ignite you. Once I had got over the upheaval of heading off to Reading, I was immediately relishing the prospect of going out to prove myself at another club and show I could be part of a new team.

There was also, however, the disappointment of the World Cup qualifying campaign to deal with, and Wales missing out after that last day defeat at home to the Republic of Ireland. Going into the last round of games I think we were in a position in the group that we would have taken, all things considered. We always wanted to be in the mix towards the end of the group stages, because prior to the Euros we were generally out of it after four or five games. Having said that, when we now look back, it was the games in the middle of the campaign that cost us, especially all the draws.

Serbia went on to win the group but we were ahead in both our games against them, and the home result was particularly tough to take with the equaliser coming so late. Throughout the group, we didn't make the most of the opportunities when we went ahead, and then away in Ireland the sending-off changed the game.

Whilst it was a positive campaign, compared to the qualifiers over the previous ten years, it was clearly so disappointing because it was all set up in that last game for us to take our journey further, but the Republic of Ireland did a job on us. We weren't able to turn our football into decent chances and as soon as they got in front it was always going to be really difficult to break them down.

Losing Joe Allen early on was massive. I think we have shown that we can still be competitive without the big players, and had got results without Gareth Bale but, even so, the likes of him, Joe and Aaron Ramsey are players that can make the difference in such a tight game like the Ireland one.

We all said after the Euros that the success in qualifying and reaching the semi-finals must not just be a one-off. It had to mean something going forward, whether that be to encourage more younger people in Wales to play football, or for the next age groups coming through to want to repeat the success of 2016. We wanted to be a generation of footballers that started consistently qualifying for major tournaments but unfortunately, with the World Cup, it just wasn't meant to be.

Yet, the bar has been set now, and I genuinely think Wales are only going to get better. You can now see younger players coming through which maybe hasn't happened over the last year or two. Look at Ben Woodburn, David Brooks and Ethan Ampadu – they are going to have plenty to offer and it's still a relatively young squad with only a few of us over 30.

The next European Championships is now the aim. We have to qualify for that and go and do well, and then look at the World Cup in Qatar. It is still a good time for Welsh football, despite the disappointment of missing out. Where it is now is the best it has been for a very long time – the staff have been magnificent, the fans have been magnificent and the players have raised their levels.

We also now need a new manager after our inspirational leader, Chris Coleman, departed for Sunderland in November 2017. The FAW will make their choice and the players will give the new gaffer exactly the same support as we gave his predecessor, the most successful manager in Welsh football history.

POSTSCRIPT

I am still enjoying international football, and featured in seven of the ten qualifiers, starting three of them. To still be in contention, I need to keep on playing club football regularly which I've managed to do for Reading since my move. I've even scored a few! I am at a point in my international career where I know I am not necessarily first choice for the Wales squad. If I deemed to be taking the place of a younger player who needs valuable game time for the future, then that is something I would totally understand. Those will be the conversations to be had moving forward with the new management team, but I certainly still love playing for Wales and would love to remain involved if I have the opportunity.

That's because, on the football front, I feel good. I feel I know my body so much better now than I used to, and I feel I know how to preserve my energy over a long season to – hopefully – allow me to continue to contribute at a high level. Mentally I am also different to the player I used to be. All the injury setbacks, the relegations, the disappointments, the criticism from supporters – it has all combined to make me a far stronger character. I know my abilities and I know my limitations. I'm not going to do a load of Ronaldo-style stepovers to beat a defender, or smash one into the top corner from 30 yards, but I still feel I have plenty to offer as a midfield player with an eye for goal who can also perform the defensive side of the role and be an influence in both boxes.

Above all, if people recognise and acknowledge that I am a player who lives his life right, is dedicated to his profession, and gives every last drop of energy and enthusiasm every time he takes to the pitch, then do you know what? That will do for me.

I am also very content away from football as well. I have a wonderful family – they are my absolute priority and I try to spend as much time with them as I can. I am also delighted to have set up a charity – the Little Rascals Foundation – which followed on from the Little Rascals play centre I jointly-own with my best mate, Ben Wootton. We always said we would go into some form of business together. We've got kids the same age, and used to take them to play centres in Oswestry and Telford. There was nothing like that in Shrewsbury so, one day we just thought it might be an idea to get something together which was closer to home. It all started from there and, from first talking about the idea, 12 months later it was all up and running.

It was nerve-racking, but also exciting. It was new to both of us, but Ben did have a background of working with children with disabilities. We set up specific sessions at the Little Rascals play centre for children with disabilities and they were proving a success but it was nowhere near enough, and so we pursued another shared aim of launching a charity. From there, the Little Rascals Foundation was born.

We decided to go down the route of launching the Foundation which aims to provide funding for vital equipment, an operation or a holiday – anything to make a child's or family's life that little bit easier. Ultimately, the plans are for a play centre purely for children with disabilities, including learning disabilities and conditions such as autism. A purpose-built facility can provide children and their families with a safe and comfortable environment to go and have fun and enjoy themselves, away from any fear or worry.

I feel strongly it is my duty as a footballer, in such a privileged position, to try to help and give something back to the local community. I'd love to get to a point where I literally just did charity work. I am in a fortunate position to be able to help people, to be able to change one little boy's or little girl's life, although we come across so many stories which are truly heartbreaking. It is very hard work to set up a charity, but we feel it will be worth it, and we are committed to helping as many children as we can.

Away from Little Rascals, I am also involved in a business, Q Financial Services. I was approached by a friend, Mitchell Gough, who always did my mortgages, and we set up the business with three other guys, and it is going really well. We set up the business plan, are all heavily involved in it and meet up every week. I am learning all the time. It has been going from strength to strength and we now have an office in Telford and five members of staff as well as Mitch. I really enjoy the business world. It is another avenue which allows me to get away from football and try and develop another skill and interest.

As long as I am fit and healthy I want to play football for as long as I can, but when all that comes to an end I would love to be able to have a natural progression into the media and the business world and a lot of what I do away from the game at the moment is trying to prepare for that.

I will do my coaching badges, because you never know what's

around the corner, and I wouldn't rule coaching out but, at the moment, the media really interests me and if I can do more and more, along with the plans for the businesses, that is where I see my future.

I certainly have no plans to hang up my boots just yet though. I still love coming into training every day and that will never change. You are a long time retired!

To play for my country has afforded me the sort of experiences I could only have dreamt of as a young boy growing up, like so many others, with the dream of becoming a professional footballer. My first ever training session with Ryan Giggs, lining up for fixtures alongside Craig Bellamy and Gareth Bale, forging so many strong friendships and travelling the world. I feel hugely privileged to have been part of the international set-up for so many years, none more so than being in that 23 for the 2016 European Championships and amongst a squad which went all the way to the semi-finals.

Those weeks in Dinard and everything associated with it offered memories which will last a lifetime and memories which I will no doubt bore everyone with in years to come when I look back on my career. For Wales to have waited so long to have reached a major tournament, and then done so well, it was an incredible achievement from everyone involved and just shows what you can do with some quality players, excellent coaching and unbreakable team spirit.

The memories that will probably linger most with me are from the supporters, who followed us in such vast numbers everywhere we went. Seeing them outside the team hotel or on our pre-match walks, getting into the stadiums so early for when we arrived to check out the pitch, the incredible level of support during the games and throughout the tournament was humbling beyond words.

Together. Stronger – never can there have been two truer words, and that fantastic backing not only helped make the experience what it was, it drove us on all the way to the last four. Hopefully, Wales will become a regular feature of major tournaments, and really impose themselves at the top table of international football but, even if that happens, France in 2016 would still take some topping.

What a summer it was. An unbelievable experience and, just as the song said, we really didn't want to go home.......

St David's Press

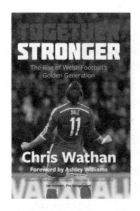

978 1 902719 481 - £13.99

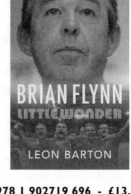

978 1 902719 696 - £13.99

978 1 902719 511 - £13.99

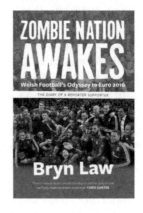

978 1 902719 467 - £13.99

978 1 902719 023 - £9.99

978 1 902719 023 - £9.99

All of Dave's royalties from the sale of Living My Dream will be donated to the Little Rascals Foundation, which supports children with disabilities in Mid Wales and the West Midlands.

The Foundation - established by Dave and his lifelong friend and business partner Ben Wootton - works to enhance the lives and increase the independence of disabled children by providing them with the opportunities to follow their dreams, be ambitious and live happy, fulfilled and independent lives.

"The Little Rascals Foundation helps disabled children lead the fun and happy lives they deserve."

www.LittleRascalsFoundation.com

 **@LittleRascalsFn**    **@LittleRascalsFoundation**    **/LittleRascalsFoundation**